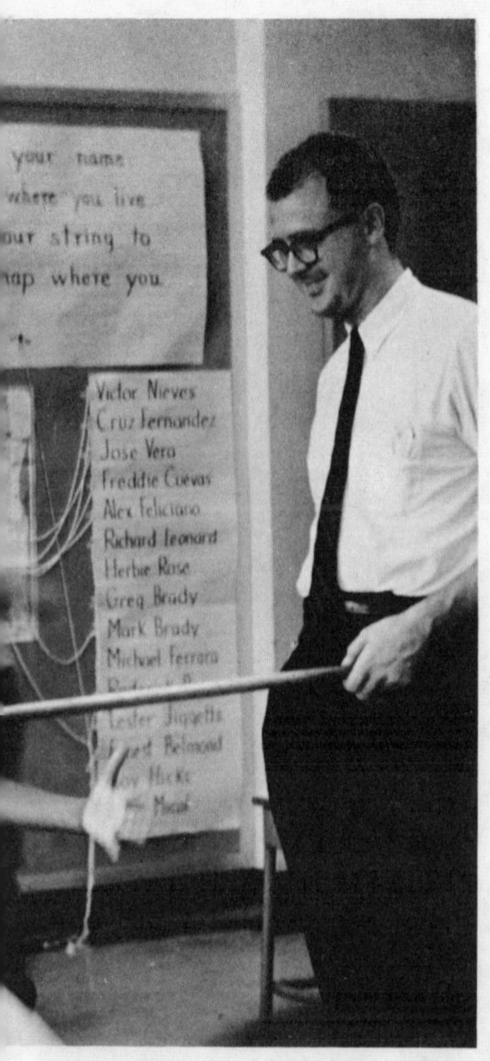

Conducted for the
Office of Economic Opportunity
and Staff of the
Office of Education

A SOCIAL CONTEXT

with disadvantaged children and youth

Gordon J. Klopf and Garda W. Bowman

Project Director and Dean of Faculties — *Project Program and Research Coordinator*

MENTAL HEALTH MATERIALS CENTER, INC.
104 East 25th Street, New York, New York 10010

Library of Congress Catalog Card Number: 66-29837

PREFACE

A study of the preparation of school personnel who work with disadvantaged children and youth, Project Aware, has revealed a series of paradigms with implications for all teacher education. The Project found no panacea in its search for effective ways of training teachers. It did discover innovation and experimentation, and trenchant polemicism concerning the theory of training was evident. The profession concerned with the education of all teachers may find the profiles of illustrative programs provocative. The valence of these programs was found in their effective methods of integrating cognitive, affective, experiential, and action approaches in the training process, of strengthening their foundations in the behavioral sciences, of developing an awareness of the child's learning process, and of evolving imaginative teaching strategies and materials.

Initial plaudits go to Donald Bigelow of the United States Office of Education, and to Stanley Salett and Sanford Kravitz of the Office of Economic Opportuntiy for conceiving the idea for the study and giving it scope and financial support.

The members of the Advisory Committee gave time, energy, insight, and direction at short notice and used vacation periods to serve in active planning and visitation roles. They are to be congratulated for preventing the Project from being colloquial and provincial.

The directors of institutes, chairmen and deans of education and teacher education programs, school officials, and state educational leadership are to be thanked for their responses to letters requesting information, for completing long questionnaires at a busy time of the year, and for providing the opportunity for Project personnel to visit their programs. Their openness and cooperation in every instance provided the data without which there would be no study.

The staff of the Project was a mosaic of personalities, skills, backgrounds, temperaments, points of view, and training. Students, freelance writers, nationally known teacher educators, researchers, retired professional educators, school and state department leadership, returning-to-career mothers, teachers searching for new roles, and national organizational leadership, representing all economic levels, meshed together to conduct the study and to produce the report. As they met, discussed, wrote, interviewed, visited, typed, traveled, studied, read, and contemplated, they found in these programs that, as Sefaris said, "the pomegranate, when broken open, was full of stars."

The Director wants to express particular appreciation to John Niemeyer, President of Bank Street College of Education, who, though not directly related to the Project, has given the focus and leadership in Bank Street to the institutionalization and integration of major innovative and basic concepts of teacher education; to Charlotte Winsor, Vice President in Charge of Planning, whose inspirational programs of teacher education, although not particularly aimed at education of the disadvantaged, provide the necessary sensitivity for considering the child as an individual, whoever he is, with particular learning needs; and to Elizabeth Gilkeson, who has been a most perceptive and intellectual mentor, truly a teacher of teachers. Lodema Burrows, the author of Chapter Two on the historical approach, has, in fact, been essential to the whole operation. A special tribute goes to the Project's Research Coordinator, Garda Bowman, and her helpful and patient husband, LeRoy Bowman. Project Aware was a concept and strategy in June, 1965; Garda Bowman had the major responsibility in making it an actuality.

GORDON KLOPF
Director,
Project Aware
July 1966

CONTENTS

APPENDICES

TEACHER EDUCATION
IN A SOCIAL CONTEXT

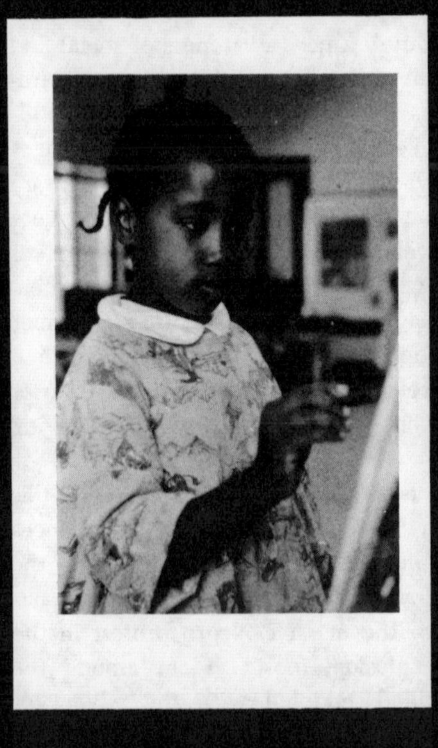

The need and the process

CHAPTER I

If we could first know where we are and whither we are tending,
we could better judge what to do and how to do it.
ABRAHAM LINCOLN

At midpoint of the twentieth century a new awareness of social and economic inequities challenged the obliviousness of previous generations of Americans. Four persons of vastly divergent backgrounds and roles contributed to the awakening of the public conscience. A Negro seamstress in Montgomery, Alabama, was simply too weary one day to stand in the rear of the bus while seats in the front were empty. A white worker in a Bowery mission wrote of the extent of poverty in the midst of affluence with a poignant pen. And two men, one a Bostonian with an Ivy League tradition, the other a former school teacher from Texas, institutionalized the protest and intensified the search for solutions. The comfortable philosophy of Charles Dickens' Mr. Bumble that "The poor, me lad, is always the poor an' nothin' else" no longer prevailed.

Concurrent social phenomena had prepared the nation for this heightened sense of responsibility. The commonality of experiences shared during World War II had helped to create a new sense of the possible in democratic living. The rising expectations of emerging nations all over the world reinforced the massive Negro protest in the United States. The population explosion, most evident among the economically deprived and unskilled, coupled with the advent of automation, resulted in the anomaly that highly skilled jobs went begging while unskilled people were seeking jobs in vain. As productivity and profits soared, the gap widened between the material abundance of the middle and upper classes and the absence of even the basic elements of existence for the nation's poor. Michael Harrington in THE OTHER AMERICA[1] estimated that there were 50 million poor in the United States, a third of whom were children and youth.

[1] Michael Harrington, THE OTHER AMERICA, Penguin Books, Baltimore, Maryland, 1965, p. 172.

Robert Lampman reported to the U. S. Senate that "a considerable number of younger persons are starting life in a condition of 'inherited poverty.'"

Within this context the educational deficits of disadvantaged children and youth were identified as prime causal factors in the self perpetuating cycle of poverty. The successful launching of the first man-made satellite by Russia had precipitated a reappraisal of American education. The U. S. Supreme Court decision of 1954 outlawed *de jure* segregation while *de facto* segregation persisted. In an atmosphere of self-appraisal, the issue of desegregation was joined with the related issue of quality education for disadvantaged children and youth in ghettoes of the inner cities, in rural schools in depressed areas, in schools attended by the children of Indians, of Spanish Americans and of migrant workers.

The question was raised whether schools, even in disadvantaged areas, are rooted in middle class values and expectations to such an extent that they attempt to prepare all children for a place in a middle class world. However, many children perceive this world as closed to them, as indeed it is in many respects, and reject the education offered. With the total unemployment rate less than 4 percent, one out of every four Negro youths is unemployed. The irrelevance of today's education to the needs and life experiences of the disadvantaged is reflected in a high dropout rate—a protest against and a rejection of the educational programs of their schools.

The circular relationship between educational deficits and poverty is not only evident with regard to vocational choices but also, and more importantly, in early childhood education. The cognitive inadequacies of those who have suffered disadvantage must be corrected in order to develop coping behavior in school as well as in the broader community. However, when children who need compensatory education are forced to attend inferior schools, the problem of inherited poverty is magnified.

In seeking answers to the fundamental question of meeting the educational needs of disadvantaged children and youth, additional questions were raised. What preparation do teachers and other school personnel need to work in schools with a large population of the disadvantaged? Should it differ from teacher education in general? If so, how?

Government recognition of the centrality of the need for basic conceptualization in this field has been a catalytic force in the design of bold new approaches. Analysis of the multifaceted problem revealed the inadequacy of merely providing more and more teachers, and more and more schools. Excellent quality of the learning-teaching process was identified as the essential component. Massive funding and consultative services by the federal government expedited the development of viable programs for assisting teachers to function more effectively in schools with large populations of disadvantaged children and youth.

As programs multiplied, Donald Bigelow of the U. S. Office of Education applied the words of Abraham Lincoln to the education for teachers of the disadvantaged: he asked first to know where we are and whither we are tending before judging what to do and how to do it. Sanford Kravitz and Stanley Salett of the U. S. Office of Economic Opportunity shared this concern, and Project Aware was created to study the preparation of school personnel for working with disadvantaged children and youth. Financed by the Office of Economic Opportunity, with the cooperation of staff of the Office of Education, the Study was conducted on a nationwide basis during the summer of 1965 by Bank Street College of Education. This report is the outcome of the research.

The sequential pattern followed in the Report is to proceed from this introductory chapter on need and process to the perspective of history; then to the present, next to a series of brief profiles and a few more intensive case studies of current programs illustrative of unique and effective approaches; next to a report on the extent and nature of teacher education for work with the disadvantaged as perceived by program directors, by participants, and by members of Project Aware visitation teams; and finally to recommendations and implications, based on the findings.

Purposes

The purposes of the Study were to describe selected programs designed to improve the knowledge, skills, and attitudes of school personnel for working with disadvantaged children and youth; to identify unique and significant elements of such programs; and to develop basic concepts and guidelines for emerging programs of this type.

Definitions

"Disadvantaged" for purposes of this study is defined as environmentally disadvantaged—that is to say, economically, socially, and/or educationally handicapped.

"Enrollee" and "participant" are used interchangeably to describe those who were being prepared to work with the disadvantaged in school situations.

Scope

The time span for the Study was from June through December, 1965.

Four populations were studied so as to survey both preservice and in-service programs as well as those financed by the federal government under special legislation. The populations were: (1) programs in colleges of teacher education and in departments of education in institutions of higher learning; (2) in-service programs in selected school systems; (3) summer institutes for teachers of disadvantaged youth financed under Title XI of the National Defense Education Act; and (4) teacher education programs financed under the Economic Opportunity Act.

Data were collected through written questionnaires and site visitations to selected programs. There were 1,127 questionnaires distributed to the four populations studied, which brought in 503 replies. Details regarding the process of data collection and analysis are given in Chapters 5, 6, and 7, in which the data are reported and analyzed.

Dynamics of the Process

A highly significant feature of Project Aware's operation was the creation of an Advisory Committee[2] of leadership in teacher educa-

[2] See Appendix A for list of Advisory Committee membership.

tion, the members of which were recommended by colleges and universities all over the country, by the sponsoring government agencies, and by the American Association of Colleges for Teacher Education. This committee assisted staff in formulating the design for the project, in devising and testing instruments, in selecting programs for site visitations, in reviewing the findings, and finally in formulating recommendations based on the findings. Members of this committee, specialists[3] from various disciplines, and staff[4] visited 59 programs in teams of two or three persons for a 2-day period in each site. The reports of these visits and the written comments of more than a thousand enrollees, were important components of the data.

After the appointment of a nucleus of staff, a 2-day consultation was held at the Princeton Inn, Princeton, New Jersey, to allow the Advisory Committee and staff to conceptualize the project, initiate the instrumentation, discuss the purposes and procedures for site visits, select programs to visit, and suggest specialists from various disciplines and from school systems to serve on visitation teams. A cadre of specialists was subsequently appointed, as well as a full complement of staff, to carry out the various phases of the project: planning, data collection, data analysis, and writing.

The next step was field testing of the instruments with the staffs of the Board of Education of Milwaukee and New York City, and at an NDEA institute in Puerto Rico. The aim was to develop an instrument that would serve both information-collecting and catalytic functions. It was hoped that the checklist questions might start a process of self-evaluation. After revision the questionnaires[5] were distributed and guidelines for Aware Visitation Teams[6] sent to 25 persons (Advisory Committee, specialists, and staff) who served on these teams. Special emphasis had been placed both at the initial consultation and in subsequent briefing sessions with specialists and new staff on the role of the team member—that is, to secure information, not to rate each program as "good" or "poor," and not to advise on operation.

[3] See Appendix B for list of specialists.
[4] See Appendix C for list of staff.
[5] See Appendices D, E, F, and G for questionnaires and letter of transmittal.
[6] See Appendix H for guidelines for Aware Teams.

The Focused Interview[7] by Robert C. Merton was among the books distributed to the Advisory Committee and to staff serving on visitation teams, and relevant excerpts from this book were sent to the Aware Team members as further interpretations of the role of researchers. However, Team members were sometimes asked by program directors to step out of their research roles and serve as consultants on program development. Such requests were complied with only when the Team member had made it clear that he was commenting as an individual, with no relationship to Project Aware.

Interpretation of the purposes of the Project to the directors of programs visited was a highly important component of the operation. This was initiated by the Director of Project Aware in his request for the visit and was further developed in the orientation session for Team members and director which occurred at the start of every visit. The criteria for selecting programs were explained: to cover as broad a range as possible geographically and to include variations in size, span of grade levels, length of program and other organizational variables, and also programmatic factors. The pattern for each visit was also agreed upon in the initial contact by the Director of Project Aware and in the orientation session for each visit. Visits included separate group interviews with staff and with enrollees as well as observation of the program in action. At the beginning of each interview with enrollees, brief written responses were requested. The replies from 1,054 enrollees are reported and analyzed in Chapter 7. The intersubjective agreement of enrollees, directors, and Aware Team members was high on several crucial issues. The availability of independent judgments from three sources was valuable as objective verification of subjective reactions.

Of the 59 programs visited[8] 35 were NDEA summer institutes, 13 were OEO teacher education programs, 9 were conducted by school systems, and 3 were conducted by institutions of higher learning without NDEA or OEO financing. Because not many of the latter two types of programs were operative in the summer, relatively few

[7] Robert C. Merton, The Focused Interview, The Free Press of Glencoe, New York, New York, 1956.

[8] See Appendix I for list of sites visited. (One program received both NDEA and OEO financing and so is listed in both categories.)

visits were made to them. Visits were made in almost every case after the program had been in operation for at least two weeks. The 25 Team members averaged three visits per person. The purpose of the multiple visits was to provide some perspective and a basis for comparison.

The reports of the site visits were analyzed from the three perspectives mentioned: the programs as pereceived by the directors, by the enrollees, and by the Aware Team members. Both strengths and weaknesses were observed, and accomplishments were analyzed in terms of purpose and rationale. Both the *why* and the *how* of the programs were reported upon periodically, as the analysis progressed, to directors of NDEA institutes at two work conferences, and to members of the Aware Teams at a series of consultations. As the dynamics of the process evolved, differences between Advisory Committee, specialists, and staff were minimized. All who had served on Aware Teams were needed in the slow and careful formulation of recommendations based on common experiences and on a joint analysis of the findings. The final chapter of this report contains all those recommendations.

The Major Recommendations are summarized below:

1. General Recommendations

That there be joint planning by institutions of higher learning, school systems, and the disadvantaged themselves.

That racial and ethnic integration be a reality at all levels of operation: staff, participants, and pupils in the practicum.

That there be openness to new ideas at various levels: administrative, teaching, community agencies, and family.

That flexibility of program development be increased without detriment to goals and standards.

That the approach be two-fold: first to seek understanding of the disadvantaged, and then to give assistance in translating such understandings into teaching behavior.

That more emphasis be placed upon developing and utilizing new instructional strategies and materials which have special reference to the disadvantaged.

That instructional content stress teaching as related to personality variables of pupils, affective aspects of learning, analysis of the special diagnostic competence required for teaching disadvantaged children and youth, as well as the foundations of social and behavioral sciences.

That programs of individual and group counseling help develop ego strength in participants.

That evaluation be an integral part of every program.

2. *For "Institute-Type" Programs*

That the size be limited to not more than 35, the span of grade levels be limited to early childhood and elementary or middle and secondary school, and the duration be extended to at least eight weeks (preferably a whole term) and residential arrangement be provided for at least a portion of the period.

That one important criterion for selection of participants be their potential effectiveness as agents for change within their own schools upon their return at various levels of responsibility, particularly at the top administration and supervisory levels, operating as teams from a given school, wherever possible.

That there be an opportunity for administrators, teachers, and auxiliary personnel (such as aides and assistant teachers) to develop roles and relationships within a context of reality.

That the staff be full-time, in large measure, and include both academicians and school personnel with experiences in working with the disadvantaged.

That programs be differentiated to meet various levels and styles of learning.

That there be three phases of the training: pre-institute, institute, and post-institute, with particular emphasis upon the application of learnings to the school program upon the participants' return.

That more emphasis be placed on parent participation in the program and continuing relationships of parents and enrollees in the homes.

That instructional process provide opportunity for experiential learnings in closely supervised practicums and home visits.

3. *For Funding Agencies and Organizations*

That follow-up be financed through stipends for group seminars, for intervisitation among schools, and for research as to the effects of such training upon pupils' learnings.

That funds be provided for training administrators, supervisors, special services personnel, and auxiliary personnel as well as teachers so that teachers may learn their new functions of diagnosis and of orchestrating adults to meet the needs of pupils.

That programs for school-family-community relationships be funded.

4. *For In-Service Programs in School Systems*

That emphasis be placed on "training the trainers," so as to maximize the impact upon the total school system.

That planners familiarize themselves with promising practices for teaching the disadvantaged, developed in other school systems.

5. *For Institutions of Higher Learning with Programs of Teacher Education*

That there be a larger proportion of other school personnel such as administrators, supervisors, counselors, curriculum specialists, and auxiliary personnel among the enrollees, who are now predominantly teachers.

That auxiliary personnel be not only trained, but also utilized in the practicum so that teachers may learn through experience effective ways of orchestrating adults within the class-room.

That instructional process include smaller classes, more emphasis on practice teaching in disadvantaged areas, and more effective supervision so as to combine field experience with analysis in depth.

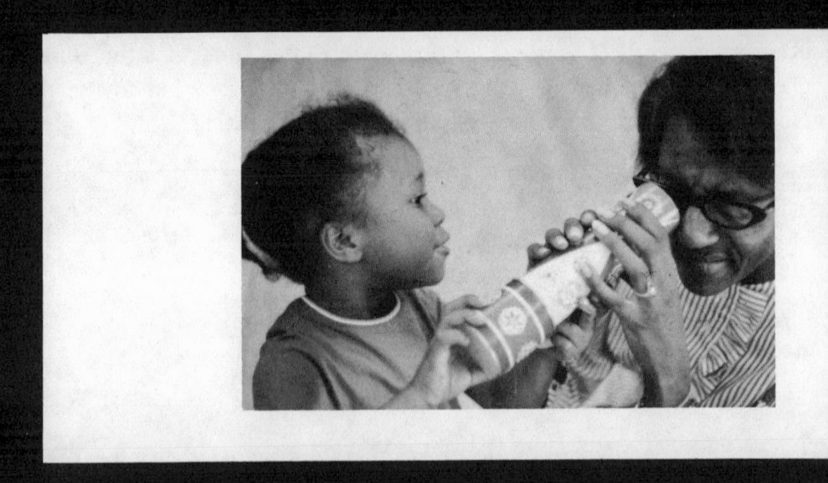

Historical setting of the preparation of teachers for working with disadvantaged children and youth

CHAPTER 2

In the United States the historical beginning of teacher preparation for working with disadvantaged children and youth is closely connected with the beginnings of all teacher education. The first attempts at formal teacher education as such can be traced to a recognition of the need to prepare adequately the children of the poor, the immigrants, and the freed slaves. The principles and methodology that were developed with these children were applied to teacher education in general. It was not until a much later time that the differences in children were recognized, and this discovery led to the development of more specific types of teacher education.

PAST PATTERNS

The First Attempt at the Preparation of Teachers To Work with Disadvantaged Children and Youth

The earliest recorded example of large-scale, organized teacher preparation in this country was the use of the Lancastrian system by the Free School Society of New York City in 1805. The New York Free School Society was established by the mayor, De Witt Clinton, and other citizens who saw a need for a means of educating "such poor children as do not belong to, or are not provided for, by any religious

ACKNOWLEDGMENT—This chapter was written by LODEMA BURROWS with the assistance of CLEMENTENE WHEELER, MARTIN HABERMAN, JOHN GRAY, GORDON KLOPF, and GARDA BOWMAN.

society."[1]* The Society began by providing one teacher and one school house for the 20 children who first responded to its initial advertisement in the daily papers. The immediate response to this modest effort was so great that the Society realized that in order to provide enough teachers for the children who wished to avail themselves of the education being offered, the Society would have to develop a plan to prepare teachers to teach in its schools.

The currently popular Lancastrian method used in England was selected as the one which would make possible the training of the greatest number of teachers in the shortest possible time. In essence, the method was to provide small-group instruction to many children through monitors. A large number of children were assembled in one room. The pupils were sorted and seated in rows of ten, with a pupil designated as a monitor assigned to each row. The teacher first taught the monitors a lesson from the manual, and the monitors took their rows to "stations" around the wall and proceeded to teach the other boys the lessons they had just learned. Such schools were highly and mechanically organized.

The Manuals of Instruction gave complete directions for the organization and management of monitorial schools, the details of recitation work, use of apparatus, order, and classification. Teachers were proscribed from varying from the manual in the minutest detail. It was assumed that by carefully studying and following the manual any person could soon learn to become a successful teacher in a monitorial school. The teacher had only to organize, oversee, reward, punish, and inspire.

Since schools with classes of more than 100 pupils were possible under the Lancastrian system, the method became popular in towns that wanted mass education at the price of only one schoolmaster's salary. Whatever limitations the method may have had, it appears to have stimulated great interest in teacher preparation, and Lancastrian training schools, such as that conducted by the New York Free School Society, are identified as forerunners of the normal school.

With the exception of the Lancastrian model schools, the earliest

* For this and all other Chapter 2 references, see the listing at the end of this chapter.

teacher-training school in America was established privately in 1823 by the Reverend Samuel R. Hall, who opened a tuition school for the training of teachers at Concord, Vermont, as an adjunct to his ministerial duties. He offered a three-year course:

> Based on common-school education, which reviewed the common-school branches; studied much mathematics, some book chemistry, and natural philosophy, logic, astronomy, evidence of Christianity, moral and intellectual philosophy, and in the third term of the third year, took up a new study which was called the "Art of Teaching."[2]

The Reverend Mr. Hall arranged for observation of teaching in the school, and for practice teaching during the winter in nearby rural schools. His was the typical training of the academy (forerunner of present-day high school) of the time, with the "Art of Teaching" added.

Publically supported institutions for the preparation of teachers in America developed slowly. Not infrequently the first step was state aid to academies, earmarked for teacher preparation. The students at these academies were for the most part being prepared to teach in the rural district schools, some of whose pupils would fit today's characterization of disadvantaged. At the time they were not so designated, nor were the teachers being prepared to meet these children's special needs. Indeed, they were not identified as having unique needs. Teachers of that time were being prepared to provide an education to develop a literate citizenry.

The first public normal school in the United States was established in Lexington, Massachusetts, in July, 1839. Cyrus Pierce, principal of the school, taught 10 subjects in a single term and 17 in the course of a year, supervised the model school of 30 pupils, acted as demonstration teacher, and, in addition, developed the professional materials for the curriculum and served as janitor of the building.[3]

There is some disagreement as to the origin of the normal school movement. Some students contend that its source was German, others that it was the logical outgrowth of the academy and related experiments, such as those of Samuel R. Hall. Certainly in the minds of the American public the early normal schools were adaptations or extensions of the academy.

Another notable European influence on teacher training in the United States in the early nineteenth century was Johann Heinrich Pestalozzi, a German Swiss, whose Rousseauian theories of education were based on the natural development of the child. Edward A. Sheldon of Oswego, New York, was largely responsible for dissemination of Pestalozzian principles in the American normal school.

The Evolution of a Normal School

Sheldon had established a school for disadvantaged children and youth in Oswego in 1848. It served "rude and untrained Irish boys and girls between the ages of five and 21."[4] By 1861 he had become Oswego's superintendent of schools. The Board of Education supported his work by creating a city normal school to train teachers in his methods.

Sheldon wrote a new course of study which eliminated much of the textbook memorization popular at the time. He prepared his students to teach according to Pestalozzi's theory and methods:

> In the above plan of studies, the object is not so much to impart information as to educate the senses; arouse, quicken, and develop the perceptive faculties; teach children to observe; and to awaken a spirit of inquiry. To this end the children must be encouraged to do most of the talking and acting. They must be allowed to draw their own conclusions, and if wrong *led* to correct them. The books should be used only for reference and as models for the lessons to be given.[5]

Visitors came in increasing numbers to see and study the new style of teaching. "Oral instruction" and "object teaching" became, for a time, the great new ideas in education as Oswego graduates were sought by city school systems and the new normal schools all over the United States.

How much the Oswego movement meant in the nation's educational history may be gauged by the change which came about in the process of instruction. Before the introduction of object teaching, the child learned by rote and recited individually. Each pupil worked at his seat, and the teacher heard him read or looked over his work.

Teaching in an organized group was an advance, but the teacher or monitor under the Lancastrian system still heard recitations of subject matter memorized from a book. It was "schoolkeeping," not school teaching that teachers were engaged in.

The Pestalozzian approach, based on sense perception, reasoning, and individual judgment, called for a complete change of classroom procedure. What Pestalozzi tried to do was to get teachers to allow children to use their senses and their minds.

The new teaching process, for the first time in the history of American education, called for a real technique of instruction. Dependence on the words of a text no longer sufficed. The oral instruction of a class required the teacher to have more extensive knowledge of the subject and new skill.

Despite the impetus of the Oswego method, the growth of state-supported normal schools was slow. By the 1860's there were only 11 state schools, 4 of which were located in Massachusetts. A few municipal teacher-training schools had also been established, among them schools in New York City, Boston, Trenton, Philadelphia, Baltimore, St. Louis, and San Francisco.

Impact of Federal Support for Higher Education

The individual states were not the only legislative bodies interested in the development of publicly supported teacher education. Congressional debates during the first 60 years of the nineteenth century reflected the concern of the federal government for the education of its citizens. The Morrill Act of 1862 ushered in a period of increasing participation in, as well as aid to, education on the undergraduate level. Its chief significance for education of the disadvantaged lay in the fact that the federal government for the first time recognized the existence of classes which educational institutions prior to that time had not been serving. Specifically, the Morrill Act authorized grants of land to establish colleges for the purpose of

> . . . teaching such branches of learning as are related to agriculture and the mechanic arts in such a manner as the legislatures of the States may

respectively prescribe, in order to promote the liberal and practical education of the industrial classes in the several pursuits and professions of life.[6]

Effects of Early Immigration on Teacher Education

The growth of the nation was placing unforeseen strains on the mechanism of public education. The expansion of cities illustrates the processes that brought about change in education, and New York City is the most dramatic case in point.

In 1805 the New York Free School Society was organized in order to provide education for poor children who could not attend private or religiously sponsored schools. These children were for the most part children of immigrant parents or children of freed slaves. Between 1805 and 1853 the Society had educated over 600,000 children and trained over 1,200 teachers, originally through private donations but eventually with financial aid from both the City Council and the State Legislature. Nevertheless, by 1842 the State Legislature of New York had found it necessary to create a public school department for the city.

Starting in 1842 the number of immigrants coming to the United States from Europe reached 100,000 or more a year, over two-thirds of whom entered the country through the port of New York and many of whom had children of school age. These immigrants, unlike the majority of those arriving before 1840, were mainly of the Catholic faith, and as Catholics they objected to sending their children to schools of the Free School Society, which taught a nondenominational Protestantism along with the three R's. During that time the Catholic Church had not yet established an adequate parochial school system of its own. These alienated Catholic immigrants frequently chose not to send their children to school at all rather than to expose them to the teaching of another religion.[7]

The education of immigrants from northern Europe brought about a significant change in the purposes, and in the problems, of the publicly supported schools. For children who had been born to the traditions of the American Revolution, it had been assumed that literacy was a sufficient goal for popular education. It was now necessary to educate alien children for democratic citizenship. Concurrent with the developing need for citizenship training, another theme was woven into public education: the idea of education as a means to upward mobility.

As early as 1833 Robert Owen had recognized that immigrant children were not reeciving an education suited to their particular needs. He proposed a special, vocationally oriented curriculum for the children of workingmen. His program met with vigorous opposition, the most vigorous from the workingmen themselves.

Immigrant parents, who were commonly laborers, wanted their children to have the same training as children of the upper classes in Europe—a classical education. The native established Americans used education as a means to universal literacy and as preparation for democratic citizenship. Teachers had to be prepared to teach so that both the goals of developing a literate citizenry and providing possibilities for upward mobility could be reached by their students.

The normal schools, while growing in number, appeared unable to prepare teachers to achieve the dual goal because of the quality of instruction the normal schools provided. Instruction was almost entirely on the secondary level and was similar to that given in the academies of the time and in the newly emerging high schools. There were few entrance qualifications and admission was denied to very few. Most entering students had only a grammar school education. The semesters were short, and the total length of the normal school course was either one or two years. A majority of the entrants attended only part of the course, some for but a few weeks.

The curriculum covered a review of elementary school subjects with an emphasis on teaching problems. A sample of the texts used were Orville Taylor's *The District Schools,* Samuel Hall's *Lectures on Schoolkeeping,* and Jacob Abbott's *The Teacher: Or Moral Influence Employed in the Instruction and Government of the Young.*[8]

Throughout the country there was a wide divergence of opinion about the uses of popular education, as well as a vast difference in the ways of training teachers. A survey of regional practices of the time just prior to the Civil War points up these differences.

The cities of the country, for economic, social, and political reasons, were leading the way in the development of new methods and a new philosophy of education. Innovations were started experimentally and allowed to grow as they proved their value or until they were supplanted by newer ideas. Thus the Lancastrian method had slowly given way to the Pestalozzian approach to teacher education, first along the northern Atlantic Seaboard, and later inland, on the trail of the pioneers.

Rural education, both in the Midwest and in the Far West, was slow to develop trends, largely because of the distances involved, the slowness of communication, the pressures at the frontier for survival, and the extreme decentralization of schools in rural areas.

In the South the class system impeded modernization of the educative process. Landowners usually provided privately for their children's education. The poor whites, a class made up of many former indentured servants who had turned to tenant farming or marginal farming in the mountains, were precluded from education by isolation and lack of money. The Negroes, under conditions of slavery, were forbidden education by law.

Preparation for Working with Disadvantaged Groups

Another group for whom the public took no responsibility in regard to education was the Indian population. Although the Bureau of Indian Affairs was established in 1834 under the control of the War Department, and in 1849 was placed under the newly formed Department of the Interior, the Indians were not considered to be citizens. In this early period the national policy in dealing with Indians was based on treaty and the tribes were considered to be quasi-independent nations, responsible for the education of their own citizens.

Following the Civil War a resurgence of interest in education was shown by the North, the Midwest, and the Far West through increased attention to teacher education. The South had to face the problems of reconstruction and, in facing these problems, had to begin laying the foundations of public education, first, on the common school level, progressing from there up the educational ladder. This process included the development of state-supported normal schools to prepare teachers to teach in the rural as well as urban public schools of the South. The need for preparing a large number of teachers was made more urgent by the necessity for educating the children of the newly freed slaves.

It was estimated that at the close of the war, of the four million freedmen, no more than a few hundred could read at all or write well enough to sign their names. Immediately after the Civil War, Negroes in the South began pressing for admission of their children to public schools. The southern schools were integrated for a brief period directly after the war, but various strategems of the white community soon segregated all southern educational facilities. The southern states borrowed the principle of "separate but equal" from a decision of the Supreme Court of Massachusetts in 1849. That decision prevented Benjamin Robert, a Negro, from enrolling his daughter in a Boston public school for white children. Although Boston abolished separate schools for Negroes six years later, the precedent remained and provided legal support for separation of the races in the South.

A problem inherent in "separate but equal" schools for Negroes was, of course, who would teach in them. The best southern teachers wished to teach in white schools. The northern school teachers who came to the postbellum South to begin Negro education were limited in number and lacked sufficient funds. A few northern philanthropists established colleges to prepare Negroes to teach in the segregated schools. Spelman College in Atlanta, Georgia, and Tuskegee Institute in Alabama are examples of such colleges.

The Negroes were not the only minority group faced with inequalities in educational opportunity. As early as 1886 the National Education Association devoted a section of its annual convention to a discussion, "The Problem of Race Education in the United States." In a series of conference speeches, three well known men spoke of the necessity for educating the American Indian, the Chinese immigrant, and the Mexican immigrant (but not the Negro) for their place in American life. Robert L. Owen, former secretary of the Cherokee Board of Education, urged:

Let Congress increase tenfold the present appropriations for the education of the wild men, who unlike the civilized tribes have not the means to educate their children, and out of these will grow in a few years a class of intelligent and useful citizens, as many have already become. They will then be absorbed into the great body of American citizenship, where all the races of men can and do meet on the level of a common right and equal justice.[9]

In spite of admonitions such as this, education for the nonwhite child in America remained inadequate and noticeably inferior to education provided for other children. The white immigrants who continued to enter the country in increasing numbers during this period created economic and social pressures which led to the expansion of educational opportunities afforded to their children. In part the economic pressures derived from the move toward industrialization which tended to concentrate the labor force—of which the immigrants were a large part—in the urban centers of the nation. The cities, sensitive to the political implications of the huge numbers of potential voters, enlarged their school systems to teach these immigrant children. Not only was this a period of school construction, but it also marked the introduction of public kindergartens and high schools.

Development of Teachers Colleges

By the end of the nineteenth century there were 167 public normal schools in the country and the number did not begin to meet the demands for teacher preparation. In some of these schools, curricula had undergone major upgrading and a few offered four-year programs.

The most significant addition to the curricula of the normal schools was psychology. The new conception of the child as a slowly developing personality demanded presentation of subject matter suited to his stage of development and a conception of teaching as the direction of the educative process. This approach replaced the former theory that teaching meant drilling the child in knowledge unrelated to the capacities of the learner. The influence of psychology thus led to increased emphasis on methodology in normal school curricula.

The availability of a normal school education brought about another change in the schools. For the first time inexpensive higher education was open to women. The percentage of male teachers began to decrease, from 55 percent in 1860 to 31 percent in 1900. According to Cubberly, the new normal-school-trained woman teacher

> brought with her to the school a new conception of childhood, a new and minute methodology, and a new enthusiasm, all of which were valuable additions, though for a time often carried to a ridiculous extreme. . . . The spirit of instruction was often lost by too strict observance of form.[10]

At the same time, the introduction of large numbers of women into the schools opened the door to a "maternal teaching style" in which the teacher relied on techniques of warmth, affection, and involvement with students as human beings rather than on a subject-centered approach to teaching.

Concurrently a number of factors began to give impetus to the establishment of teachers colleges as a new approach to teacher education. The rapid increase in the number of high school graduates had provided candidates; an awareness of the importance of the quality as well as the quantity of schooling had created a public interest in the developing teachers colleges; and the entrance of teacher preparation into university programs had lent it respectability.

The increase in the number of high schools following the Civil War created a demand for college- and university-educated high school teachers. A university chair of education was established in 1873, and by 1890 there were almost 250 such chairs. With the increase in the number of university departments, education began to be accepted as a serious subject of study.

The Spread of Vocational Training

Industrial expansion continually increased the demand for skilled workers. Throughout the last two decades of the nineteenth century there had been vocational schools to supplement the apprentice system, but these had met with firm opposition from the growing labor union movement. Labor stated that such schools turned out "half-fledged mechanics," while other critics warned that vocational schools would "deprive children of general education already too brief to begin with."[11] The unions feared that to relinquish control over apprenticeship would be to relinquish a hard-won right crucial in the struggle for higher wages and improved working conditions.

By 1910 the attitude of the unions had been modified by Samuel Gompers. The unions accepted the principle of vocational training through public education but reserved for themselves the right to influence the kind of training that was to be given.

Unsupported, the labor unions would probably not have been as influential in this matter as they were with the backing of the farmers' institutes, which had long supported the idea of vocational education for farm children. The agricultural institutes worked endlessly for county normal schools that would train farm-oriented rural teachers.

The Wisconsin branch of the farm society was extremely militant and attacked the state's education system as being a "cold-storage institution of dead languages and useless learning which costs several millions of bushels of wheat each year," when it could have been concerning itself with relevant knowledge. The society announced, "The rotation of crops is as inspiring as the position of the preposition; the economy of the horse and cow as close to life as the duties of the President and the causes of the Revolutionary War."[12] Such pressure brought about sweeping changes in the curricula of the rural normal schools just as the establishment of city vocational schools on the secondary level brought about changes in the curricula of the teachers colleges serving urban areas. In both cases the changes were directed toward preparing teachers to provide education that would be more relevant to the lives of their students. In both rural and urban situations these teachers were being trained to work with children who in some respects could be termed disadvantaged.

The Effect of Compulsory Attendance Laws

Local laws regulating school attendance became common by the end of the nineteenth century, although there was great variation in compulsory school age, length of attendance required, and means of enforcement. The degree of America's commitment to universal education is evidenced by the fact that between the end of the Civil War and 1918 every state passed a compulsory education law of some kind.

A by-product of the compulsory education laws was a change in the character of pupil population. Children whom the schools had not been expected, or prepared, to serve previously must now be educated. Formerly, retarded and physically handicapped children had dropped out of school when it became apparent that the program was not appropriate to their needs. Their required attendance under the new laws forced differentiation of school purposes and curricula, as well as specialized preparation for teachers who would teach them. The seeds of education for the blind, the deaf, and the mentally defective, planted before the Civil War by men like Gallaudet, began to bear fruit. By 1918 over 100 special schools had been established.

As the need for such special education became apparent, the teachers colleges throughout the country began offering, first, institutes for the retraining of existing teachers in methods and curricula for the handicapped. Later the teachers' colleges introduced courses into the regular teaching curriculum, and finally developed entire programs leading to degrees in special education.

The compulsory attendance laws also refocused attention on the question of including groups traditionally excluded from the public schools. By 1920 the Census record shows that, despite child labor laws in effect at the time, a million children between the ages of 10 and 15 were gainfully employed in shops, factories, and on farms, and therefore were not attending school. At the same time, only 70 percent of all Negro children between ages 7 and 15 were enrolled in schools; only 67 percent of Indian children and 85 percent of Chinese and Japanese children in the same age group were enrolled.

Further Attempts to Educate the Disadvantaged

INDIAN CHILDREN AND YOUTH: Earliest of the disadvantaged, the American Indians had not yet achieved either assimilation into the population or a satisfactory program of education for their children by mid-twentieth century. Until the Civil War they had the unique disadvantage of being considered citizens of quasi-independent nations, outside the responsibility of the United States. The policy change in 1862, when the Indians became wards of the government and as such were transported to reservations, only ushered in a more painful period.

Official concern for Indian education dates only from 1889, when the Commissioner of Indian Affairs set forth several principles of educational policy, among these that Indians must be prepared for assimilation through compulsory education, and "must conform to the white man's ways, peaceably if they will, forceably if they must."[13]

The study of Indian affairs by the Institute for Government Research, published in 1928 and popularly known as the Merriam Report,[14] was perhaps the first significant turning point in Indian education. The report described the tragedy of the land allotment system, which had deprived the Indian of so much of his economic land base that it forced continued dependence upon the federal government. It described the antiquated teaching methods in the federal boarding schools, the regimented life, the severe and punitive discipline, and the exploitation of even the very young Indian children for institutional labor.

As a result of the Merriam report, the focus on Indian education shifted from off-reservation boarding schools to day schools on the reservations, within the Indian community. However, funds were extremely limited and school facilities were primitive and inadequate. Much emphasis was placed upon the "civilization" of the Indian and the teaching of English. Assimilation of the Indians was to be fostered through federal agents on the reservations, to help the tribes adjust to farming and reservation life, and through education. The incongruence between segregation and assimilation did not seem to be recognized by the authors of the policy. Not until 1924 did the Indians finally gain citizenship.

In 1934, as an outgrowth of the Merriam Report, Congress passed the Indian Reorganization Act, incorporating many of the policies of Commissioner John Collier. James Officer lists four major objectives of the Collier program:

1. Give the Indians a greater sense of participation in the school program.
2. Modify the curriculum of the Indian schools so that it better serves the educational needs of the students.

3. Encourage, rather than discourage, pride among Indians in their native accomplishments.
4. Provide Indian Service teachers with special training which will enable them to understand better the Indians they are teaching.[14]

Officer identifies eight changes that occurred in Indian education as a result of the implementation of these four aims. The eighth concerned teacher education:

In-service training programs were begun for Indian Bureau teachers. These training programs, held during the summer months, offered courses in tribal government, Indian language, Indian art, history, and other subjects closely connected with the work of an Indian Bureau teacher.[15]

The in-service training programs have been continued up to the present time by the Bureau of Indian Affairs. However, in some cases they have emphasized orientation to the Bureau as an organization rather than orientation to the teaching of the Indian child.

Before World War II nearly all educational efforts for the Indian had centered on the federal school. Mission schools, which had been a large contributor to Indian education before the Johnson-O'Malley Reorganization Act of 1934, were held back in their efforts by the provisions of this act against compulsory religious training and the interpretations given to the intent of these provisions by officials of the Bureau in the field. Mission schools like Ganado Mission (Presbyterian) on the Navajo Reservation, or St. John's Mission (Catholic) on the Pima, and many others, have made important contributions to the quality of education on Indian reservations and to the development of techniques for teaching the Indian child.

Although its full effect was not felt until after World War II, the Johnson-O'Malley Act of 1934 provided the means for the development of public school education on the Indian reservations. This act provided federal funds for the education of Indian children in the public schools through the state departments of public instruction or the school districts. This law, along with Public Laws 815 and 874, made it possible to set up public school districts on Indian reservations, build public school plants, and operate them largely with federal funds while retaining local district control. Funds for Indian education were also made available to the public schools in surrounding communities, and arrangements were made to house many Indian children in dormitories in towns near the reservations and send them to the local public schools. For many Indian children this was their first experience in integration.

A fact of great significance that emerged from this growing concern with the education of Indian children before the end of World War II is that the problem was approached from the viewpoint of improving facilities, changing the locations of schools, redesigning the curriculum for the students, and attempting to involve the parents in education. Very little attempt was made to change the education of teachers who were to teach Indian children and youth. Aside from the few in-service courses provided by the Bureau of Indian Affairs, there were no courses taught or special programs set up in teachers colleges or university departments of education to prepare teachers specifically to teach Indian children.

HISPANOS—THE SPANISH-SPEAKING AMERICANS: The history of the Hispanos is an interesting parallel to that of the Indians. In the western part of the country, Latin Americans constitute one of the largest and least assimilated ethnic groups. This multigroup minority includes descendants of very early settlers living in areas taken over from Mexico, a mixture of Spanish-speaking and Indian peoples, and more recent immigrants from Mexico and other Latin American countries. The oldest of these groups is the Hispanos, of mixed racial parentage—Spanish and Indian—whose history dates back to the days of the Spanish conquest. Because the Southwest had been their traditional home for four centuries, they became Americans by acquisition when the southwestern territories were ceded to the United States after the Mexican War of 1846–1848. Their life patterns still mirror the style of Old Mexico.[16]

Between the turn of the century and the end of World War I more than a million Mexicans emigrated to the United States as laborers, many of them becoming migratory workers. Half a million of these Mexicans remained in the United States and so their children became citizens by birth. Prejudices against the darker-skinned Spanish-speaking people blocked the path to American-style success. The slums of southwestern cities filled with the immigrants. For these residents, education was available in slum schools but economic conditions and attitudes of alienation kept many parents from seeing that their children took advantage of this minimal education. For the Spanish-speaking Americans who were migrant workers, education for their children was not only minimal, it was constantly interrupted by the moves the families made in following the crops.

The plight of these immigrants was complicated by economic fears of American laborers, leading to further prejudice and discrimination. This was aggravated by the entry into the United States of illegal immigrants, the "wetbacks," who swam or waded the Rio Grande from Mexico to work at starvation wages, undercutting the legal immigrants' opportunities for employment, stability, and education. The *braceros*, Mexican immigrant workers legally under contract to agricultural or industrial employers, constituted another kind of economic threat to the legal immigrants. The *braceros* were coming to the United States only to earn money quickly so as to return with it at once to a country with a lower standard of living. This situation made *braceros* willing to accept a lower wage scale and, again, undercut the job opportunities for Mexican-American residents.

Children from these groups snatched whatever education they could, usually in the poorest schools in the district, which were staffed with teachers who had no apparent preparation for teaching children with a Spanish language and tradition. Thus the lack of emphasis on teacher education for working with this group of children and youth roughly parallels the deficiencies in teacher preparation for working with Indians.

CHILDREN OF AGRICULTURAL WORKERS: Negroes, Indians, and Spanish-speaking groups were not the only ones who received inadequate educational opportunities during the first half of the twentieth century. Part of the American tradition is high mobility of the population. This country was settled by the restless and the adventurous, by the pioneer moving westward, seeking new land and a new life. The trappers and the mountain men are good early examples of people for whom movement was a way of life. More recent immigrant groups have been impelled to mobility less by adventure than by self-preservation.

During the depression years of the 1930's countless families were driven from drought-ridden and worn-out farms in Oklahoma and

Arkansas. They headed west, hoping to find in the fertile valleys of California a chance to make a living. This internal migration was of unprecedented size in American history. The newcomers, lacking money to buy or rent homes, camped on and lived off the land. For the most part, education was neglected by the local authorities, who did not have room in the schools for the newcomers or tax money to build and staff new schools; and by the migrants themselves, to whom the extra hands of children in the fields and orchards represented more pay.

As the depression ended and war production began, some of the migrants found jobs in industry, becoming permanent residents of West Coast states. Some of them, through personal disorganization, disease, or defeat, dropped out of the labor market and onto the relief rolls. A percentage remained migrant workers, however, forming the nucleus, along with Mexican-Americans, of present-day migrants who follow the needs of the crops.

The education of migrant children is at best disorganized. Although the need for migrant workers at certain times of the year is great and the economy depends on them, in general they are not welcome and their arrival in a town is looked upon only as an invasion offering an opportunity for the store owners and restaurant and garage operators to exploit them. In most communities some effort is made to provide temporary schooling for the children. Since compulsory education laws vary from state to state, and since it is difficult to keep records on so mobile a population, there are often gaps in the education of these children which are never closed.

Prior to 1960 teachers colleges did not offer special courses for preparing teachers to meet the needs of these migrant children. The teacher was left to cope with the sudden influx, and equally sudden disappearance, of these children as best he could. For the most part they represented so many names added to his register for a brief while, and he could summon no specific guidance from his college preparation to help him determine the needs they brought with them.

Other disadvantaged agricultural workers existed in the country who were not migrant workers. Throughout the first half of the century in rural areas, particularly in the southern and border states, remnants of the class system of education prevailed, affecting both the marginal white and Negro farmers. Rural public schools consistently paid lower salaries to their teachers than did urban schools. In the southern and border states, which had historically paid lower salaries than the rest of the nation, the lower salary scale for rural teachers took on added significance. The least prepared teachers taught in these rural schools. Often such positions were filled by teachers with little or no academic preparation for teaching.

This situation produced marginal education for the children of poor white families, but the Negroes had a further handicap. The segregated schools serving Negro farm children were generally taught by Negro teachers who had previously attended segregated schools and who had been prepared for teaching in segregated colleges, instructed by Negro faculties who themselves were products of this same system. This cycle tended to perpetuate inadequate education for Negro children of agricultural workers.

Educating for Particular Needs

A famous and far-reaching attempt at reform in rural public education was made in the 1920's by Marie Turner Harvey in Missouri. A local school board hired Mrs. Harvey, an experienced country-school teacher, to rehabilitate its one-teacher school into a model of the best in rural education. This she proceeded to do over a period of 12 years. She began by securing community cooperation in rebuilding the schoolhouse and a cottage for herself so that she would not have to "board around" with local families. Lawrence Cremin relates how she developed a completely new curriculum integrating the work of the students with the life of the community. The school became as much a learning and social center for the neighborhood adults as it was for the children. The experiment was publicized through a book by Evelyn Dewey, NEW SCHOOLS FOR OLD. Mrs. Harvey was asked to join the faculty of Northeast Missouri State Teachers College, where her theories concerning rural education were incorporated into the curriculum. Graduates of this program were influential in its further dissemination throughout the Midwest.[17]

Another example of reform in education, this one in a city system, was started in Denver and spread rapidly throughout the country. It took the form of the development of curricula by a new method, initiated by Jesse H. Newlon, superintendent of the Denver school system. He shared "the standard progressive belief that it was the responsibility of public schools to serve all comers, and that to do so required drastic curricular adjustments in terms of changing social circumstances."[18] This commitment to universal education, coupled with a profound faith in the average classroom teacher, led to the institution of teacher-staffed system-wide curriculum committees to devise a completely new curriculum relevant to the needs of all the children in the schools.

The process of curriculum reform, involving successive committees of teachers, was lengthy and thorough but eventually culminated in revised syllabi that were published as the Denver Research Monograph Series. These were bought by many school systems in other countries as well as throughout the United States. At the end of five years of experimentation, Dr. Newlon was appointed director of the Lincoln School at Teachers College, Columbia University, a position from which he was able to influence more directly the preparation of teachers, rather than to affect teacher performance solely at the in-service level.

Extension of the Educational Ladder

While similar experiments in education were taking place, the ladder of American education was extending in both directions. The concept of kindergartens as the first rung had become firmly established by 1918. At that time a biennial survey of education reported that of 4.5 million American children between the ages of 4 and 6, approximately 10.4 percent attended kindergarten. This percentage increased over the next thirty years until it had risen to 89 per cent by 1950.

Higher on the ladder the junior high schools were becoming established. In the same report of 1918 the Bureau of Education estimated that there were 577 junior high schools in the nation, with more than

116,000 students enrolled. The organization of junior high schools, to meet the particular needs of the early adolescent and to provide a bridge from elementary school to high school, continued.

During the same period there was a movement to establish more high schools. By 1918 there were 25,000 high schools with an attendance of over 1,600,000 youths. These high schools offered two programs: the terminal program aimed at vocational training and the classical program providing preparation for continued study in colleges. These were generally offered in the same building for economic reasons. It was only in the large cities that there was a tendency to make available high schools serving different functions to differing segments of the community. At first the teachers in the high schools were holders of college degrees in the subject they taught, with little preparation in teacher education. As high schools increased in number, teachers colleges began developing courses specifically for the preparation of high school teachers. In a similar way the teachers colleges responded to the need for preparing teachers of kindergartens through the development of specific early childhood programs.

Changes in Teacher Education

The expansion of educational opportunity in American life during the past 50 years has brought changes in teacher education, which has become increasingly specialized in preparation for the various grade levels and for the special requirements of the handicapped or exceptional child, and has increasingly differentiated between rural and urban teaching as a central focus. These changes were direct outgrowths of the following factors: the phenomenal growth of education in the period following World War I, when each successive year more children spent more time in a wider variety of schools; the diversity of children to be educated; and the experimentation in education, which was related to the progressive movement. Another factor was the progress made toward centralization of schools. In 1920 there were 200,000 local school districts, but after that time the number declined with consolidation, so that individual schools were able both to afford better programs and to demand better prepared teachers. Yet another factor was the increased attention to the needs of children and youth—an outgrowth of the development of educational psychology and the child study movement. This innovation stands as the unique contribution of teacher education during the first fifty years of the century.

Certain patterns clearly emerge from the history of teacher education that are relevant to the preparation of teachers for working with disadvantaged children and youth. Chief among these is the proclivity of the schools to start with the needs of the people living at the time. Teacher education then follows by attempting to prepare teachers to educate people according to their needs. A second noticeable pattern is the tendency of educators to "experiment with children" and to "experiment with the taxpayer's money"[19] in the public schools before changes are made in teacher education.

It is because of these trends that the preparation of teachers for working with disadvantaged children and youth has to be examined in historical perspective. Without an awareness of these developments the changes of the past 15 years cannot be clearly understood.

CURRENT TRENDS

Implementing Universal Educational Opportunity

Despite the signs of educational ferment reflected by the changing programs for teacher education in the first half of the twentieth century, and despite the enormous strides made toward seeing that almost every American child attended schools and learned to read and write, it became increasingly apparent that Americans were not satisfied with the education their children were receiving.

The technological and material advances that combined after World War II to produce the highest standard of living in the world for the majority of Americans threw into sharp relief the discrepancy between what the many could enjoy and what was obtainable by the poor.

Admittedly there has always been poverty in the United States. During the depression of the 1930's it was the common lot to be poor. After World War II, however, the rising cost of living created much sharper distinctions between the poor and the middle class.

Before the depression of the 1930's, poverty for white persons had been closely related to immigrant status. Generally the European immigrants brought with them to their new country high aspirations, a strong family unit, and a strong cultural heritage that provided ego support and a sense of identity. These assets enabled them to make the transition to new ways of life in one or two generations. The Negroes, who had been imported into America, were systematically stripped of their family unity, their identity—personal and cultural—and their aspirations, as a process of enslavement. Therefore they were unable to make a successful transition.

Significant immigration ended after the second World War. Replacing it were two new phenomena: an explosive birthrate and a gigantic increase in internal migration. These factors called for sharp increase in the number of teachers to be educated and in the number of schools to be erected to accomodate the expanding child population. The educational efforts of the early fifties were directed first of all toward meeting these quantitative needs.

The war had the effect on minority groups of increasing their awareness that they were being called upon to assume the responsibilities of citizenship while being denied access to the benefits enjoyed by the majority of Americans. Equality in educational opportunity was a major goal in securing their rights. In 1954 the Sweatt decision of the United States Supreme Court opened all state-operated graduate schools to Negroes, including graduate schools of education. Three years later in the *Brown v. Board of Education of Topeka* decision, Chief Justice Earl Warren wrote, ". . . in the field of public education, the doctrine of 'separate but equal' has no place." Major precedents were set for change.

An international incident—the launching by Russia of the first man-made satellite on October 4, 1957,—focused national attention on the quality of education being provided in American schools. The resulting criticism extended to the field of teacher education and preparation of teachers for working with disadvantaged children and youth.

Changes in the Preparation of Teachers for Work with the Disadvantaged

The intensive criticism of the schools came from all segments of the nation and affected all levels of schooling, from kindergarten through schools of teacher education. The educational community also examined its achievements critically and, after evaluation and analysis, began to seek ways to bring about improvements. According to Harry Rivlin, Dean of Teacher Education, City University of New York,

> The major responsibility for educational change rests with the education profession. We do not have to discuss whether we should accept this responsibility, for, if we do not accept it, others will. If the education profession is not capable of accepting the responsibility for educational change, it is no profession, regardless of how many resolutions are passed declaring it is.

He proceeded in the same paper to explore ten areas in education which needed the attention of the profession. In highly abridged form these may be summarized as follows:

1. The ending of segregated schools and the opening of schools and colleges to all, equally, which means discovering and developing talents in children that were not fully cultivated previously, without disruption in learning for any children.
2. Educating children in large cities who have less educational background and sometimes less academic ambition than children formerly enrolled in these schools, through changes in curriculum, changes in methods of teaching, and changes in the organization of schools.
3. Learning ways to prepare teachers to educate children who do not wish to be educated and finding ways to prevent children from dropping out of school.
4. Devising ways to implement change for more and better education of all children without bankrupting the community that has to pay for it.
5. Learning how to make a career in education competitive with other careers which offer more money, increasing the supply of teachers and learning how to get along with fewer thoroughly prepared teachers.

6. Deciding how to make curricula relevant to the learner; finding answers to the perennial problem of what we should teach to whom and how it should be taught.
7. Recognizing education as a major line of defense; seeing that federal support, as through the National Defense Education Act, really does improve education and strengthen national defense.
8. Understanding a massive upgrading process to produce people to fill jobs which truly exist; not the unskilled and semiskilled jobs which are being automated out of existence.
9. Learning to develop a dialog between parents of school children (including the disadvantaged) and the profession, so that both groups can communicate their goals to each other.
10. Responding to pressure for increased educational efficiency in ways which really improve the effectiveness of what it is that our students are learning and becoming, without sacrificing quality.[20]

The profession undertook a massive program to improve teacher education through a wide variety of institutions. In-service training programs were started in schools for teachers already in the field. Institutes for advanced education of teachers were sponsored by educational institutions and supported by federal funds. Experimental programs, with teacher education components in the schools, were mutually sponsored by local school systems and colleges of education. Some teachers education institutions began offering courses on both the undergraduate and the graduate level in teaching the disadvantaged.

Identifying the Disadvantaged

Before steps could be taken to prepare teachers to improve the education of disadvantaged children and youth, these children had to be defined and identified. In 1964 the legal definition in Public Law 88-665, section 1101, of "culturally, economically, socially, and educationally handicapped" was interpreted to mean children from families outside the mainstream of American culture; or whose circumstances of poverty precluded their taking advantage of educational opportunities; or who have been discriminated against by American society; or who for external reasons have not been able to develop their potential. Such children could be found in the crowded inner-city schools, in rural schools, and in suburban schools where *de facto* segregation existed.

The disadvantaged children and youth of the inner city were generally in-migrants: Negroes moving from southern rural regions to the cities of the North and West; Puerto Ricans migrating from the islands to the mainland urban areas; Appalachian whites going to mid-American cities. The rural disadvantaged were the Indians who remained on reservations; Spanish-speaking Americans living on ranches and farms in the Southwest and West or migrating from farm to farm; and poor whites on isolated, worn-out farms. The common denominators are poverty, discrimination, and defeat.

Some of these groups have been discussed in previous sections. Two additional groups are noted here because they have emerged as major disadvantaged groups within the past fifteen years.

THE RURAL-TO-URBAN MIGRANT—Aside from the migrant worker who follows the crops, the American population encompasses a significant number of internal migrants. These are primarily the people being displaced from the rural community because of increased automation in farming and the change from small, family-run farms to larger, mechanized farms that are operated as big business. Internal migration has involved 10 percent of the population since the end of World War II.

As an example of this group, migrants from Appalachia come to the cities in the late fall, hoping to find employment during the winter that will give them enough extra money to go back home and live through the summer. The leap from the eighteenth century culture of the mountains to the twentieth century culture of the large cities produces culture shock, often followed by apathy and alienation. Hilda Taba makes this statement about the educational implications of such culture shock on children:

The problem of acculturation is more difficult for the minority children, for in their case the problems of isolation, language, conduct, and the difficulties with content coverage are multiplied. Elam describes cases resulting in a total inability to respond . . . the consequences of acculturation shock which causes them to cease responding altogether. They evade the responsibility because to function is to fail. The safest thing is not to respond at all. Milder cases are observed in which children 'tune out' when directions are given.[21]

Some inner-city teachers in centers like Cincinnati, St. Louis, Chicago, and Toledo are learning new methods to reach and then to teach these in-migrant children through in-service training programs set up by the individual school systems.

Some urban Negroes are in-migrants. Outside the South, economic and social conditions force Negroes into *de facto* segregation, which affects their educational opportunities. The concept of neighborhood schools coupled with segregated housing brings about the following results, according to Michael Harrington:

Housing is perhaps the most crucial element in racial poverty. As long as Negroes and other minorities are segregated into neighborhoods, the impact of all civil rights legislation is softened. It is possible to have a public school policy for integrated schooling, but if the school districts are themselves a product of residential discrimination, the schools will continue to be Jim Crow.[22]

Caught in the vicious circle of segregated, inferior housing, inadequate education, and low-paying service jobs, Negroes, after nearly 350 years of life in America, in general, retain the self-image of a low-status, nonproductive people, defeated and alienated.

In mid-twentieth century the civil rights movement has effectively demonstrated to the country that most Negroes are not willing to move "with all deliberate speed" toward school integration. The answer, in the nation outside the South, has been to look at school organization and districting. Bussing of children from ghetto schools to integrated or all-white schools has been attempted. District lines have been redrawn to integrate existing schools. New school complexes are being built on the edges of the ghettoes. The concept of the neighborhood school is being retained in some areas only for the earliest grades, and a 4-4-4 plan is replacing the 6-3-3 ratio in order to make earlier integration possible. Methods of assigning teachers to schools are being examined to assure that all schools will have a complement of quality staff.

Services in ghetto schools and in schools with a high percentage of Negro children are being increased. School boards are implementing remediation by increasing staff. They are redesigning curriculum to include Negro history and culture. Studies of learning styles and patterns are being made. Testing for intelligence and achievement is undergoing rethinking and revision in order to increase validity for cultural subgroups. Textbooks are being published with interracial illustrations and an interracial approach, to give Negro children a healthy, more positive self-identification. The education of teachers and other school personnel to meet the needs of Negro children has had the increasing attention of many local and state systems, and unprecedented financial support from the federal government.

The present forward thrust to improve education for disadvantaged Negro children is dominant because of the force of protest. Already it has had far-reaching effects in the education of other disadvantaged groups.

THE PUERTO RICANS—The Puerto Ricans are a unique minority since they are United States citizens coming to the States as inmigrants, although they are treated like immigrants when they enter the large American cities. Glazer and Moynihan sum up the Puerto Rican's relationship with his home island and his migrant status:

> The links between the New York Puerto Rican and the island are close and complex, and quite different from the relationship earlier migrant groups had to their homelands. Puerto Rico is part of the United States and there is no control over movement between the island and the mainland. Puerto Rico is brought relatively close by air, and air passage is not too expensive. One index of movement is entries into and withdrawals from New York public schools. In 1958-1959, 10,600 children were transferred from Puerto Rican schools, and 6,500 were released to go to school in Puerto Rican schools. Going back is not, as it was in earlier migrations, the return of someone who has made a small competence that will look big in the homeland, although there is more and more of this movement. Going back is too easy for it to have such great significance.[23]

The inadequate schools in the ghetto areas to which Puerto Ricans migrate compound the problems Puerto Rican children face in getting a good education. Some of their problems are based in their difficulties with learning a new language. The New York City Board of Education reports, "On October 31, 1958, of the 558,741 children in our elementary schools, there were 56,296 children of Puerto Rican ancestry whose lack of ability to speak or understand English represented a serious handicap to learning."

Several theories have been advanced explaining the slow rate of language assimilation. One suggests that the attitude of the schools in Puerto Rico toward teaching English has been ambivalent. English is required in schools there, but little agreement exists about when English should be started and how much time should be devoted to teaching it. Another theory sugggests that the freedom Puerto Ricans have to come and go from their homeland makes them less willing to make the effort to become proficient in a second language. Other theories are that darker Puerto Ricans tend to cling to the Spanish language in order to differentiate themselves from the Negro minority and to escape some of the discrimination that results from being mistaken for a Negro. Another hypothesis suggests that the adolescent male Puerto Rican, who retains the highly developed sense of masculine pride from his Island-Spanish culture, does not attempt English, when his speech might be imperfect or accented, for fear of exposing himself to ridicule.[24] Glazer and Moynihan state,

> We can only speculate about the reason why Jews and Italians coming into the city at roughly the same ages, with much less formal knowledge of English, should have made a rather better linguistic adjustment. Of course, in the years of the heaviest Jewish and Italian migration, the school-leaving age was much lower, children often began working at 12, and the problems that the schools face today (which are severer with older children) were reduced. In other words, the children who could not learn English 40 years ago got out before the problem became too noticeable. But we can only guess at the difference—no one seems to have gone back to see what schools did when whole districts were filled with Yiddish-speaking and Italian-speaking children.[25]

Hilda Taba suggests that perhaps one reason for the failure of inmigrant children is a form of culture shock that teachers are not trained to recognize. Therefore, they do not try to mediate between the old and the new culture.[26] In New York City, which becomes the home of three-fifths of the Puerto Ricans who reach the United States, the school system is attempting to remedy this situation—for example, through publication and distribution to teachers of social studies curriculum supplements that relate life as it is lived in Puerto Rico to life lived in the city. In-service courses in Spanish are offered to teachers. Departments of Education in local universities have started programs to place student teachers in ghetto schools so that they can have first-hand experience working with Spanish-speaking children.

In these examples the established pattern can be seen repeating itself. The problem is identified; the first attempts at remedy are made by the local school systems that face the problem, which leads ultimately to changes in teacher education. The development of programs for educating teachers of Indians on reservations is the final example of this trend.

THE INDIANS—Because of the widely differing cultural backgrounds and value systems of the Indian child and the typical middle class teacher, education has been a difficult path for the Indian to follow. He has found that all too often it is the Indian who is expected to do all the changing to conform to the values of the teacher, the schools, and the community. It has frequently been difficult for him to maintain his identity and ego strength under these conditions. Many educated Indians regard their less educated tribesmen as "those" Indians —as though they were a completely different group. And yet the man who reflects this prejudice will often admit a longing for the values he has tried to leave behind, and a desire to reclaim his Indian identity.

Partially in recognition of these problems and partially from a desire to increase the more tangible results of the educational process (e.g., reading ability and language and mathematics skills), special training for teachers working with Indians has been markedly increased in the past few years. The Bureau of Indian Affairs has extended its in-service and preservice training programs and has sought to increase the depth analysis of the teaching process as it relates to the Indian child. A summer training program is held each year in Brigham City, Utah, for Bureau personnel. In addition, in-service workshops are encouraged at the agency or subagency level. Unfortunately, spokesmen for the Bureau of Indian Affairs admit, an understanding-in-depth of the processes of interaction with the Indian child is seldom achieved.

Many colleges and universities conduct workshops and courses during the summer months that attempt to relate the cultural background of the Indian child to teaching methods and an understanding of his personality dynamics. Some of these courses have utilized the knowledge and skills of experienced teachers of Indians and the interpretations of the trained psychologist and anthropologist, as well as the newer media available in recent years. Others have been taught pedantically by instructors whose only contact with the Indian child has been through the pages of a book. Nearly all such inadequately prepared instructors have lacked insight in depth into the mind and life of the Indian.

A recent review of college and university catalogs indicates 17 specific Indian education courses offered by four institutions, with related courses of value to the teacher of the Indian child offered by approximately 12 other institutions in the West. In addition, several institutions list departments or staff in the Indian Affairs or Indian Education areas but no course for the teacher of the Indian child. In 1962, G. D. McGrath, R. A. Roessel, *et al.*, listed courses and ongoing research activities in 12 southwestern institutions.[26] At the present time 15 states have departments of Indian education or have designated officials to work in this area. A systematic and objective start has been made in the preparation of teachers to work in schools serving disadvantaged Indian children and youth.

As was to be expected, the college and university courses in teacher education preparatory to working with Indian children and youth are located in states with a high proportion of Indians, just as programs of teacher preparation for work with the inner-city child are located in urban areas. Martin Haberman notes that the system of teacher education is built on the historical assumption that programs should be determined separately, institution by institution, and should be geared specifically to the population to be served. The implication is that teacher preparation for working with disadvantaged children and youth is not a separate discipline, but that the content changes according to the population to be served. A teacher prepared to work with West Coast migrant children might not be equally effectively prepared to teach urban in-migrants or Appalachian children.

Recent Trends in Teacher Education

Teacher education programs for preparing school personnel to work with disadvantaged children and youth have been heavily oriented toward the sociological and anthropological aspects of the group ultimately to receive the education. The teacher being prepared is usually different from the children culturally, economically, or socially, and often in all these ways. Yet it is a basic premise that new understandings of the culture of the particular disadvantaged group are necessary if the teacher is to bridge the gap from the home culture of his students to the school culture and the culture of the larger society.

Because the teacher of the disadvantaged, typically, does not share a common cultural background with his students, and because he has middle class values which his students have not acquired, it is assumed that he may have attitudes which form a barrier to his acceptance of his students, a barrier to which they may react negatively. Many programs, then, are designed to change the attitudes of the teacher toward the disadvantaged. These affective aspects of the programs, however, are difficult to evaluate. William Kvaraceus in NEGRO SELF CONCEPT states:

> One rather significant finding, however, which we can be somewhat sure about, is the fact that education has relatively little impact on attitudes and behavior. Coleman's study of adolescent society, Jacobs' study of college education, and the research reported by Sanford indicate that most students enter schools, whether it be high school or college, and leave it without any visible change except that they are four years older.

He continues:

> Some are changed, true, but only, as Jacobs points out, when the total collegiate atmosphere is consistent and pressing or, as Sanford indicates, due to the particular personality of the particular person. In almost any instance, however, the change is to produce more of the same; that is, the intellectual becomes more intellectual, the nonconformist becomes more deviant, the conservative more entrenched in conservatism. The school serves to reinforce what is already present.

If this is true, the standard approach to classroom instruction cannot achieve desired change in attitude because the standard approach tends to reinforce the student's self-concept. Kvaraceus concludes:

> Therefore we would propose a new approach. We would suggest that the utilization of the idea of deliberate effort to change the self-concept of students (in educational courses) will appreciably affect their total education as well as their personal experience.[27]

Bloom, Davis, and Hess suggest that a major change in the teacher's self-concept means a shift from his conception of himself as the operative agent in a status-giving and selective system to that of the operative agent in a system which develops each individual to his highest potential. These authors suggest that in order to accomplish this change, teacher education programs will have to shift their emphases. One such shift is teaching teachers how to place increased stress on the higher mental processes of problem solving rather than keep existing stress on information learning. Another places the emphasis on basic ideas, structure, and methods of inquiry rather than on amassing minutiae of subject matter. A third emphasis must be placed on learning how to learn. Additionally teachers must be taught how to develop disadvantaged children's interests, attitudes, and personality which will lead to their finding satisfaction in the things they do, bringing meaning and fulfillment to their lives.[28]

Much of the educational research and study of the past decade has been directed toward exploring the problems of the disadvantaged, their causes, and possible courses of remedial action. Frank Riessman in THE CULTURALLY DEPRIVED CHILD has made such a study and has identified the inductive learning style of disadvantaged children, which can be utilized by teachers to strengthen the learning-teaching process.

Different styles of teaching as well as of learning have been explored. David and Pearl Ausubel identified the maternal style of teaching the disadvantaged. "Teachers in segregated schools may also tend to be overly permissive and to emphasize play skills over academic achievement. They are perceived by their pupils as evaluating them negatively, and concerned with behavior rather than with school work."[29]

Jules Henry discusses the origin of the maternal style.

From where comes the belief that teachers should be parents? The answer is, from the circumstance that our children *do not have enough parents,* because parents are unable to do all that has to be done by parents nowadays. Two technologically driven parents are not enough for technologically driven children, and technological drivenness has made the two-parent family obsolete. The schoolteacher who acts like a parent is society's answer to the obsolescence of the two-parent family.[30]

Miriam L. Goldberg takes the position that no single teaching style can be effective with all students. She states, "Children from disadvantaged backgrounds, though highly variable, nevertheless represent a describable pupil population in need of teachers who are uniquely good for them."[31] She quotes Ryan (1963) in defining the dimensions of teacher style in terms of these continuums: from friendly-warm-understanding to aloof-restricted; and from stimulating-informative to dull-routine. Using Ryan's and others' research as a starting point, Goldberg develops a model of the hypothetical teacher who can successfully teach the disadvantaged, suggesting three attributes of the model which can be taught to teachers-in-training. They are (1) mastery of subject matter, (2) understanding of the major concepts of the behavioral and social sciences and their relevance to teaching disadvantaged children, (3) a repertoire of teaching strategies which hold promise for working with disadvantaged pupils.

To prepare such teachers adequately, Goldberg suggests the need for development of new courses, for an emphasis on laboratory experiences to develop emotional closeness, and for criteria to select candidates who will successfully adapt to teaching disadvantaged children and youth.

The discussion of learning styles and teaching styles is carried further by Elizabeth Gilkeson of Bank Street College of Education. In a paper delivered before a conference of NDEA institute directors at Tufts University in 1965 she recommended that teachers be educated to recognize their own teaching styles and children's learning styles and then to develop ways of making the two styles fit.

Teachers have to learn how to help children attain the skills and competencies that are not seen as important in their own cultures, according to Gilkeson, through the process of developing motivation for attaining new goals and aspirations. Such support for building the transition between the home culture and the school culture can be given the child by the teacher who learns how to—

1. Establish empathy with the child so that he knows how the child perceives his world and himself; recognizing the child's style of thinking, his stage of cognitive development, his attitude toward discovery, his fears and dependencies, and his skills and satisfactions.
2. Join a child at his own level in order to lead him out to maximum strengths and satisfactions; investing in his learning, and building in the child a positive self-image as well as trust in the adult teacher.
3. Develop a design of new experiences for the child to lead him to learn the modes of thinking and behaving necessary for his stages of development and for coping with his expanding world.[32]

For successful teaching the teacher must be taught to diagnose the learning needs of disadvantaged children and youth, to develop strategies for facilitating their learning, and to fit the strategy to the individual diagnosis. Such an approach to teacher education for working with disadvantaged children and youth relies heavily on clinical experiences for the teacher-in-training. Only through extensive, closely supervised practicums can such a combination of knowledge, understandings, and skills be developed.

The provision for clinical experiences with disadvantaged children and youth as a vital part of teacher education seems to be becoming a trend. Vernon Haubrich describes an early experiment sponsored by the City University of New York, Hunter College Department of Education. In Project 120, education majors volunteered for student teaching placement in disadvantaged inner-city schools, with the stipulation that, if successful, they would be given the opportunity to join the staff of the school in which they had worked. The Hunter experiment used a team approach that closely coordinated the work of master teachers, school administrators, and the student teachers under college supervision; and provided intensive community experiences to supplement the student teachers' in-school activities.[33]

Experiments similar to the Hunter project are being conducted throughout the country, demonstrating another trend in teacher education for work in disadvantaged schools. This is the increased cooperation between departments of education in colleges and universities with the local school systems. Such cooperation takes place on many levels, affecting teacher preparation, in-service training of teachers in the field, and continued learning on the part of the college faculties. Increased interchange of ideas and experiences between theorists and practitioners of education and the assumption of joint responsibility for the preparation of new teachers are in many localities a direct outgrowth of the programs developed to prepare teachers for working with disadvantaged children and youth.

Issues Raised in Preparing Teachers for Work with the Disadvantaged

As increased attention has been turned in the past few years toward educating teachers to work with disadvantaged children and youth, fundamental issues have been raised about what specifically should constitute this kind of education. First of all, there is the question of limiting the definition of *disadvantaged.* Many teachers have assumed that membership in a minority group constitutes in itself a state of disadvantage. The tendency to make this assumption has its roots in the convenience of applying labels to groups of people and of so labeling all persons within that group—in this instance, as disadvantaged. Such an approach is not only unrealistic, but damaging as well to the persons thus labeled.

William Stringfellow defines "disadvantaged" in terms of social deprivation:

> The Negro revolution is the eye of the hurricane, but it is not the whole storm. It is the most intense focus of contemporary social crises but that crisis involves many other citizens: all those who have . . . been cast off in America—all those for whom the promises of freedom and humanity and society remain unredeemed in America in the twentieth century.[34]

There are some special-interest agencies and groups that have for years been working to improve human relations in the society and in the schools. The National Conference of Christians and Jews, for example, has sponsored workshops and seminars designed to develop within teachers the ability to promote positive intergroup relations. However, not until comparatively recently have many teachers colleges and departments of education in the universities seen the need to incorporate such training into their programs and to develop effective means of implementing it. Gertrude Noar suggests that

> The teacher candidate needs to understand not only what makes the child tick but also what motivates himself. Somewhere, sometime, during his years in college, he should experience a self-confrontation. This may not be easy to arrange. It is likely to happen if study of the nature and genesis of prejudice is included in one or more courses. . . . There is no longer any doubt that the very nature of our culturally pluralistic society imposes on the college the necessity of so preparing teachers that they are free of irrational prejudices and can see their responsibility for helping children to become people free of racial, religious, and social class bias.[35]

Nevertheless, the majority of educators agree that freedom from prejudice and the development of understanding of the disadvantaged children provide only a partial answer to the educational needs of these teachers. Specifically differentiated skills for teaching disadvantaged children and youth have to be developed. Repertoires of strategies, techniques, and materials for the practical implementation of new insights into teaching behavior have to be taught if the teacher is to be able to structure the learning-teaching situation so that the disadvantaged child can truly develop to his highest potential.

In order for these strategies, techniques, and materials to be evolved, further questions have to be answered about the nature of disadvantage. Currently at issue are such questions as: should the disadvantaged child be expected to learn as much as the middle class child? Should he be required to learn the same kinds of things? Martin Deutsch has identified differences in the home environment of the disadvantaged preschool child which contribute to gaps in his cognitive map that render him less able to cope with the learning situation when he gets into the classroom. Some of these environmental deficiencies are: a minimum of visual stimuli (few pictures in the home—furniture, toys, and utensils that are few in number and lacking in variety of form and color), lack of varied manipulative materials, and exclusion from stimulating encounters with natural phenomena that were available to poor children in previous eras. Further, Deutsch points out, the slum home tends not to be verbally oriented, causing difficulties in the child's auditory discrimination. Nor does the slum home provide extended training in memory, expectations of rewards for performances, or recognition by the child of adults as a source of information, corrective feedback, and reality testing.[36]

The lack of opportunity for learning in the slum home has serious implications for learning ability in the school. The researches of Piaget and Hunt tend to show that learning depends upon a heirarchical system of prerequisite learning, and the lack of this learning during the early developmental stages causes a deficit which the teachers of disadvantaged children must develop strategies to overcome. Deutsch suggests a kinesthetic approach as one useful technique. The use of the Montessori materials and techniques, or similar techniques geared to developmental learning, are other approaches that teachers might usefully learn.

Some educators, basing their theories on Deutsch's findings, tend to classify most disadvantaged children as nonverbal. Basil Bernstein studied differences in language development between the lower and middle classes and has hypothesized that entirely different language systems exist within each of these classes. The language of the lower classes he characterized as "restricted"—made up of short, grammatically simple sentences that are condensed and limiting, containing symbols of a low order and generality. The middle classes use an "elaborated" language, more accurate and grammatically correct, which is precise and can express a wide range of thought. Bernstein suggests that the differences in language systems between these two segments of society can cause a failure in understanding as individuals attempt to communicate between the two classes.[37] Teachers therefore have to understand the "restricted" language of disadvantaged children and to construct situations that will enable these children to develop the use and understanding of the "elaborated" system. This can be accomplished when the disadvantaged children are recognized, not as nonverbal but as verbally different.

The home environment of disadvantaged children and youth is seen by educators as exerting other influences on the child's ability to learn in school. The current trend seems to be to explore as many avenues as possible that could lead to the teacher's getting to know the home life of the child. Home visits, field trips in the neighborhood of the school, Saturday morning trips to the laundromat in the school neighborhood to watch children and families interacting—are all techniques for observing the life conditions of disadvantaged children; parent conferences, in school or out, are encouraged. The danger here, some educators feel, is that the teacher may not bring to these encounters the highest form of professionalism, so that information gained through the use of such methods may be used for the benefit of the child's in-school learning.

Teacher education programs have to devise methods for developing within future teachers a professional approach to understanding disadvantaged pupils, according to Herbert R. Schueler:

> This requirement that the teacher understand his pupil extends beyond the classroom, for the behavior of each pupil is determined not alone by the social and psychological environment of the classroom but by what he is as a product of his own innate makeup and his interacting environment both in and out of school. The teacher, therefore, must understand his pupil and the social and familial forces that produced him and are continually shaping his development. . . . While this principle may seem self-evident, it becomes most crucial when the teacher is himself not a member of the economic and ethnic level of his students and therefore cannot use his own experience of growing up and living as a basis for understanding and communicating with his pupils.[38]

The teacher, according to Schueler, in his study of the home life of the children whom he teaches, must be careful to collect relevant, useful information free from value judgments based on his own experiences.

Another question in teaching disadvantaged children is whether they come to school ready to learn. The prevailing assumption is that due to gaps in their experiential background they do not. The question perhaps should be restated: Do children from disadvantaged backgrounds come to school ready to learn what the school has traditionally taught? If it is agreed that they do not, then there are alternative approaches to the problem. One is to bring the school and the child into contact at an earlier stage in his development and build a program to ready him for the traditional schooling. A second is to permit him to enter school at the normal age but to redesign the traditional program for early childhood in order to meet the needs of the entering disadvantaged child.

The need for redesigned programs is applicable to children in their middle school years as well, the period at the ages of 11 to 13 when children often begin to become alienated from school. It would seem that teachers need to be prepared to meet this situation and deal with it effectively, not merely through programs of remediation but by reshaping the existing program for the child so that it becomes relevant to his life and times.

Certain characteristics, then, emerge as fundamental to all education for disadvantaged children and to the preparation of teachers to work with them. The education offered to these children should be appropriate, relevant, and meaningful in order for the child to learn. It has been suggested that the teen-age boy who drops out of school may be showing more realism and more intelligence than a comparable boy who remains to finish the twelfth grade. Assuming both boys to be disadvantaged, and both to have been exposed to a high school education designed to prepare them for a society that is effectively closed to them, such analysis of their responses may be correct.

An unresolved issue in the education of disadvantaged children and youth is the question of hetrogeneous or homogeneous grouping. Teacher education programs generally stress the importance of child development and the need for an individualized approach to children's learning. However, the schools commonly group homogeneously. Various rationales are advanced for this practice: it permits children to work together at more nearly the same rate; it frees the teacher from the necessity of designing a variety of differentiated programs for many children; it is an administrative convenience. In a recent survey in a disadvantaged inner-city school, the staff of 40 teachers was asked by the principal which grouping for their classes they would prefer; 38 voted for homogenous grouping, stating as their chief reason that "it made teaching easier." This response might not have been so remarkable had it not occurred at the end of a faculty meeting on the subject of the needs of disadvantaged children.

Kenneth Clark suggests that the real harm in homogenous grouping is:

> . . . that these groupings tend to require that children be seen in terms of group characteristics rather than in terms of their individual characteristics. This would seem to be true equally for the bright children as it is for average or dull children. Furthermore, it is questionable whether it is possible to establish a homogenous group of children on any grounds other than the arbitrary selection of some single aspect of the total complexity which is the human being.[39]

Yet another issue relating to the education of teachers for disadvantaged children and youth is whether behavior change in teaching can come about in the absence of learning that has an experiential basis. This is a crucial question when programs are being designed for teachers of the disadvantaged. Should the program be heavily weighted toward the practicum and field experiences or can the learning process be facilitated best through lectures and reading followed by informed, in-depth discussions in small groups? The discussion used to center on how much of the process of preparing teachers to work with disadvantaged children and youth should be affective and how much should be cognitive.

However, a third concept has recently been introduced into the cognitive-affective debate. That component is action. Some educators have taken the position that there need be no dichotomy between affective-cognitive, but rather that these elements are mutually supportive in the learning process. Others have enlarged this viewpoint to include integration of affective, cognitive, and action components. Before these questions can be answered definitely, further study needs to be conducted.

The question whether preservice or in-service training is more effective has not yet been answered. At this point in time, when teachers are so urgently needed for work with disadvantaged populations, both courses must be pursued. Teachers without special preparation who are working in schools with disadvantaged children and youth need to be reeducated, while teacher candidates should be made aware of the possibilities of working in this area of education and be prepared to explore them.

Since the federal government has recently given such wide support to institutes sponsored by teachers colleges and university departments of education, it becomes important to determine how the institute approach to preparation can be developed in order to produce maximum results in the reeducation of teachers for working with disadvantaged children and youth. Is there an optimum size for an institute? What is the best ratio of staff to participants? What is the ideal length of an institute program—six weeks, eight weeks, one semester? (Or is it possible at all for a short-term institute to accomplish reeducation of a teacher for work with disadvantaged children? If so, to what degree?) Should the staff of an institute include representatives of the appropriate subculture? Should enrollees be integrated? Should the institute comprise an intensive, total experience for the enrollees, including residence at the institute? These are but a few of the questions to be answered.

Even though institutes and other programs have proliferated, it is extremely difficult to assess the extent to which teacher education institutions are involved in the preparation of teachers to work with disadvantaged children and youth. As recently as 1963 Bernard Asbell reported that only three departments of education in the entire nation offered a program designed to educate a teacher specifically to teach the disadvantaged.[40]

The study conducted by Project Aware in the summer and autumn of 1965 revealed that the situation has rapidly changed. One hundred and one school systems and 193 colleges and universities from every region of the nation responded to the survey, indicating that they were currently involved in programs related to some aspect of this kind of teacher education. Only six of the 101 school systems reported that they saw no need for such education and only 12 institutions of higher learning saw no need.

Specific programs reported in operation during the summer of 1965 included 89 school systems sponsoring in-service training programs, 61 NDEA institutes for preparation of school personnel to work with the disadvantaged, and 59 preservice programs in teacher education institutions. A total of 209 specific programs were identified by the Aware Study. The full extent and nature of these programs are amplified in Chapter 5 herein. Some of the issues raised above are referred to in the recommendations of the Project Aware Study in Chapter 7.

It is too early to predict whether the problems involved in the education of the disadvantaged will result in a totally new, or different, or separate teacher education program for preparation of school personnel to work with disadvantaged children and youth or whether existing programs will merely be changed by adding, subtracting, or modifying particular courses. From a historical perspective, as this chapter has demonstrated, it appears that teacher education programs tend to evolve through minor mutations related to the needs of time. The cumulative effect results in the eventual labeling of these mutations as new programs. However, it is no longer possible to rely for a prediction on the patterns of the past, since the recently introduced factor of massive federal support may facilitate more rapid change.

That start has been made. American society has recognized the problem. The educational institutions have begun diagnosis and treatment through the education of teachers specifically to teach disadvantaged children and youth. Although certain predictions cannot be made concerning the directions this preparation will take in the future, one fact stands out. The disadvantaged are not disappearing from the American scene. A Ford Foundation survey made in 1960 identified one-third of the urban school population as disadvantaged at that time. It was predicted that by 1970 half the learners in the city schools would be, by any reasonable definition, disadvantaged.[41]

References

1. Elwood P. Cubberly: PUBLIC EDUCATION IN THE UNITED STATES, Houghton Mifflin Company, Cambridge, 1962, p. 125.
2. *Ibid.*, p. 375.
3. R. Freeman Butts and Lawrence A. Cremin: A HISTORY OF EDUCATION IN AMERICAN CULTURE, Holt, Rinehart, & Winston, New York, 1953, p. 251.
4. Cubberly, *op. cit.*, p. 385.
5. Edward A. Sheldon: COURSE OF STUDY, Oswego Schools, 1859–1860.
6. E. P. Cubberly and E. C. Elliot: STATE AND COUNTY SCHOOL ADMINISTRATION SOURCE BOOK, The Macmillan Company, New York, 1915, p. 85.
7. Rush Welter: POPULAR EDUCATION AND DEMOCRATIC THOUGHT IN AMERICA, Columbia University Press, New York, 1962, p. 84.
8. Butts and Cremin, *op. cit.*, p. 449.
9. National Education Association: PROCEEDINGS (1886), p. 192.
10. Cubberly, *op. cit.*, p. 401.

11. Lawrence A. Cremin: THE TRANSFORMATION OF THE SCHOOL, Vantage Books, New York, 1961, p. 36.
12. *Ibid.*, p. 48.
13. U. S. Department of the Interior, Bureau of Indian Affairs: THE UNITED STATES INDIAN SERVICE, A Sketch of the Development of the Bureau of Indian Affairs and of Indian Policy. U.S. Government Printing Office, Washington, D.C. 1928, p. 49.
14. Lewis Merriam *et al.:* THE PROBLEM OF INDIAN ADMINISTRATION, The Johns Hopkins Press, Baltimore, 1928, p. 21.
15. *Ibid.*, p. 25.
16. Peter I. Rose: THEY AND WE, Random House, New York, 1964, p. 43.
17. Cremin, *op. cit.*, pp. 291–295.
18. *Ibid.*, p. 302.
19. *Ibid.*, p. 276.
20. Harry N. Rivlin: "The Profession's Responsibility for Educational Change," in CHANGES IN TEACHER EDUCATION, Official Report of the Columbus Conference, Eighteenth National TEPS Conference, The Ohio State University, Columbus, Ohio, June 25–28, 1963, National Education Association, Washington, D.C., 1964, p. 20.
21. Hilda Taba: "Cultural Deprivation as a Factor in School Learning," in EDUCATION IN DEPRESSED AREAS, Ed. A. Harry Passow, Teachers College, Columbia University, New York, 1963, p. 154.
22. Michael Harrington: THE OTHER AMERICA, Penguin Books, Inc. Baltimore, 1962, p. 79.
23. Nathan Glazer and Daniel Patrick Moynihan: BEYOND THE MELTING POT, The M.I.T. Press, Cambridge, 1963, p. 100.
24. Glazer and Moynihan, *op. cit.*, p. 127.
25. Clarence Senior: THE PUERTO RICANS, Quadrangle Books, Chicago, 1965, p. 39.
26. G. D. McGrath, R. A. Roessel, *et al.:* HIGHER EDUCATION OF SOUTHWESTERN INDIANS WITH REFERENCE TO SUCCESS AND FAILURE, Cooperative Research Project No. 938, Arizona State University Press, Tempe, Arizona, p. 10.
27. William Kvaraceus, *et al.:* NEGRO SELF-CONCEPT: IMPLICATIONS FOR SCHOOL AND CITIZENSHIP, McGraw-Hill Book Company, New York, 1965, p. 36.
28. Bloom, Davis, and Hess: COMPENSATORY EDUCATION FOR CULTURAL DEPRIVATION, Holt, Rinehart and Winston, New York, 1965, p. 2.
29. David P. and Pearl Ausubel: "Ego Development among Segregated Negro Children," in EDUCATION IN DEPRESSED AREAS, Ed. A. Harry Passow, Teachers College, Columbia University, New York, 1963, p. 124.
30. Jules Henry: CULTURE AGAINST MAN, Random House, New York, 1963, p. 312.
31. Miriam L. Goldberg: "Adapting Teacher Style to Pupil Differences:

Teachers for Disadvantaged Children," in MERRILL PALMER QUARTERLY, Vol. 10, No. 2, April 1964, pp. 161–177.
32. Elizabeth Gilkeson: "Is There a Mousetrap?" paper delivered at Conference of NDEA Institute Directors at Tufts University, Medford, Massachusetts, September 24, 1965.
33. Vernon F. Haubrich: "Teachers for Big-City Schools," in EDUCATION IN DEPRESSED AREAS, Ed. A. Harry Passow, Teachers College, Columbia University, New York, 1963, p. 247.
34. William Stringfellow: INTEGRATED EDUCATION, November 1964, p. 47.
35. Gertrude Noar: "The Times Call for Courage," in JOURNAL OF TEACHER EDUCATION, December 1964, p. 3.
36. Martin Deutsch: "The Disadvantaged Child and the Learning Process," in EDUCATION IN DEPRESSED AREAS, Ed. A. Harry Passow, Teachers College, Columbia University, New York, 1963, p. 170.
37. B. Bernstein: "Language and Social Class," in BRITISH JOURNAL OF PSYCHOLOGY, Vol. 11, September 1960, pp. 271–276.
38. Herbert R. Schueler: "Teachers and Resources for Urban Education," in OFFICIAL REPORT OF NATIONAL COMMITTEE ON TEACHER EDUCATION AND PROFESSIONAL STANDARDS, Washington, D.C., 1963, p. 228.
39. Kenneth B. Clark: "Education Stimulation of Racially Disadvantaged Children," in EDUCATION IN DEPRESSED AREAS, Ed. A. Harry Passow, Teachers College, Columbia University, New York, 1963, p. 152.
40. Bernard Asbell: "Not Like Other Children," in REDBOOK, October 1963.
41. State TEPS Chairmen and Consultants: "The Urban Associations' Responsibility for Recruitment, Preparation, and In-Service Education of Big City Teachers," in REPORT OF 13TH ANNUAL MEETING, National Education Association, Washington, D.C., 1965, p. 10.

Profiles of selected programs

CHAPTER 3

OFFICE OF ECONOMIC OPPORTUNITY PROGRAMS

The impact of Office of Economic Opportunity teacher education programs exceeded many expectations. Although relatively few participants were involved, the highly imaginative quality of the programs provided a new sense of direction amid the complexities and frustrations of the educational scene in the mid-sixties.

Fragmented planning and intergroup tensions are outward symptoms of a divisiveness that pervades the entire fabric of life in these United States. The Office of Economic Opportunity programs were addressed to one of the prime causal factors of this condition—lack of communication among the various groups and elements in our society. The programs selected for description here* dealt with various facets of this problem: lack of communication between colleges and school systems, public and parochial schools, teachers and parents, and also among various diverse groups in terms of ethnic and socioeconomic background.

In Nashville, Tennessee; Detroit, Michigan; Riverside, California; Boston, Massachusetts; Princeton, New Jersey; and Racine, Wisconsin, joint sponsorship of teacher education programs demonstrated the feasibility and the value of such cooperation.

In Tempe, Arizona, and Boston, Massachusetts, teacher-aides of different ethnic backgrounds were prepared to assist and supplement the task of teachers in the classrooms. They provided far more than technical help for the professional. Frequently coming from the same ethnic background or social class as the pupils, these teacher aides

* These summaries are based upon (1) the sponsoring agency's plan of operation, (2) the director's final report, and (3) the Aware Team's Report.

provided a link between the school and the disadvantaged child, strengthening the child's self-image in the process. The aides themselves gained in self-confidence and stature because they were functioning in a new and constructive role.

The dynamics of intercommunication were demonstrated at many levels in Riverside, California, where teachers, parents, school dropouts, and high school students served as co-panelists in interpreting the needs and frustrations of the youth of today to the teachers of tomorrow. A unique feature of this program was the appointment of a prison inmate among the school dropouts as a teaching assistant. This youth commuted from jail to class, communicating the negative reactions of disadvantaged youth to their rejection by today's economy with a vividness no lectures or readings could convey.

The brief summaries of representative OEO programs presented here attest to the vision and yet the essential practicality of the approaches. Sometimes hastily conceived and not uniformly strong in organization, these programs nevertheless seemed to contain three essential ingredients: a clear sense of direction, willingness to experiment, and true commitment to the stated goals.

TEACHER-AIDE TRAINING PROGRAM: ARIZONA STATE UNIVERSITY, TEMPE, ARIZONA

As acculturation continues to take place, there has been a change in the aspirations of some American Indian groups. What had appeared to some scholarly observers to be a reluctant acceptance of alien value systems has begun to shift to a reaching out for the techniques and training of the wider culture that will help the Indian become aware of the potentiality of life in the larger society, while at the same time permitting him to strengthen his own cultural traditions.

An excellent example of this movement is the Teacher-Aide Training Program instituted this past summer at Tempe, Arizona, by the Arizona State University and its Indian Training Center. Here, members of four tribes, the Maricopa, the Navajo, the Sioux, and the Pima, met together for eight weeks in residence to receive preparation that would enable them to assist more effectively in preschool and kindergarten classrooms in their tribal communities upon their return.

There were 58 women, among them a group of unmarried young Sioux and a woman in her fifties who had never finished high school; the majority of them were heads of families. Within the tribe Indian custom decrees the woman's role as the central one. As a property owner, she is the final arbiter not only in family affairs, but in matters affecting her tribal community. It was therefore highly significant that so many Indian women discovered within themselves the courage to dare the unknown and step off the reservation to attend the program. As one Pima folklore lecturer said when she spoke to the group: "I am like a rustic bridge. My feet are in the waters of Indian culture; my head and hands belong to the non-Indian world."

A problem to be faced by aides returning to classrooms on their reservations was that of identifying with the classroom teacher. The gap between the Indian mother and the white teacher can only be bridged by education and understanding. With the advent of financial support in the form of federally funded Community Action Programs, specific training that would help the Indian teacher-aide to operate at an effective level with increasing confidence and ego strength became a possibility.

Under the aegis of OEO, staff leadership developed the program and set as its objective enabling teacher-aides to operate more effectively by

- providing a firm grounding in knowledge and approaches relevant to the preschool classroom,
- establishing foundations for effective working relationships between teachers and teacher-aides,
- providing the cultural information necessary in order to understand the Indian child, and insight which can better transmit to the Indian community the goals of education for all.

In pursuit of this objective the program stressed workshops and discussions on child development to inculcate a deeper understanding among participants of this branch of the behavioral sciences. Behavior earlier seen as difficult or intractable could then be related to growth patterns, and more appropriate measures to meet it could be undertaken.

An invaluable part of the child study program, in the view of the staff, was the laboratory school on the University campus, where 25 Pima children 4 and 5 years of age provided the participants subjects for demonstration classes and made possible a gradual introduction into their role and responsibilities as assistants in the classroom.

The Pima children, whose families lived on a reservation only 10 miles out of Phoenix, learned to express themselves verbally. Observations of their conversations, games, and play gave the participants valuable clues and insights into the nature of all Indian children.

In further exploration of the basic similarities of the behavior of all children, field trips were taken to the Head Start program at Guadalupe, where Spanish-speaking children were being taught. Two other trips for observation of other tribes living on the Sacaton and Salt River reservations extended bases for comparison.

Reinforcement was provided the Indian participants as they expressed a need to become more proficient in English, through informal classes in grammar and syntax given by one of the staff. Language support for the children came through stories read aloud, games, parties, and by trips to the zoo, University Farm, and local shopping centers.

For many participants this program was the first experience in the "outside," off-reservation world. Living in a college residence hall and developing relationships with white people on a basis of equality had not been possible before the Institute. Some participants, normally very reticent, viewed some other tribal members and a staff member who had expressed a degree of bias toward one tribe with a realistic but somewhat jaundiced eye, according to one observer. One tribe with a strong culture and sense of self-identity was seen to have advantages in size and reputation over others of a more modest type. The program provided opportunity for participants and staff to work toward strengthening their relationships through the breaking down of stereotyped thinking.

In the Aware Team Report and also in post-institute impressions from the staff, some interesting problems were mentioned. Among them were certain difficulties in communicating to the host University the needs of a subprofessional group that does not meet admission requirements. This situation resulted in artificial regulations and problems connected with *a priori* residential standards. Some problems also arose in connection with the use of University recreational facilities. This aspect of the program seemed to require attention. However, it may be noted that this was a pilot program and there were no administrative precedents to rely on.

The teacher-aides were found to be at a higher level of social maturity and academic capability than expected by the staff. With the motivation and enthusiasm elicited from participants, this pilot program should have far-reaching implications and application to home and community activities. The Aware Team discovered that the teacher aides functioned well in a wide variety of activities requiring individual initiative, as well as under direct supervision. They were adept at operating equipment such as duplicating machines and visual aids and developed ability and enjoyment in the preparation of instructional materials such as transparencies and art media, or techniques such as rhythms and dances. Many teacher-aides, depending on their receptivity, provided excellent interpretation of Indian culture to the Indian child, in this way serving as a stimulus for the child's developing self-concept. Attention paid to tribal and folklore traditions had awakened in the Indian participants themselves an increased awareness of the value of their own culture. Because of their influence, tribes need to screen potential teacher-aides carefully, the staff believed.

The Aware Team suggests that its observations of the program at Arizona State University show that the positives in the program auger well for future development of this kind of preparation, and, indeed, further programs of a similar type are now under way at Tempe.

DEMONSTRATION OF THE ROLE OF THE NONPROFESSIONAL IN EDUCATION: UNIVERSITY OF CALIFORNIA EXTENSION, RIVERSIDE, CALIFORNIA

The assumption has developed in American education that only certified professionals are capable of teaching children in schools. Now that the demand for teachers cannot meet the need, educators are beginning to look at this assumption and to design programs to test its validity. The University of California Extension at Riverside proposed to demonstrate the role of the non-professional in elementary and preschool education. It was predicated on the hypothesis that it is severely limiting to assume that only professional teachers can help children learn.

A further consideration was that problems in learning are often problems in communication, particularly when the teacher has a differing set of values from that of the children. It was hypothesized that non-professional teaching assistants may be able to modify the traditional teacher-student relationship. The child does not completely identify the teaching assistant with the formal authority structure because of his non-professionality and/or youth. Moreover, the child may be more receptive to being taught by someone from his own background with whom he can communicate freely and identify. Still another objective was to attempt to demonstrate that student self-motivation can be developed when the children cooperate in the planning of curriculum and in teaching it to other children.

The non-professionals in the program were grouped into teams comprised of a high school student, a high school dropout, a college student, and a mother. Each of these teams worked with a teacher in the classroom each morning, participating with the children in planning curriculum and activities, observing, and actually teaching. Both professional staff and nonprofessionals devoted their afternoons to a variety of activities; team meetings for discussion and planning, evaluation sessions for the total group, study seminars and weekly contacts by nonprofessionals with children's families. The teaching assistants served as "linkers" both between families of children and the school and between children and teachers. A highly innovative aspect of the program was the involvement of parolees. One teaching assistant actually spent weekends in jail and was released to the project during the week.

The summer school phase of the project was of six-week duration. This was the portion of the program visited by the Aware Team. Other phases included 12 weeks of part-time preparatory work by staff, beginning in April. This preparation involved administrators, certified teachers, and college students in: (1) discussing objectives for the summer; (2) familiarizing themselves with the project area;

(3) selecting team members; (4) developing administrative and instructional plans; and (5) observing the children in the target area for the purpose of comparing their achievements with those of children from more privileged neighborhoods. The 12-week phase ended with a 3-day residential workshop in which staff assessed its progress and formulated common goals through human relations training.

Following the summer session, two weeks were allocated to evaluation by professional staff and by nonprofessionals. During these two weeks they organized data collected during the summer school session (interviews of teachers, teaching assistants, pupils, and parents; achievement scores; and statistical summations). They also wrote a monograph giving an account of the project in detail, including an evaluation, and formulating conclusions relevant to the field of elementary education.

The Aware Team was impressed with the innovative nature of this program, which used a multilevel, intergenerational approach to the problem of communication. The staff seemed quite open to ideas, suggestions, and points of view other than their own. This openness was communicated to the nonprofessional enrollees, who participated with enthusiasm and purpose in the afternoon sessions. Other areas of strength identified by the Aware Team were the pretesting and posttesting program and the general tone, which conveyed excitement and dedication.

The Team reported that staff felt the need for exploration of a more structured curriculum and believed that a materials center for the production of materials, games, and lessons might have been usefully added.

A major problem area seemed to be definition of the role of the teaching assistants and their use in the classroom. The Team suggested that this problem needs rethinking before such a project is attempted again. Involvement of the total team, not just the nonprofessionals, in the community at large was considered another essential to success of the program.

The location, on site, facilitated achievement of the purpose of this program.

There was evidence that learning was taking place among both the children and the total staff—the certified teachers as well as the staff teachers. In relation to children's learning, the Aware Team suggested that a more selected series of units or lessons directed to the children's specific learning disabilities would have improved the cognitive aspects of their program. The cognitive aspects of the enrollees' program might have received more attention had their roles been more clearly defined.

The affective aspects of the program were perceived by the Aware Team to be outstanding, as demonstrated by the openness between staff and teaching assistants and in the planning sessions with children.

The highly experimental nature of this program calls for further study and clarification but, given the hypothesis of the program and the special qualities of the children, enrollees, and staff, the Aware Team felt that all concerned were significantly involved in an effort to make some basic discoveries about the interactional nature of the learning-teaching process.

HARVARD-BOSTON SUMMER PROGRAM IN URBAN EDUCATION: HARVARD UNIVERSITY GRADUATE SCHOOL OF EDUCATION CAMBRIDGE, MASSACHUSETTS

What is educational change and how does it begin? As in the case of other innovations and reforms, change must initially be based upon an individual's or a group's recognition of a problem and upon the concomitant perception of a particular structure which may contribute to the solving of that problem. The rising national concern about the problem of urban education gave impetus to the development during 1965 of the Harvard-Boston Summer Program in Urban Education.

This program was sponsored by the Harvard University Center for Research and Development on Educational Differences in conjunction with Action for Boston Community Development (ABCD), and the Boston School System, funded by OEO. The Center was established in the fall of 1964 to investigate the relation between education and human differences, with the ultimate goal of making educational policy and practice more truly responsive to the wide range of differences among individuals. ABCD was founded by a committee of private citizens who were concerned with the proliferation of approaches to the community problems of Boston and who wished to provide a central coordinating agency for action programs.

The Center's sponsoring committee was convinced that, in order to be consistent with the basic purpose it was necessary to focus its attention on the children of the disadvantaged section of the city and examine in particular their educational problems. The beginning was to be concerned with improvement in the quality of teaching these children were receiving in the urban schools. Thus the concept of the Harvard-Boston Summer Program in Urban Education was evolved. This concept was based on three assumptions, which the directors stated as follows:

1) Teacher education is changing.
2) Curriculum and teacher education are underdeveloped arts.
3) Most teachers lack the skills for self-evaluation, causing past patterns to become set.

The program included a six-week enrichment experience for 330 Boston elementary school pupils, and an extensive seven-week clinical training program for 97 experienced teachers, principals, and guidance counselors. It was housed in an area serving a population mixed both racially and economically, in the John F. Kennedy School in Jamaica Plain, Boston.

A unique feature of this program was the Planning, Teaching, and Observation Cycle (PTO). In essence, this meant that the participants were divided into three teams of approximately 24 each, of whom 8 were planning while 8 others were teaching and the remaining 8 were observing. Each subteam of 8 persons went through two complete PTO cycles, with a week of the cycle devoted to each phase: preparation, teaching, and observation. Each subteam had a teaching team leader, an observation team leader, and a guidance counselor assigned to it. In the preparation stage, subject matter specialists from the staff worked with the team.

Each phase allowed the participants to assess a different aspect of the teaching process. For example, the observation phase provided both discussion of criteria for classroom observation and an analysis session at which the team agreed upon strategy for presenting its evaluation to the teacher under observation. The teacher then had an opportunity not only to evaluate himself, but also to evaluate the team's presentation of its critique.

The principals taught in the first PTO cycle and served as supervisors in the second cycle. The guidance counselors assigned to each team held individual and group guidance sessions with the pupils, as well as being responsible for contacting the parents. The Director of Guidance attempted to mesh guidance with the subject matter being taught.

The PTO cycles were only one part of a tripartite design, the two other parts of which focused on a laboratory for curriculum development and understanding the city child through an imaginative program of social studies that stressed the discovery method. According to the directors of the program, there was little stress upon self-understanding except as it relates to the participants' perception of their own teaching methods.

The approximately 300 children in this program ranged in age from 7 to 12. The youngest pupils had completed the first grade and the eldest had completed grade six. Large teams of pupils containing two or three age levels allowed for flexible grouping and assignment to subteams according to the needs of the children or of the subject being taught.

The efforts of participants to develop curriculum for the children were related directly to the children's needs and life situations. This necessitated an intensive study of the children with whom the participants were working in order to analyze their observation and to design lessons to fit the diagnosis.

The Harvard-Boston Program was a design on the professional level to facilitate change in teacher behavior. In some circles it is fashionable to speak glibly of change in education at this time. However, positive change is not easily achieved. Because of the relatively conservative role of the American public school and of American teacher education, even minor changes come about only as a result of widespread recognition of the need for change. This recognition must be accompanied by an enormous effort to define and implement a plan which may fiill the need acknowledged. Adoption of the innovations inherent in the Harvard-Boston approach to teacher reeducation, it seems reasonable to assume, is by no means a minor change. Therefore, the nature and amount of thinking and work that must necessarily precede any attempt to adopt this kind of team teaching must be unusually great. Such efforts the Aware Team observed, were evident in the Harvard-Boston Summer Program.

The Aware Team, while being impressed with a number of aspects of the program, raised questions about this effect on the children in the practicum. While the program delved into the list of limitations and strengths of team teaching, how much had it cost in pupil achievement? An integral part of the program, namely, the cyclical changing of teachers, led to a certain discontinuity for the children. Did the instability of having a team of teachers for one week replaced the next week by another team, and the following week by still another team, affect these children? Various studies of disadvantaged children have revealed that for some, uncertainty in many facets of their existence is the only way of life they know. Is it the function of the school to perpetuate this condition or to provide the stability of a known and knowing adult with whom a long-term working relationship may be developed?

Undoubtedly this method of rotation was an effective instrument for teacher reeducation. However, in view of the evidence that a prime need of disadvantaged children is stability, the Aware Team questions whether the children's need is not too central to the problem to be subordinated to the need to give teachers a variety of experiences.

The program, which called for self-evaluation, curriculum development, team teaching, and child study, although excellently conceived, was of such complexity that a limitation of its scope seemed advisable to the Aware Team, whose members were also of the opinion that, if such a limitation was *not* desirable, then the overall duration of the program should be extended.

In summary, the Aware Team concurred in finding that the theoretical and practical aims of the program had been most effectively conceptualized. The Team further noted that the ability of both leadership and staff was impressive. The formula itself, members agreed, needed to be tested in a given school—perhaps for a term, and preferably for a school year—before any final judgment as to its potentiality could be reached. Such a long-term trial would help to offset the effects of constant rotation of teachers. Indeed, teacher rotation could, over a year's time, become a positive factor, exposing the children to opportunities to develop meaningful relationships with a greater number of concerned adults than disadvantaged children normally have in a one-teacher classroom.

The program, while encountering difficulties inherent in a pilot effort, succeeded in the area of educational involvement and in the linkage of university with public school system, according to the staff and to the Aware Team. These achievements were welcomed by the program directors as a giant stride forward, an authentic opportunity for innovation and advancement.

DEVELOPMENTAL CAREER GUIDANCE IN ACTION PROGRAM: WAYNE STATE UNIVERSITY AND DETROIT PUBLIC SCHOOLS, DETROIT, MICHIGAN

This pilot program, jointly sponsored and directed by Wayne State University and the Detroit Public School System, focused upon the training of teams of school personnel for the purpose of raising the occupational and educational aspirations of a selected group of disadvantaged students from six schools in an inner-city Detroit school district. Further, participants in these teams will continue to meet monthly with the project staff during the 1965–1966 school year. Of the 6 schools that participated, 3 were elementary and 2 were junior high schools which fed the district senior high school. This program of preparation of school personnel differed from the usual in-service guidance programs in focusing upon the need to change the attitudes and values of elementary school children in order to raise their vocational sights. A rationale for such an approach is given in the Project Plan of Operation which states that "children early begin to develop preferences for types of occupations." Consequently it is at the elementary school level that a developmental guidance program must begin and, of course, be continued in the junior and senior high schools.

The project consisted of two phases: the first, a three-week workshop at Wayne State University for 50 enrollees and guidance personnel from the 6 participating schools. In the second phase of the program, which will take place during the following school year, these workshop teams will work together in their own schools, at which time a guidance consultant will be placed in each participating school to assist the workshop teams in the application of their learnings. The program and its effects will be systematically evaluated. Only the first phase of the program, which took place this summer, is the subject of this report.

The workshop at Wayne State attempted to give its participants a realistic view of the current employment picture and to help them understand and communicate better with minority youth. Participants were encouraged to develop more explicit ways of helping students in their schools. They attended lectures on current economic and social trends and were oriented by field trips to employers in business and industry, to institutions of higher learning, and to community agencies. The 50 enrollees were divided into four groups for the field trips, then regrouped into small workshops in which the teams from each school met together to discuss and synthesize their findings.

There were large group meetings with consultants to discuss such areas as curriculum and guidance. Each enrollee interviewed an unemployed adolescent dropout in a counseling laboratory and questioned the youth about his perception of school, life, and work. The enrollee then wrote an analysis of the interview and discussed the implications of his findings with his work group. Enrollees were expected to prepare and present a report of a program of action for their school.

An attitude survey was administered to the participants before and after the workshop. It revealed definite changes in participants' perceptions. They seemed to have become more aware of the need to help minority youth prepare for employment and more cognizant of job opportunities available to qualified minority youth. The participants indicated dissatisfaction with their school's curriculum and services. Furthermore, evaluations completed by cooperating schools and social agencies revealed widespread acceptance and enthusiasm for the program.

When asked to give an overall rating of their experience at the workshop, 90 percent of the participants gave a rating of *excellent*, while 10 percent gave a rating of *good*. All said that they would participate again in such a workshop. They found the field trips, the panel-exchange of views, and the interviews with unemployed adolescents valuable. Participants commented on the good organization of the program and on the interest and enthusiasm of the project director. They believed, however, that selection procedures for applicants could be improved. The comments given here were taken from the final report of the program.

The Aware Team visited the project before the workshop began and was impressed with the intelligent preparation for the program and with the spirit and good relations among the personnel. The program appeared to be a promising one, offering help both to the participants through a team approach and to the disadvantaged youth in the Detroit public schools.

INSTITUTE FOR KINDERGARTEN TEACHERS: GEORGE PEABODY COLLEGE FOR TEACHERS, NASHVILLE, TENNESSEE

George Peabody College, experienced in the education of teachers at the nursery and kindergarten level, was asked by the Nashville School System to develop an eight-week summer institute for 39 teachers who will be teaching in a new preschool kindergarten program for 750 disadvantaged children in Nashville during the school year 1965–1966. Until that time Nashville had had no public kindergartens. The institute, conducted by George Peabody College, was the first extensive program for the preparation of kindergarten teachers in Tennessee. Peabody, which has been involved in other programs for disadvantaged children, has its own demonstration kindergarten on campus, as well as a fully equipped and staffed learning resource center with a curriculum laboratory. The 39 enrollees, selected by the

Nashville School System, varied in age and amount of teaching experience and were about equally divided between Negro and white.

The institute program stressed the fusion of theory and actual practicum experience. Background material was presented in seminars on economic and educational deprivation and related aspects (psychological, sociological, anthropological, and psychological). Participants were encouraged to examine their own values, attitudes, and prejudices. Direct laboratory experience with children was provided. The enrollees first observed demonstration class kindergartens and attended seminars with the teachers of these units; then participated with the children of these classes on an individual basis and in small groups; and finally taught in the demonstration units under close supervision. Materials and methods seminars directly related to the laboratory experience formed the third element of the program.

What seemed most impressive about this program to the Aware Team, staff, and participants was the precision with which it had been planned. Outstanding features of this institute were the excellent working relationships among the staff, its uniformly high competency and flexibility in meeting the needs of the enrollees, and the strong *esprit de corps* making possible extensive group interaction and exchange of information between the Negro and white participants.

The Aware Team interview with staff revealed the belief of staff members that they had learned much from the Negro teachers about attitudes of Negro children. The idea advanced by the Negro teachers that the disadvantaged child learns a second language at school and must continue to speak his first language at home was "intriguing," according to the staff. These remarks are significant in that they point clearly to the need for contact with Negro children by teacher education institutions.

In this institute a variety of effective approaches was utilized: lectures by subject specialists, demonstrations by teachers in kindergarten classes, small group discussions, full group seminars, and experiential learning through teaching and individual projects. The small group sessions presented an opportunity to discuss specific techniques and problems and they encouraged self-analysis on the part of the enrollee. The individual projects involved the making of an institute notebook containing notes about curriculum development, examples of the work of participants, bibliographies, and lecture notes that seemed to the enrollees to have practical value for them as teachers.

An aspect of the program that provided negative comment by the various observers—Aware Team, staff, and participants—was the choice of the kindergarten classes that were used as demonstration units. Peabody has its own demonstration kindergarten on campus, and as the program was originally planned, the resources of this kindergarten as well as those of two demonstration kindergartens which were to be set up off campus in disadvantaged areas were to be utilized in the institute. However, the off-campus kindergartens were cut from the budget and, instead, a variety of kindergarten programs were substituted, so that the Peabody kindergarten was only one of several (including day care centers, community agency kindergartens, and Head Start programs) that were used by the institute. The Head Start classes had a majority of inexperienced teachers and proved unsatisfactory for the purposes of the institute. It was therefore recommended that the practicum setting in which enrollees could observe and teach be organized by the College and taught by master teachers. Such demonstration units would make it possible to improve selection procedures so as to provide truly disadvantaged pupils and integrated classes.

An aspect of the program which appeared to the Team to require further implementation was home-community relations. More time could have been devoted to working with parents in the demonstration classes and in visiting disadvantaged neighborhoods, community leaders, and agencies. The Aware Team recommended some coordinated programs between the metropolitan Nashville School System and the College to meet the city's needs by employing the know-how of the Peabody faculty. The College staff of the institute will be used as consultants in the fall of 1965, when the majority of enrollees will be teaching disadvantaged children in kindergarten classes.

There was evidence of curriculum experimentation at this institute. What seemed evident, however, was the need for still further research in experimental situations in order to find new and meaningful ways of assisting teachers of early childhood programs in disadvantaged areas. The need for research of this kind extends beyond this project.

Summary of OEO Programs

In summary, the major strengths of the OEO Teacher Education programs, as perceived by the Aware Teams, lay in their high degree of innovation and flexibility, and in their responsiveness to the needs of both the participants and the community.

The principal weakness identified by the Aware Teams lay in some of the administrative details rather than in the conceptualization. The involvement of community leaders in the planning, while an asset in most situations, occasionally caused conflict when lay leaders attempted to make decisions of a professional nature related to education.

A dramatic example of experimentation in a new direction was the preparation of teacher-aides, which gave impetus to the development of a new paraprofession with both educational and economic advantages. The educational advantages lie in freeing the teacher to function at the level of his professional skills and in increasing the proportion of concerned adults to children in the classroom. This latter advantage is of particular importance to disadvantaged children, for whom individualized care is deemed essential. The economic advantage lies in the creation of a new job market, as this type of semiskilled job cannot easily be automated out of existence. Machines can never be substituted for human care of human beings. One difficulty faced by unskilled workers in the past has been that the serving professions have offered few opportunities for any but the highly skilled.

Flexibility, a quality frequently requested by participants in other types of programs studied, was evident not only in the design of the OEO programs but also in the multilevel composition of the enrollee group. No rigid requirements ruled out the combined attendance of administrators, teachers, counselors, and teacher-aides.

Responsiveness to the needs of the participants was reflected in the evolving curriculum—a striking feature of the OEO programs. Responsiveness to the needs of the community was evident in the involvement of community representatives in the planning, and in their continuing responsibility for conduct of the program. The OEO programs have, in fact, provided a link between educational leadership and the community and have served also to strengthen interagency cooperation in government.

NATIONAL DEFENSE EDUCATION ACT INSTITUTES

During 1965 nearly three and one-half million dollars of National Defense Education Act funds were devoted by the U. S. Office of Education to offering "a specialized program of instruction designed to assist teachers in coping with the unique and peculiar problems involved in teaching disadvantaged children and youth." More than 2,000 teachers participated in 61 summer institutes at an average cost of 100 dollars per teacher per week. More than 16,000 applications were completed, revealing the extent of the interest in and the need for this kind of teacher education.

In their *Summary of Director's Final Reports** Louis Urgo and Roderick Hilsinger of the U. S. Office of Education stated: "The variance of their (the Directors') approaches and the range of their recommendations indicates that NDEA institutes are, indeed, something quite different from regular summer teacher education programs."

One unique feature of these institutes was the precision and insightfulness of the planning. The U. S. Office of Education had issued *A Manual for the Preparation of Proposals* which was conceptualized by educators on the local educational scenes. It served not only to guide but also to stimulate. What these programs may have lacked in flexibility, they gained in a sense of direction and in generally high standards of performance. They shared with the OEO programs a pervasive climate of excitement and verve, apparently as a result of being part of an experiment.

* See Appendix J for complete report.

The institutes summarized in the following section were selected to illustrate a variety of programmatic approaches and to provide broad geographic representation. Each one is in itself a model for the college and the community of which it is a part, as, indeed, were the 61 NDEA summer institutes for their respective communities.

NDEA INSTITUTE FOR TEACHERS OF DISADVANTAGED YOUTH: DISTRICT OF COLUMBIA TEACHERS COLLEGE, WASHINGTON, D. C.

The glamour and excitement of the nation's capital is centered on Capitol Hill and the White House. The men and women who work in these two seats of power are, for the most part, citizens with residences outside the 61 square miles of the District of Columbia. However, within the District of Columbia 763,956 people live, most of them connected directly or indirectly with the functioning of the federal government. Washington, D. C., is their home. Their children are born there and go to school there. Among these people is an increasing population of those described as disadvantaged.

In this city as in other large cities of the country, the areas that are disadvantaged desperately need large numbers of well-prepared teachers to staff the schools. But there are not enough good teachers to meet this need. Principals report that only a few teachers are available who have the special preparation and the professional enthusiasm to become effective teachers of disadvantaged youth in the Washington schools. The vast majority of teachers seem to avoid this challenge and seek assignments in schools in middle class areas. In part, this can be explained by the fact that most teachers do not have the special skills and understandings necessary for them to function satisfactorily in disadvantaged areas.

The NDEA Institute for Teachers of Disadvantaged Youth was held for six weeks during the summer of 1965 in an attempt to alleviate this situation. Under an institute grant, the District of Columbia Teachers College, in cooperation with the city schools, carried out a program designed to provide a number of urban teaching specialists to work with the disadvantaged.

From an application group of 492, fifty secondary school teachers were selected. Twenty-six youths who had completed the seventh grade were selected by counselors to be pupils at the institute. They came from Shaw Junior High School and Banneker Junior High School, both a part of the Model School Division (Cardoza Area) of the District of Columbia Public Schools. These schools are in the group considered the most disadvantaged in the city. At least 5 of the pupils were nonreaders; the remainder represented as wide a distribution of ability as might be encountered, and all were disadvantaged. All except one lived within 10 blocks of the school.

The District of Columbia Teachers College was uniquely prepared to develop an institute because of the long experience it has had in working with the schools and other community agencies dealing with the disadvantaged. Operating within the framework of the public school system, it was able to employ the services of public school personnel who might not have been available to other institutions.

Experienced master teachers of disadvantaged youth from the schools of the inner city were employed as instructors for the institute. To this staff was added reading and speech improvement experts who had been working with the disadvantaged in the public schools. These master teachers received backup support from the curriculum department and from the administrative staff of the schools.

Obtained as visiting lecturers were prominent persons familiar with the problems and needs of disadvantaged youth. Major emphasis was placed on utilization of the talents of local people who were working effectively in this area, among them police officers from the juvenile division, school personnel assigned to the Model School Division, recreation department personnel, city social workers, and others of the city whose daily work and familiarity with the local situation the staff believed could not be duplicated by outside lecturers.

The college library, the shelves of which were stocked with current sociological and psychological publications, was only one of many facilities available for use by participants. Organic to the institute was a reading laboratory and a speech improvement laboratory. These provided an opportunity for working directly with the disadvantaged youth within the institute. Community agencies were used for first-hand experiences in working with pupils. There were discussion sessions in the area of human relations as well as sessions on curriculum, new instructional materials, and methodology in each teacher's subject area. Provision was made for supervised independent study.

The staff reported that, in general, the program operated effectively as planned. The following minor adjustments were made to solve problems as they arose.

In response to evaluations by the participants, the discussion period was shortened by 20 minutes, while the workshop period on teaching was lengthened by 20 minutes. This additional time in the workshop enabled more discussion and preparation of those lessons which were to be presented to the pupils, who met daily with the workshop teachers.

The staff of the institute quickly discovered they were operating a parallel school for their 26 disadvantaged students. The original proposal had focused on the activities of the participants and had not planned an adequately organized educational program for the children. The teacher relationships with the pupils became a major strength of the program, according to the perceptions of the participants and staff. A description of this parallel school, the practicum, is in order, to explain the adjustments made and to provide a basis of understanding for what the director of the program believed to be the value of the practicum to the participants.

The children attended the institute from 11:00 a.m. to 2:00 p.m. Lunch was provided. At the end of each day each child was given 50 cents to cover the expense of transportation. From 11:00 to noon, groups of children went to each workshop to provide a demonstration class. From 1:00 to 2:00 p.m. the children were taught individually by the participants. Two participants were assigned as a team to one child. To insure continuity of learning for each pupil, one participant accepted major responsibility for the pupil's development, with the other participant acting as assistant. This arrangement enabled either participant to be released for additional laboratory instruction without seriously disrupting the child's program.

The participants reported that working with one child for an extended time enabled them to gain great insight into the backgrounds and characteristics of disadvantaged children. Participants began to take "their" children home on weekends and in many cases took them to plays, to museums, and on trips. Home visitations were expected of all teachers. When the teachers were on field trips, parallel trips were conducted for the children. The use of pupils, both in the workshops and in the individual tutoring sessions, furnished the setting for the development of psychological insights.

Virtually all the participants became affectively involved with the children they were tutoring. Along with the visits by the children to the homes of the participants, many provided personal trips on weekends. Near the end of the institute, staff became concerned with the problem of terminating these relationships and during the last week children were reassigned to another team of teachers to modify the emotional effect of termination.

The staff reported that with the extensive personal attention the pupils received, they showed noticeable improvement. One instance involved an extremely withdrawn nonreader. At the beginning no amount of cajolery could induce him to say a word. Persistent supportive techniques were employed by one of the participants, who was a counselor, and the youngster began feeling more secure. Soon he was participating with the others. This was regarded by the enrollees as a good example of what they were attempting to do with all the children, and it led to discussions in the general sessions concerning the relationship of emotion to learning.

It was the unanimous belief of the staff that emotional interaction with the disadvantaged youngsters produced a change in many enrollees' perceptions and in their attitudes toward such children. One weakness of the program, as stated in the institute's final report, was in not providing each participant with his own pupil rather than assigning two teachers to one pupil.

Another finding of the institute staff was that many teachers who are successful in disadvantaged schools are themselves unusually "action oriented." Their ability to work with children and to teach is often more highly developed than is their ability to express themselves in theoretical constructs.

In the 11:00 to 12:00 workshops, a small group of children formed the class. This class was used by the master teacher to demonstrate new materials and methods. It was also used for an advanced form of practice teaching by the participants. Gradually, according to the staff, this practicum led the participants to develop a role-playing technique whereby each participant could communicate his concepts of educational approach by demonstrating with the children in front of the group. He would then use the demonstration as a discussion vehicle for bringing out insights in methodology. With this highly selected group of teachers the quality of teaching performance reached extremely effective levels, the director reported. The participants declared great satisfaction with this phase of the program.

The use of children was absolutely essential to such an approach. The success or failure of new materials and techniques became immediately apparent. The staff concluded that lesson structures cannot be clarified unless one demonstrates how pupils will be utilized in the lesson. The behavior of the teachers and the emotional climate they generate are an integral part of the lesson, particularly for disadvantaged children.

One evaluation of this device occurred near the end of the institute, when the pupils volunteered to put on a skit to entertain the teachers. With no participant direction they gave an imitation of the classes, using a series of children as the teacher. It was evident to staff and participants that many of the children who were playing teacher had perceived and learned the newer techniques of instruction which had been demonstrated.

Field trips were usually rewarding to participants for observing the slum milieu. Participants reported discovering that theoretical discussions tend to oversimplify the situation and do not have the impact of direct experience. The trips, however, were related to preliminary theoretical presentations and to later discussions for maximum effect.

Since virtually all participants were themselves from disadvantaged schools in the inner-city area, a field trip to the curriculum center of a nearby advantaged school system proved to be the most disturbing trip of all for participants, staff stated. Most participants said they had not realized the extreme contrast between the facilities and life style of the suburban area and of the inner city. The staff perceived a noticeable increase in militancy in the tone of discussions following this trip. The Aware Team reported that this aspect of the program and others as well seemed to be a product of confident and evocative conceptualization.

The Aware Team saw as a strength the fact that District of Columbia Teachers College is under the aegis of the Board of Education of the District of Columbia. However, certain deficiencies marked its program. Perhaps a comparative lack of emphasis on techniques that have been developed in private institutions would be one. The Team believed that this deficiency led to an in-group pride on the part of participants and staff, hence a limitation on the scope and depth of the work of the institute.

The Team also considered the effects of reversing the ratio of teachers to pupils so that each teacher would have more children with whom to work. The relationship witnessed at the institute practicum was not at all similar to the relationships of children to teachers in the regular classroom.

The range of participants, the Team believed, could effectively be extended up the line (principals and senior high school teachers) and down (elementary school teachers). This arrangement would afford a greater variety of participants the institute learning experience and would present differing points of view.

According to the staff the program seemed to gain momentum and direction as the participants became involved with the children and the teaching process. (The original design had been highly organized and had included the children, who arrived on the first day and were present throughout the six weeks.) The staff freely admitted that they did not expect the institute to revolutionize the teaching that was taking place in the inner-city junior high schools. However, both staff and participants believed that significant learnings had taken place and that these 50 teachers were better prepared to meet the needs of the pupils in their schools.

NDEA SUMMER INSTITUTE FOR SECONDARY TEACHERS OF DISADVANTAGED YOUTH: GOUCHER COLLEGE, BALTIMORE, MARYLAND

The Goucher College institute was unique in several respects. It was characterized by a nondirective approach that placed responsibility directly on the enrollees. It provided a parallel learning situation for the teachers and practicum students, wherein the teachers observed students struggling with the same problems of self-expression and literary exploration that they themselves were involved in. Through these observations and by the skillful use of group dynamics and role-playing, the institute sought to achieve new insights into teacher and pupil behavior. The program involved 30 Baltimore high school teachers of English and Social Studies, chosen in teams from 8 schools in the inner-city area; and 22 high school students from these schools.

It was hoped that all participants would be able to live on campus. However, this was not feasible and about half of the enrollees commuted, but it was observed that they devoted increasingly more of their free evening time in association with those living on campus. Also in residence on campus as part of the program were the 22 high school students. These students were selected on the basis of being disadvantaged (with reference to economic position, family conditions, and housing) and of having shown signs of average to good academic ability as registered on one or more test scores but not reflected in actual scholastic performance. These were underachievers whose performance was apparently affected by the social conditions under which they lived.

The presence of the students as young people to observe while under instruction and to learn to relate to and identify with in the total aspects of community living served well the basic purpose of the institute as set forth in the Plan of Operation: "To broaden the teachers' awareness of student potential, their recognition that, while their students may be 'disadvantaged' when it comes to possessing certain skills and manifesting certain kinds of motivation, these students sometimes actually have, because of their background, talent and drive which make them highly educable."

The six-week institute program consisted of three daily class experiences. In addition, there were evening lectures, panels, and film programs for one or two evenings each week, averaging about three hours of required evening time per week. The first class, which met for 1½ hours every morning, was a group discussion situation based on a combination of T-group method and the concept of Carl Rogers.

The purpose was to allow each participating teacher to rely on his own insights and knowledge about the multiple factors of teaching inner-city youth; to learn that he himself (without a basic reliance on "authorities" or "experts") has the capacity and strength to be his own authority and expert about inner-city teaching.

This round-table class developed as a result of a weekend planning conference held by the staff eight weeks before the beginning of the institute. At this conference it was decided, in the light of the widely differing academic backgrounds of the teacher-participants, that the ordinary lecture-discussion methods would simply produce a situation in which those participants who were "intellectual" and articulate would become more so and those who considered themselves ordinary and inarticulate (many of the latter, out of direct experience, really did have important knowledge to share) would have this self-depreciatory attitude increased. Also, stress was placed on the fact that the self-images and ego strengths of the teachers who work in inner-city schools need to be positively reinforced.

The staff concluded that each day of the institute provided a group experience which proved that primary insights and actions came not from the staff members but from the participants themselves. The staff member in each group was not present as a resource person but rather as a relatively silent, sympathetic listener or tone-setter. It was understood that substantive discussions on inner-city teaching and related problems would take place and also that books would be mentioned, recommended, even assigned by group members to each other. It was planned that all these components would develop in accordance with the desires of the members of the group; not directed by any authority or any one person in the group. It was assumed that frank self-examination and emotional conflict would occur, as in T-group situations. However, in the setting postulated, these developments would occur in the context of mutual examination of inner-city teaching, and with the group feeling that there was substantive business on the table, the tendency to dwell in personal emotional areas would be minimized.

Five groups composed the institute, consisting of about 12 persons each, including a staff member. Of the five groups, one was made up exclusively of participants. The other four comprised equal numbers of teachers and high school students. This situation was the result of the difference in numbers between teacher and student participants and also of the staff's desire to observe the differences between the two kinds of group experiences. While there were no specific assignments, the key books and articles that were read seemed to have meaning for participants, since the reading grew out of their own expressed needs and they were self-assigned.

In operation the major difference between the all-teacher group and the combination teacher-student groups was that in the former the discussion was more manifestly intellectual and more directed to problems shared by teachers, while in the latter the teachers' experience derived much more from direct communication with the student participants and observation of their attitudes and personalities.

The second class of the day was English. Two days of one week and three days on alternate weeks this class was devoted to observation of the student English class, followed by an evaluation hour. Three days of one week and two days on alternate weeks this class was an English course for teachers in poetry and poetic theory, with emphasis on writing poetry. In the first instance the teachers (broken into subgroups of 15 each) observed a master teacher working with the 22 tenth and eleventh grade students. Throughout the six-week period the students in the observation class discussed poetry by William Carlos Williams and E. E. Cummings and selected prose works by Ernest Hemingway, Richard Wright, and George Orwell. At the same time they discussed poetry they themselves were writing in relation to the material read and to their personal experiences in and outside the institute. The continuing six-week observation of these classes was important for its demonstration of a method of free discussion, guided by questioning (though never dominated by teacher synthesis) in an atmosphere of acceptance of whatever the student wanted to contribute.

In the latter instance the teachers read and discussed the same books the students were reading, with the emphasis on the personal relationship between the teacher participant as a person and on poetry itself. Poetry was written by all the participants as they wished and this material (duplicated) became the focus of many class analyses. In this class the instructor refused to play the role of lecturer or even of a resource person. A list of books was provided for the course but no assignments were given; the only guidance from the teacher was a suggestion that the participants could, if they liked, write poetry or prose, and if they did so, might arrange conferences with the instructor.

The English observation class, as had been intended, made a profound impression on the participants, which was evident in their written evaluations. Yet, as the director pointed out, it was the hard work and the penetrating discussions of their own English class which laid the foundation for the success of the observation class. It was largely because they themselves became directly and personally involved in the literature the students were studying that the participants were able to identify with the students' need to speak seriously about the literature. Thus they were able to witness the students' growing sophistication about the concepts and techniques of the writers being studied. Underlying their expressed satisfaction with the observation classes were the frequent frustrations and the sometimes painful self-exposure that took place within the teachers' own English class.

The third class, Sociology and Role-Playing Techniques, was planned and taught jointly by a sociology professor and a dramatics instructor who is a social worker with the Baltimore Department of Welfare. Three days a week were spent with the sociologist in a course in urban sociology employing the lecture-discussion method. Material covered inner-city family, economics, housing, and minority group problems, with considerable use of outside speakers. For two days a week the dramatics instructor involved the group in role-playing, creating "scenarios" concerned with inner-city social problems and having the teacher-participants act them out. Following these activities, the attitudes revealed would be discussed. The goals of this joint course were twofold: (1) participant insight into personal experience in relation to inner-city environment and (2) demonstration of how role-playing methods can be combined with social science subject matter and with more conventional lecture and discussion techniques.

A successful outgrowth of the sociology course was a series of voluntary small-group sessions with a psychiatric social worker whose major role in the institute was to interview and counsel the participants. Here enrollees brought up their own counseling problems with inner-city disadvantaged teenagers. Under the leadership of the social worker, they discussed and analyzed cases.

A further result of this course was the formation of a committee of teachers who intend to continue planned role-playing (sociodrama) that will dramatize the problems and challenges of teaching in the city. This group mounted a trial production for the institute on its final day. Its members have made contact with a local television station that is interested in broadcasting both the production and a discussion of the group purposes. They seek to perform before Parent-Teacher Associations and teacher groups throughout the year.

Evaluation of the institute experience by the participants revealed a marked development of sensitivity and a strengthening of self-concept. The teachers came to feel their importance and the reality of their own capacities to perceive and to act. Persons who somehow considered themselves "dedicated" or "sensitive" and yet felt alienated, subordinated, or rebuffed in the world in which they normally lived, here found themselves in a community where people would listen to them and take them seriously.

Group rapport in the Goucher Institute was excellent as a sense of community developed within teacher and student groups as a whole. Joint softball games and picnics were organized voluntarily, by participants and staff; teachers and students attended plays together. The Aware Team commented on the willingness of the staff to live on campus and work with the group from 8:00 a.m. to 10:00 p.m. if necessary.

Some criticisms were leveled at the institute by some enrollees and by the Aware Team. The social studies teachers wanted demonstration lessons in their subject. Some of the teachers felt that the students were not typical because they did not evidence any serious emotional, behavioral, or reading problems. Others felt that there should be school administrators among the enrollees. The Aware Team observed a need for a longer institute, perhaps for eight or ten weeks. The Team noted that the use of the nondirective approach seems to take longer to produce changes. There was a suggestion that a historian might be added to the staff for the social studies teachers or that the institute be limited to English teachers. The Aware Team saw the need for an additional staff member and recommended that a public school administrator or teacher be added to the staff.

The staff felt that they would make no major changes in the design of the institute. They would have preferred to include some participants from other parts of the country and to have all the enrollees live on campus, even if this meant making provisions to house the families of some. The staff was in agreement with the Aware Team that a longer session of eight weeks would be desirable. The director would revise his student selection procedures because the schools involved removed all disciplinary cases from the lists of students considered for the institute.

The success of the Goucher Institute lies in its clear demonstration of one critical factor—an atmosphere of freedom in class and in related out-of-class experiences—an atmosphere in which the student commits himself to participating only if he really wants to and where there are clearly no penalties if he seems not to be participating. This atmosphere results not only in improved self-image and authentic motivation but also in actual work done, in skills and concepts learned and retained. The volume of poetry and prose written by the participants, teachers, and high school students is tangible proof of the success of this approach.

The teachers had an opportunity to see students from their own school area as enthusiastic, highly motivated, highly educable. They could then go back to their own school ready to make an increased commitment to the education of such youth. In the view of the director, this new attitude was more important than the sociological knowledge, techniques, and enrichment of subject matter that might be derived from the institute experience.

NDEA INSTITUTE FOR TEACHERS OF DISADVANTAGED CHILDREN AND YOUTH: JACKSON STATE COLLEGE, JACKSON, MISSISSIPPI

There is tenseness in the air of Mississippi, a result of prejudice and lack of trust. As the winds of change move down, reluctant segments of society gird themselves to fight for the familiar past. Change is taking place in spite of trouble. A small college for Negroes in the heart of Jackson has become a symbol of change and hope, a force in the attack on disadvantagement and human disintegration that is the result of poverty and bias.

Operating on the philosophy that the Negro teacher in the South must be helped to see himself as a worthwhile individual and one capable of a definite contribution to society, the director of the summer Institute at Jackson State College and the staff took on the task of designing an eight-week institute for teachers of disadvantaged children and youth. The institute selected 30 elementary and high school teachers ranging from preschool through grade 12. These participants were themselves the product of disadvantagement, living in the small towns that dot rural Mississippi. The participants were to become the "textbooks" that would describe, in a manner no book has ever done, the disadvantaged Mississippi child. The participant in the institute, however, did not have to rely solely on his memory of children with whom he had worked. In the practicum of the institute the participant discovered, through close contact with one child and his community, how this individual child thinks, plays, and learns and how his parents think, feel, and learn.

Because much of Mississippi is a closed society, it was reasoned that broader contact with the larger world was imperative for the participants in the institute. Arrangements were made for conference calls enabling participants to converse with such people as Norman Cousins, John U. Munro, Allen S. Hortman, and Daniel Schreiber. These discussions offered an opportunity for participants to respond to the ideas of the speaker, to challenge and question him. Ideas which lingered inchoate in their own minds were given a chance to be fleshed out and thus probed in a way not previously possible. This aspect of the institute was seen to be a distinctive, truly innovative facet of a program described by the Aware Team as imaginative and well conceived.

Field trips were augmented by tours to colleges, research centers, and other points of interest in Mississippi and New Orleans. It is significant that some participants expressed reluctance to travel on field trips away from the institute. The Director reported that they told her they feared their school boards would remove them from their jobs if they "saw too much and got ideas." The Director responded to this fear by personally explaining the purpose of the trips to the various boards and superintendents of schools, getting their assurance that no participant's position would be jeopardized by his expanding horizons.

Other field work involved having the teachers help the 60 disadvantaged children in the practicum by examining their speech patterns and then helping to improve them. The nonverbal communication of the children was studied, as was the children's tendency to stereotype thought and language.

A balance was preserved between the time given to field experiences and the time used for acquisition of background knowledge and skills. One of the techniques employed in cognitive learning was extensive use of outstanding fiction and nonfiction paperbacks. Ideas for field work, to ascertain how the concepts of Negroes and whites are undergoing change, came from these books. Much emphasis was placed on the examination of values. Trips were made to different communities of disadvantagement to speak with the residents, to observe what the community and social agencies were doing to counteract existing difficulties, and to visit the disadvantaged child in his school and classroom.

The Aware Team reported that great effort was made in the institute to refresh the teacher in the core subject matter needed by his pupils and to extend that core with the vital margin of knowledge that teachers need to have. It was believed by the institute staff that such extension of knowledge is a necessity to the teacher of the disadvantaged child, who must be an exceptional teacher to compensate for lack of family and community resources. The institute, by providing an unusual cultural and intellectual experience, demonstrated to teachers the progress that could be made through study and observation.

The selection of enrollees was seen to be a strength of the institute. The process used insured enrollment of individuals in leadership capacities from each of the educational districts of the state. It was anticipated that the sphere of influence of these people will affect existing conditions within their home districts both in matters of education and culture.

In its reaction to the program the Aware Team was impressed with the organization of the project and its scope. The Team remarked on the excitement generated in participants by the director and the staff. The Team found the main strengths of the institute to be an enhancement of the self-concept of the participants, the process of selection, and the faculty itself. The consensus was that the plan for the institute was both imaginative and sound, based on what seemed to the Team to be a real understanding of the conditions existing in Mississippi. An attempt was made to carry over institute learning into the regular teacher education program of Jackson State College by the involvement on the staff of key people from the Department of Education of the College.

The director reported that a feature of the institute which met with favorable participant response was the invitation to guest speakers to live on campus with participants and to be available for informal discussions. Participants commented favorably on the opportunity to explore the thinking of guest speakers in greater depth than is possible when a speaker comes for only a day.

It was the opinion of the Aware Team that participants needed additional time to explore in detail aspects of the program of special interest to them. They also agreed that if the sweep of the Institute concept had been less broad, participants might have been able to explore a few facets in greater depth. The reasons underlying the suggested changes stemmed from the concern that the participants were in class six days a week, from 7:00 a.m. to 5:30 p.m. Every minute of these days was planned, and participants had little time for discussion with one another or with staff except in the evenings. Reflection and study also had to be crowded in after dinner. The Aware Team observed that the pace seemed exhausting.

The range of reading materials, the Aware Team reported, was extensive—more comprehensive than the Team anticipated, considering the location of the college. The readings were correlated and integrated into the total experience and there was evidence that the participants were utilizing the library. Other aspects of the program contributing to the stimulation of cognitive development, as perceived by the Aware Team, were the field trips, the overall planning, and the tie-in to the ongoing program of the college. The emphasis on the humanities provided the participants an opportunity to see relationships in a way they had not seen them before.

This, the Team reported, was a good institute, whose "light will shine" throughout Mississippi. The Team further commented on the willingness of participants to attend classes on Saturdays. They attributed this to the understanding and dynamism projected by the director and to the impact she has had on Negro education in the state.

NDEA SUMMER INSTITUTE FOR ADVANCED STUDY FOR TEACHERS AND SUPERVISORS OF DISADVANTAGED YOUTH: WESTERN MONTANA COLLEGE, DILLON, MONTANA

On the eastern slope of the Continental Divide in the State of Montana there are seven Indian reservations, totaling 8,343,929 acres. Both North Plains and Plateau Indians live on these reservations: Blackfoot, Crow, Confederated Salish and Kootenai, Assiniboine, Gros Ventre, Sioux, Northern Cheyenne, and Chippewa—about 30,326 individuals in all. The statistics on this population are significant. Forty to 50 percent of the employables are unemployed; low levels of occupational skills are evident; average family income is $1,500 or less per year; average age of death is 42; more than 90 percent of housing is substandard; the average level of education is through the fifth grade, while a large number of school-age individuals are not registered in any school.

The director and faculty of the NDEA Summer Institute for Advanced children and youth at Western Montana College recognized that one line of attack on the environmental problem of the Indians in their region was through the improvement of education. The specific thesis of this institute was that successful teaching of Indians requires understandings, appreciations, recognitions, and approaches that are uniquely Indian and that have to be learned by Caucasian teachers. Implicit in this approach to the education of Indians is the need for teachers to unlearn stereotyped and preconceived ideas of Indian culture and misunderstandings of the potential role of the Indian in American life.

The program of the institute was organized around three courses: Improvement of Instruction—an American Indian Workshop; Special Problems—Understanding the American Indian; and Indian Culture of the Northwest. The first, American Indian Workshop, included the presentation and seminar discussion of current classroom instructional problems particularly applicable to the Indian child, as well as practicum experience for each participant at the Montana State Children's Center. The course on special problems (Understanding the American Indian) was taught by a variety of special lecturers most of whom were Indian teachers and workers who shared the particular knowledges and techniques of instruction especially applicable to Indians. Another course, Indian Cultures of the Northwest, was devoted to the history and culture of the Indian tribes in the region, with emphasis on understanding their social organization, tribal government, the land estate, political strength, philosophy, religion, literature, music, folklore, naturalism, arts, crafts, and science. This course offered extensive field trips (one lasting four days) to Indian reservations and visits to archeological sites.

The staff was composed of the director, an associate director, himself an Indian, 2 other full-time faculty and 3 part-time faculty members. Of the 50 participants, who came from 17 western states (except for one from New Jersey), all were committed to working with disadvantaged Indian children and youth. Only 2 had not at least a bachelor's degree; 27 had more than 3 but less than 10 years of teaching experience; the remainder had more than 10. The median age range was 35–39. Forty were married, and men outnumbered women by more than two to one.

It is not possible to describe adequately the impact of this program without reporting one factor which affected the total institute. The participants, the faculty, and the Aware Team all indicated that the administration of the College did not appear to support the institute and through negative actions made the participants feel unwelcome on campus, made the work of the faculty extremely difficult, and created a climate of coolness that was reflected in the participants' attitudes toward the institute. No one was able to provide a reason for this circumstance, particularly since the original attitude of the administration had been to have the biggest and best institute possible. Concurrent with the operation of the institute was the regular college summer school program, to be followed by Boys' State (a convocation of male, teenage, statewide leadership in the form of a mock state government), which was to be held on campus. Preparations for the Boys' State included the complete overhauling of food facilities, and this placed a further hardship on the institute.

The program was well divided among lectures, seminars, field trips, and practicum. In the group sessions participants reported the combination of these four features to be the main strength of the program. The staff was more selective, reporting that in their opinion the practicum and demonstration classes were of the greatest benefit. They recognized the importance of the field trips to reservations but felt that they were poorly scheduled because they conflicted with lecture sessions. The schedule difficulties were a result of the uncertain dates of tribal activities. Such dates are set by medicine men, often with little advance warning. The Aware Team, however, while recognizing the value of these aspects of the program, stated that in their perception the Indian staff member made the greatest impact on the participants, imparting his understandings in regard to the emotional, motivational, and cultural problems of Indians.

Because of the inadequacies of the facilities on campus, the participants suggested that the institute would be improved if it were moved off campus onto a reservation. They believed that there they could more closely share the life of the Indians, and through living with them, make a continuing study of their life style, learning patterns, motivations, needs, and aspirations. They further pointed out that it would be easier to move the library and other materials to the reservation than it was to transport the participants themselves in buses to the practicum schools. These observations were made after participants had visited reservations on field trips, had made home visits to the families of children with whom they were working in the practicum, and had developed community schools. Therefore they were well aware that they were opting for more rigorous living conditions for themselves, although such possibilities seemed preferable to them than the realities of the campus situation.

The participants discussed with the faculty the possibility of such a change of site for the institute and reported these discussions to the Aware Team. The faculty's reaction was that it would be considered a possibility for a future institute but it was not practicable in the time remaining to this one. In a conversation following the institute's close, the director stated that he wished he had been able to effect the change during the summer, since he believed it would have improved the learning potential of the participants. However, the Aware Team's reaction was that the participants, by openly sharing with the staff their desire to live with the Indians and a willingness to participate in their lives as much as possible, showed remarkable growth in understanding, not only of their own, but also of the Indians' situation.

The participants' satisfaction with the practicum experience was not completely shared by the Aware Team. The Team indicated that the amount of direct teaching contact with children might usefully have been increased. They also suggested that demonstrations of teaching methods might have shown some of the more recent development in teaching techniques, use of materials, and approaches to children's learning problems. Without more definite plans for post-institute follow-up it is not possible to determine what concrete learnings the participants incorporated in their own classroom teaching when they returned to their schools. The possibilities of positive change in the participants' attitudes and resultant behavior toward individual Indian children when they return can be more safely predicted. That such changes were taking place was evidenced not only through the work with the children in the practicum, but also in the willingness of the participants to have the institute held on the reservation.

A definite conclusion that can be drawn from the experiences of those involved in this particular institute is that the attitude of the host institution plays a major role in the impact of an institute.

The Aware Team suggested that hard work by the staff and goodwill on the part of participants cannot wholly compensate for less than wholehearted support by the host institution.

NDEA INSTITUTE FOR KINDERGARTEN, ELEMENTARY AND JUNIOR HIGH SCHOOL TEACHERS AND SUPERVISORS OF DISADVANTAGED CHILDREN AND YOUTH IN URBAN SCHOOLS: MUNICIPAL UNIVERSITY OF OMAHA, OMAHA, NEBRASKA

Educational authorities have increasingly urged educators to respond to the need for intensive cooperation between the public school systems and the teacher education institutions which prepare teachers for working with disadvantaged children in schools within the system. Such mutual exchange of thinking and planning is being attempted throughout the nation with varying degrees of success. The NDEA Institute conducted by the Municipal University of Omaha in the summer of 1965 provided an example of a community where cooperation had been in existence for some time but where the local school system and the University department of teacher education agreed to extend it. They embarked on a major project of retraining 50 of the most influential teachers and supervisors in the schools of Omaha serving disadvantaged children and youth.

The Omaha Public School system had previously established a compensatory education program, Assistance to Intercultural Development (AID) that included an in-service training structure for teachers of disadvantaged children. The dean of the Municipal College of Teacher Education and the director of the institute, with the encouragement of the former president of the university, studied the needs of the schools and drafted a proposal for a summer institute to expand the effectiveness of the AID program. This institute, they believed, would be most useful if it concerned itself with two major areas in the teaching of disadvantaged children: (1) study of child development and behavior, and (2) study of methods for stimulating the functioning of language and the improvement of reading skills.

Since there was little precedent for this kind of institute, it was agreed that the design should be truly experimental. The plan of operation provided for as much flexibility as could be allowed within the regulations of the NDEA. The director reported that this concept called for a staff who could function in the institute program in such a manner that emphasis on teaching the disadvantaged children and means of retraining teachers would remain in balance.

This balance was to be achieved through a careful combination of cognitive content and experiential learning. The content was provided in two courses: (1) Reading Problems of the Disadvantaged and (2) Psychological Development and Sociological Characteristics of the Disadvantaged; as well as through lectures by guest authorities and staff. Experiential learnings were to be introduced through a Materials Development Laboratory, a Child Study Laboratory, and enrichment trips—all of which were integrated in the practicum experience. Further, the school system of Omaha provided one school to house all aspects of the institute program. This, the Aware Team stated, was a factor facilitating the participants' ability to focus on the total experience.

The participants, 50 in all, were from Omaha, and had a median age range of 35 to 39. Twelve were male; 38 female. Thirty participants were married. The majority had bachelor's degrees; 16 held master's degrees, and one, a supervisor, held more than a master's.

The director reported that it became apparent to him and the staff early in the seven-week institute that in order for the staff to be aware of the needs and responses of all the participants a structure would have to be provided for feedback from participants to staff. This took the form of a participant committee that would prepare a newsletter based on participant contributions, to be distributed whenever enough material had been assembled to fill one or more pages. A first copy of the newsletter, "Breakthrough in the Barrier of the Disadvantaged," had been prepared by the staff as an orientation device prior to the institute sessions. The staff selected a committee to carry on the publication of the paper. Participant response was beyond the staff's highest expectations. The newsletter was usually distributed at the afternoon closing session, and on the few days when the paper was not published for want of material, the room echoed with the moans of participants.

The committee publishing "Breakthrough" had promised the other participants that articles would be printed as received, unedited and uncut. These articles covered participants' concerns with their learnings, their changes in attitude, their feelings about the institute, the staff, and other participants. The newsletter featured cartoons, line drawings, and institute-oriented wit, as well as serious discussions of matters of mutual concern. Lively debates among participants were recorded in successive issues. One of these concerned the feeling of one participant that her whole set of middle class values was being threatened by things she had learned in the institute. This evoked a number of pro and con reactions given space in later issues.

The staff and the Aware Team agreed that, while a daily newsletter is not the only device that can provide feedback in an institute, for this institute it was a most felicitous selection. The institute structure also provided other means for feedback—through individual and group conferences and seminars and the formation of committees to involve participants in responsibility for institute functions. Some of these were the housekeeping committee, the social committee, the library committee, and the evaluation committee.

Because the director of the institute did not have major teaching duties, he had enough time in his schedule to be available to participants, either in committee groups, or individually, for continuing discussion. This was considered by participants, staff, and Aware Team as contributing to the success of the program.

An example of this openness on the part of participants and awareness on the part of the staff is illustrated by the unique manner in which field trips were arranged for participants and children in the practicum. One staff member met with participants to discuss methods by which they could discover the kinds of trips that would be most beneficial to their teaching program with the individual child with whom they worked in the practicum. Every participant then reported the destinations he and the child desired. Trips were arranged by the staff for individuals and groups according to the needs expressed by participants. This procedure made possible a large number of trips over the seven-week period. More than 70 were taken, in all. Two of them were total institute experiences for staff, participants, and children in the practicum. More generally they were taken in small groups, and the available resources of the community were thoroughly explored. The different age levels of the children did not rule out their attending the same trips. This led to learnings shared between younger and older children, with opportunity for increased communication among children of different ages.

The practicum was conducted in an Omaha Public School. It was originally planned that this would be a demonstration school, but the school teachers and participants objected. They felt that, for the participants to be able to develop the most positive working relationships with classroom teachers and children, they needed to have more freedom to participate than was implied in the title "demonstration school." The final interpretation of the purpose of the practicum was that the institute should provide a laboratory school with disadvantaged children in attendance, where participants could try out ideas and procedures and disadvantaged children could have an enriched summer school experience.

The variety of teaching styles used by the laboratory school teachers was seen by the participants as adding a further dimension of enrichment to their program. They had opportunity to observe a number of ways of working with children, to compare and evaluate them, and to attempt to adapt the best parts to their own ways of teaching. Meetings with staff and participants in small study groups following practicum sessions permitted this kind of exploration to take place, as well as learnings in child development.

The fact of having the library and classrooms of the institute (where the lectures, films, discussions, and development of materials took place) in the same public school building with the practicum was viewed by participants, staff, and the Aware Team as being extremely practical and a factor that built cohesiveness into the institute experience. The director reported that in spite of the relatively large number of participants, no factions formed which were divisive.

The emphasis on materials development helped the participants discover their own ability to create useful classroom teaching devices. For the most part, the materials developed were not new, but in many instances they were new to the participants. Prior to the institute sessions, only a few had known about the overhead projector, to name just one. During the seven-week period all participants not only had opportunities to become familiar with this machine, but also to develop "projectuals" for use with the projector, and to use these materials with children in the practicum.

Similarly, five participants had previously owned 8-mm. film cameras but none of them had ever considered the possibility of using them as teaching aids in the classroom. During the course of the Institute these five made and edited films for use in the practicum and later in their own schools.

A highpoint of the institute's final week was a display of all materials produced by participants. To this exhibit were invited supervisors and other teachers from the participants' home schools. Their response was enthusiastic and added to the participant's reported feelings of accomplishment.

A feature originally included in the planning of the institute but about which the director and staff had initial misgivings was to enroll in the institute supervisors and teachers from the same school as participants. Misgivings proved groundless. The uneasiness anticipated among teachers performing in front of their principals did not develop. Both teachers and principals accepted the institute as an opportunity for learning together and for devising ways and means of improving their own performances as related to their roles. Strategies of change were jointly worked out in the institute that participants intended to put into effect in the school year.

The Aware Team unanimously reported that this institute had definitely succeeded in fulfilling its objectives and in meeting the expressed needs of the participants at all times during the institute. One team member suggested that perhaps no single thing attempted during the institute was really new, experimental, or original in itself, yet the total impact of the institute was both creative and experimental. Existing concepts and methods were skillfully combined to evolve new approaches to teacher education for working with disadvantaged children and youth, and they were directly aimed at problems faced by the particular participants.

Since all the participants had come from the Omaha area schools, follow-up of the institute should be comparatively easy. The staff plans to distribute questionnaires to participants in January, 1966. At the same time, supervisors and administrators of participants will be surveyed to find out what changes in participants' teaching behavior have been observed. The participants' evaluation committee also planned for a reunion and follow-up evaluation in February.

Reports of these follow-up plans are not yet available; however, all connected with the institute, and the visiting Aware Team, believed that positive changes had been accomplished. If this proves to be true, then the concept of cooperation between the school system and the University department of teacher education will indeed be strengthened and expanded.

NDEA INSTITUTE FOR TEACHERS AND SUPERVISORS OF DISADVANTAGED CHILDREN AND YOUTH: GLASSBORO STATE COLLEGE, GLASSBORO, NEW JERSEY

A trend in American education today is to amplify the extent of the school's involvement in the home and community so as to produce a more dynamic exchange of experiences and insights that can extend the school's understanding of the child and facilitate his progress. This trend can be seen as a counter response to the pattern followed until the late 1950's by public schools, which was to draw away from the familial, communal ties established earlier in a simpler, rural society into the demesne of professional expertise. But that withdrawal left educators without sufficient information on which to base conclusions regarding the needs of a growing number of students under the school's authority. Perceiving their role within a limited curriculum, educators functioned as though middle class children presented the total spectrum of their concern. Rejected as alien, the prime misfit became the disadvantaged child, product of a culture which rendered him invisible through neglect.

The fact that this trend has been reversed has left much to be done in guaranteeing effective public education to all. Certain educational institutions have recognized that close cooperation with adjacent public school systems can lead to mutual benefit in knowledge of disadvantaged children and in improvement of strategies to teach them.

New Jersey's Glassboro State College and some nearby community school systems are engaged in this cooperative process. Responsive to the now recognized need for supportive interpretation of the disadvantaged and the implicit requirement of teacher reeducation, the College sponsored a summer institute with four adjacent school districts: Camden, Bridgeton, Salem, and Vineland. Cooperative planning was developed when these four cities expressed concern with problems of educating their disadvantaged youth. Each of these cities represented an area in transition, with many newly arrived Spanish-speaking Americans from Puerto Rico and some longer-established Negro families among its citizenry. Camden and its sister city, Bridgeton, reflect the change that has come to many areas of exurbia. Formerly communities where upwardly mobile families moved as they sought to improve their status, as well as to escape the deterioration besetting the nearby metropolitan center, Camden and Bridgeton have now become areas of disenchantment. Small industries have moved in that employ semiskilled workers. The rural outskirts of these cities have long been the site of one phase of the pork industry, where midwestern pigs are fattened before preparation for the eastern market. This industry primarily employs low-paid Puerto Rican labor, replacing the former Negro tenant-workers who have been attracted to better-paying unionized jobs in the local industries.

In shacks and shanties offering no indoor plumbing or heating, and with a central spigot shared by many families for water, these Puerto Rican newcomers go about the business of readying pigs for market—a process that includes gathering garbage from nearby Philadelphia, cooking it in open outdoor vats, and shoveling it into the pigs' troughs.

Tall rows of trees planted in front of the pig-fattening farms effectively screen them from the view of the passer-by. Negroes live in small, isolated ghettoes in the towns.

Children of these families were admitted to the local schools, but the neighborhood school plan of organization effectively kept them from sharing schools with middle class children, who attended neighborhood schools near their own homes. Schools attended by the middle class children came to be preferred by teachers. Teacher turnover was noticeably higher in the schools with high populations of disadvantaged children and youth. These children were labeled "difficult," "hard to teach," and "problem children."

The summer institute for teachers and supervisors at Glassboro State can be seen as a strategy to change the situation in these schools.

In planning the institute, an assumption was made that the possibility of change is enhanced when teams of teachers from the same local school districts with similar problems undergo a positive mutual experience. Backed by an administrative philosophy emphasizing college service to public schools, a six-week program was initiated enrolling 71 participants from the four nearby communities—most of them teachers, a few of them administrative and supervisory staff. Through this process, returning teachers, with the support of their supervisors, could presumably influence their colleagues.

The participants represented a wide instructional level, kindergarten through 9th grade, which necessitated particular skill on the part of the director in making possible appropriate cognitive learnings during the first two weeks of the institute along with a practicum and field experience relevant to the primary, intermediate, and junior high school teacher groupings.

Two centers for practicum were established: one at Bridgeton, for participants from that local district, Vineland and Salem; and another at Camden. Children at each center were screened for the program. Sixty children defined as needing enrichment and representing the three instructional levels, rather than those having serious remedial or emotional problems, were selected. The principal purpose of the practicum was to enable each teacher to establish a relationship with one or two children in greater depth than is usual in the classroom.

Field trips were taken by participants and their practicum students to cultural-recreational sites, among them the Cumberland County Fair, Philadelphia International Airport, and the Atlantic Coast for swimming and a picnic. Visits were undertaken to community agencies as well as to children's homes to help familiarize participants with the children's life, their conditions, and related problems.

Although it had been anticipated that parents themselves would participate in activities at the two centers, afternoon trips and a recreational program afforded periods of time together too short to develop a fruitful parent-participant relationship, particularly since parents were working or were unable to find substitutes for home responsibilities.

Programmatic emphases, through lectures, group discussions, and readings, lay in three areas: (1) understanding of psychological and sociological dynamics affecting disadvantaged youth; (2) exploration of promising instructional techniques; and (3) development of an effective school program for these children. With the curriculum expanded to approximate the sum of his experiences both within and without the school, participants were more readily able to relate a child's experiential background and social behavior to attitudes and difficulties in learning encountered in the school setting.

Throughout the program of the institute, instructional methods and techniques related to the teaching of reading provided a major focus. Research done by Anne Anastasi at Fordham University, and by Martin Deutsch at New York Medical College among others, reveals a relationship between disadvantagement and reading ability particularly at the lower grade levels. Various interpretations suggest possible causes—among others, a home environment unstimulating to verbalization and/or a meagre variety of experiences inhibiting the child's ability to observe, compare, or relate. The need of children to develop bilingually in two different culture modes may set up yet another barrier to successful linguistic competence. A number of resources at Glassboro State College were particularly well suited as approaches to this problem area.

One such resource, a Glassboro State College faculty member who is a national authority on reading, acted as visiting lecturer and discussion leader on reading problems during the institute's initial on-campus phase. In these meetings stress was placed on both developmental and remedial reading programs and how to implement them. Promising practices were explored in using (1) children's natural language patterns to improve language expression, (2) first-hand experience as a learning technique, (3) remedial techniques to offset deficiencies in communication skills, and (4) modification of current texts, which tend to lack relevancy for the disadvantaged.

In further development of these techniques, participants evolved a series of activities entitled "Things I Am Going To Try." These were activities and materials for their use during the regular school year as a result of their participation in the institute.

Another resource available to institute participants was material published through the Curriculum Development Council for Southern New Jersey. The Council—a nonprofit educational organization of public school districts associated with Glassboro State College for "purposes of study and action research in selected curriculum areas"—through its publications acts as a medium for an exchange of ideas and experiences developed by committees of teachers in the local schools. In a number of staff presentations, ways to develop an improved reading readiness program were presented along with ways of systematizing a teacher's observations of the child's linguistic background and ability.

The institute gave little emphasis to the theoretical approach to learning, emphasizing substantive content and teaching skills as a foundation for curriculum development and interaction between teacher and pupils. In the view of the Aware Team, however, greater emphasis could have been placed on intellectual content, with greater cognitive learnings in sociology and cultural anthropology. Certain methods judged by enrollees most productive for work with the disadvantaged were those aimed at providing a curriculum based on concrete day-to-day experiences, the use of role-playing, open-ended questions, and discovery.

Small-group and individual activities geared to the disadvantaged child's shortened attention span and need for individualized attention allowed a freer, less-structured atmosphere in the classroom. With many of the participants coming from schools where middle class stereotypes about different socioeconomic groups prevailed, the institute provided an exercise in extending the teacher's empathy for those from different backgrounds. In the words of one participant, "I taught in the neghborhood for years but never really saw it before."

It had been noticed that many teachers of somewhat limited experience tend to self-assign certain methods for introducing subject matter into the content of the classroom. Ways that will provoke spontaneous interest or response are increasingly omitted from the orthodoxy of style that has been developed. One of the tasks this institute set for itself was to demonstrate imaginative techniques calculated to effect a release from earlier, presumptive sets. For instance, one morning the director, as he was informally visiting the practicum classes, brought a game into the classroom. It consisted of 15 matches arranged on the table. Challenging the children, the director asked them to make alternate moves withdrawing one, two, or three matches in turn from the table. The object was to leave enough matches so that the last turn would not force the player to remove the last match. The children's alerted interest in response to this challenge did more, as an example, to awaken teachers to other exciting possibilities for use in their own classrooms than many hours spent in examining more conventionel approaches. As the children discussed and projected a series of hypothetical moves, trying out various approaches to the problem, teachers were able to see a vindication of their growing realization that these children function most effectively in experience-oriented activities. As one teacher said, "Their self-reliance and ability to appraise a situation is surprising."

At Glassboro the effort expended in the institute on extending the functions of the school into areas that needed attention and were not receiving any provides a base for more ongoing programs to help solve problems in these areas. Needs that were formerly the concern of only a few teachers now can be formulated as mutual problems to be shared by the wider school-community. From a less isolated vantage point, teachers in the schools can, if they will, start to concern themselves more effectively with possible solutions to some of their educational problems.

NDEA INSTITUTE FOR ELEMENTARY AND SECONDARY TEACHERS OF DISADVANTAGED CHILDREN AND YOUTH: BROOKLYN COLLEGE, BROOKLYN, NEW YORK

Bedford-Stuyvesant, a densely populated section of Brooklyn, has within the past decade experienced a radical ethnic population shift. Today, 70 percent of the citizens are Negro and another 10 percent are Puerto Rican, as opposed to the predominantly Jewish and Italian residents of only a few years ago. While Bedford-Stuyvesant is not the only ghetto in Brooklyn (let alone New York City) it perhaps demands more immediate attention than most sections of the city, for 53 percent of its population is under 30 years of age.

An educational institution is obliged to become responsible for and involved in the quality of educational opportunities offered to residents of its neighborhood. Realizing this, Brooklyn College undertook, as a part of its obligation to Bedford-Stuyvesant children during the summer of 1965, a six-week institute for improving the preparation of elementary and secondary school teachers to work with the disadvantaged children of this section of the city.

Situated a 25-minute subway ride away from Bedford-Stuyvesant, Brooklyn College initiated this institute to affect the attitudes and improve the skills of 36 public school teachers enrolled in the institute who came from nine states (including 23 from New York City). All of these teachers would return to their own inner-city classrooms to work with children of similar background.

The objectives and purposes of the Institute as stated by the Director were fourfold:

1) To extend knowledge and understanding of educational problems emerging in the urban community.
2) To extend knowledge and understanding of the psychological and sociological influences on the development of disadvantaged youth and children.
3) To increase skills in understanding and communicating with culturally deprived children and youth.
4) To increase skills in developing materials and using new research findings for meeting academic deficiencies of culturally deprived children and youth.

In an effort to reach not only the greatest number of children and youth from the Bedford-Stuyvesant area but also to provide a broad and effective teaching program, Brooklyn College developed a "triangular" program. One section of the program, the storefront school, was held in a former shoe store. The previous tenants had left behind an enormous sign in the shape of a sneaker on which the word "Keds" was still legible. The director of the institute commented that one letter and lots of hard work had changed the emphasis from Keds to Kids. The second section was held in a nearby housing project; the third in a local hospital, working in conjunction with Job Orientation in Neighborhood (JOIN) in a program for hospital aide trainees.

The inductive approach to teachers' learning was one of the most significant instructional techniques employed by the institute. This attempt to move from the empirical to the theoretical proved highly stimulating to the participants.

As an example of this approach one participant, a nun, discovered the needs and interests of the children and then built a project for them based on adult models in community life with whom they could identify. Though her experience in working in an "outside" situation was rather limited, she was determined to answer her own urgent questions regarding disadvantaged children and youth. "Why do they have trouble with reading? Why are they slow learners?" She soon discovered that the disadvantaged child was handicapped by a low self-concept and therefore expected to fail.

After making this discovery she provided herself with a camera and conducted tours with her pupils to local police stations, firehouses, and hospitals. In these places she took individual pictures of the children talking with Negro police captains, fire marshalls, and surgeons. The children then compiled a scrapbook using the pictures as illustrations for stories they wrote about themselves. The children, she reported, gained immeasurably in self-esteem, while she as the participant learned more about the goals and needs of the disadvantaged child from actual experience.

That the participants were foremost in the minds and thinking of the director and staff is graphically illustrated by the fact that when asked, "If you were to plan such a training program, what specifically would you change?" not one enrollee stated she would change the selection of the staff, and only two stated they would change in any way the organization and/or administration of the institute.

The nondirective approach in group sessions was emphasized at Brooklyn College. Enrollees were not only permitted, but were given latitude to experiment. The senior staff members of the institute were careful not to discourage the participants, even when they felt a "faster" way was possible. This restraint enabled the participants to involve themselves in discovery, and in this way to gain valuable experience and insight into the children with whom they were working.

Another learning tool for participants was a daily log each kept of his students (at no time was the ratio greater than 1 to 4). This log was to be used at the end of the institute to evaluate not only the children's progress, but, much more importantly, the participants' attitudinal change.

The first week of the Institute was devoted to orienting enrollees to the various facets of the program. Visits were made to the schools attended by the children in the practicum. Key school personnel talked with participants about the previous school experiences of these children. A field trip into the Bedford-Stuyvesant neighborhood and visits to several community centers were also made.

The field work of the institute was based on the assumption that being disadvantaged results in part from the child's lack of supportive relationships with adults. Participants were encouraged to develop positive, helping relationships with children through structuring meaningful, rewarding learning experiences for them. The negative feelings the children may have associated with school buildings and the learning process were avoided by the use of more informal facilities located in the children's immediate neighborhood. Seven participants worked with 25 children, aged 6 to 14, in the storefront center; 24 enrollees worked with 76 children, aged 6 to 16 at the community center of the housing project. In conjunction with JOIN, four enrollees worked with 14 dropouts, aged 17 to 21, who were employed in a hospital.

Oral and written language skills and reading were stressed throughout the entire program of the institute. Efforts were made to utilize the neighborhood and the larger community as well as the daily experiences of the children to build vocabulary and develop conversational and story-telling skills. Emphasis was placed on helping children build their own reading interests. Excursions to museums, zoos, the United Nations, libraries, botanic gardens, and other points of interest around New York were exploited for their educational benefits. Word games, Monopoly, "Link Letters," stick puppets, masks, live animals of field and stream, magnets, sewing, cooking, baking, weaving, and crafts work were among the media used to involve the children and get them to talk and read about the people, places, and things that interested them.

One of the strongest features of the entire field teaching experience was the attempt to involve the parents in what the children were doing, the Aware Team reported. Participants met with parents either in the practicum centers or in their homes, or communicated with them by phone where posssible, to help them understand the activities in which the children were engaged.

The work with children was supervised *in situ* by the senior staff members, who were in the field daily. Diagnostic procedures were suggested, as well as methods of approach to learning difficulties. In addition to the field supervision, an hour-long practicum seminar was held each afternoon. These sessions sometimes included all the participants working with one supervisor; sometimes partial groups met for discussion, depending on need. The ways of using a log as a learning tool were discussed. The director stated that these seminars also functioned as activities through which participants might become familiar with group process.

During the fall months an effort will be made to follow up the work done in the institute. All paraticipants will be canvassed by questionnaire to ascertain what changes have come about as a result of their summer's work and what obstacles they have overcome by incorporating these changes into their classroom behavior. Those participants teaching in New York City will be interviewed to determine in greater detail what they experienced upon their return to their classrooms.

In the opinion of the Aware Team, the strengths of this program were its unusual practicum experiences, which reached the truly disadvantaged and, through small, informal class situations, provided ample opportunity for innovative approaches to teaching. The responsiveness of the institute staff to the needs of the enrollees was illustrated by their willingness, even eagerness, to adjust schedule in order to provide more free time for study and reflection. The Aware Team observed that the keeping of a daily log by the participants had definite merit. Moreover, the pervasive enthusiasm regarding the new and deep insights gained by the participants created an atmosphere of unity and purpose that did much to smooth the introduction of public to parochial school teachers, and in many cases created conditions for a new understanding of one for the other.

It was the Team's opinion that the conceptual skills of the director of this institute could have been used more effectively. Too much of her time was taken by routine administrative duties because of the absence of an administrative aide.

One weakness and its remedy, not only perceived by the Aware Team but also noted by the director, would call for employment of a psychologist for individual and group counseling to improve both staff interaction and staff-participant interaction.

A program such as that implemented by Brooklyn College was considered by participants, staff, and the Aware Team as being ambitious and in some aspects idealistic. However, perhaps through such innovative ideas the sought-for goal may be reached.

NDEA SUMMER INSTITUTE FOR SUBURBAN JUNIOR HIGH SCHOOL TEACHERS AND SUPERVISORS: HOFSTRA UNIVERSITY, HEMPSTEAD, L. I., NEW YORK

Historically, a major supplier of teachers for Long Island communities, Hofstra University is located on Long Island within a few miles of a score of communities that share the problem of educating ever-increasing numbers of disadvantaged children. The University recognized its responsibility to work with local schools in programs of teacher reeducation aimed at helping the schools offer educational opportunities for disadvantaged children. Its summer institute for suburban junior high school teachers and supervisors was designed, in the words of its director, "to be propleptic to the design and implementation of a regular in-service program of teacher education for disadvantaged children on Long Island." The outstanding characteristic of the Hofstra Institute was its intensive program of cognitive learnings in cultural and social anthropology, sociology, and psychodynamics. The objective was to establish the conceptual framework for understanding the disadvantaged. It was the rationale of the Hofstra program that affective changes in teaching behavior can be brought about through cognitive learning, and the program consisted in large measure of lectures and seminar discussions, with little provision for practicum experience.

There were daily lectures from 8:15 a.m. to 12 noon which the entire group of enrollees attended, while every afternoon they met in groups of 10, with a different staff member each week, for seminar discussions based on the content of the morning lecture. In addition, the institute offered a course for the teacher-participants, Pedagogical Structure and Materials and Methods, to help them incorporate their general learnings into their teaching behavior. For the supervisor-participants a course in the dynamics of social and educational change was given, in order to provide the knowledge and specific techniques that would facilitate their efforts to have a direct effect on the school system.

The participants of the institute were all from junior high schools on Long Island. Of the 40 who were accepted, 30 were teachers; 10 were curriculum coordinators. All of them had had at least 3 years of experience in working with disadvantaged children. Wherever possible, teachers and supervisors were selected in teams from individual schools. Most of the participants were men, outnumbering the women three to one.

While the institute program did not offer a practicum experience, provision was made for observation of a demonstration class that was conducted daily during the last two weeks of the institute. The class was made up of 25 junior high school students from the Wyandanch public schools who were brought to the campus and taught by a demonstration teacher. Every participant had an opportunity to work with a child in the class on an individual basis. A snack break for the pupils was arranged, at which time they could meet and talk with the enrollees in a relaxed atmosphere. At the beginning of this campus demonstration class, the institute presented each student with a notebook individually stamped with his own name for class use. Polaroid pictures were taken of each child and the prints mounted in their notebooks.

The strength of the cognitive program lay in its interdisciplinary approach and in the high quality of the staff. Many had had extensive experience teaching in Harlem and other disadvantaged areas. The Aware Team found them to be dynamic teachers as well as scholars. Staff members sat in on each other's lectures and each one integrated his special area into the total program of general learnings. The Aware Team reported that there seemed to be no doubt among the enrollees that they had increased their awareness of the needs of disadvantaged children.

A central idea of the program was that there was a need for understanding, first, through study of the formal disciplines; and after this, the application of their understanding to methods and techniques. The staff pointed out that the development of substantive insights often changed the nature of what the enrollees considered to be their needs. The following comments from participants illustrate this point: "It is amazing . . . at the beginning I looked for techniques that would work for a lifetime. Now I know it is not possible," and "We came here to get teaching techniques. At the beginning we were frustrated. Now we see that we must get basic understandings in the behavioral sciences *first.*"

The rapport between the staff and the enrollees was exceptional and the morale of the entire institute extremely high, the Aware Team observed. The institute had imparted to the enrollees a sense of hope and excitement and a freshness of outlook as evidenced by enrollees' reactions. In the words of one participant, "We have people here (staff) who are searching for the truth as much as we are. We get caught up in this search." Another commented, "The faculty members were individual models of creativity and commitment." Participants remarked on the flexibility of the administration, illustrated by changes that were made in scheduling more time for small-group discussions as a result of their evaluations.

Relationships of some depth and intensity developed among staff and enrollees. Respect and enthusiasm seemed to be mutual between the two groups. Staff members were freely available for consultation. Staff expressed appreciation of the freedom and autonomy they were encouraged to exercise and cited this as evidence of the democratic leadership of the director. The participants commented on the efficient administration of the program and on the consideration and respect with which they were treated.

The Aware Team found the facilities at the institute good. The university does not yet have dormitories and therefore could not make provisions for the enrollees to live on campus. A separate dining hall was provided so that participants and staff could meet together for lunch.

The director and his staff gave support and encouragement to many participants in their desire to go back to their schools as knowledgeable agents of change. There had been many informal discussions on how best to reach the power structure. This particular aspect of the program was emphasized in the afternoon sessions with the supervisors. In these sessions the problems and techniques of educational change were studied as well as the theories on which curriculum planning is based. Emphasis was placed on curricular aims and content for the disadvantaged. Methods of dealing with the problems of curricular innovation under state, local board, and administrative staff structures were explored, and ways of facilitating faculty administrative planning and implementation of programs were discussed. Methods of securing the cooperation of parents and others in the community for educational innovations were included in the instructional content, as were methods of establishing effective guidance programs for disadvantaged children. In addition, sources of data required for the design, implementation, and evaluation of educational programs for these children were identified and data-collection procedures were described.

The Aware Team questioned the assumption of the director that heightened understandings of the life conditions of the economically and socially deprived child will automatically transform inappropriate methods and teaching strategies into more appropriate ones. In its report the Aware Team expressed the belief that neither the conceptual framework nor the instructional procedures were designed to assist the participants in translating their understandings into teaching behavior, or in developing ego strengths.

In his final report the director stated that the afternoon materials and methods sessions for the teachers were not as meaningful for the participants as the lectures, because the "specificity of teaching gimmicks, the need for which most of the participants had anticipated, lost its importance when posed against the broader meanings of the academic subjects of anthropology, sociology, and psychology. . . . The sharing of minor classroom techniques became," he said, "less important to the enrollees."

While the director found that the number of readings required was slightly unrealistic, there was evidence from the comments of participants that they did not intend to cease reading when the institute was over. Most of them purchased many of the books they did not have time to read during the institute for study during the fall.

The director found the two-week demonstration class to be the least effective of the learning devices attempted at the institute. The classroom situation remained an artificial one. The children in the past year of working with the demonstration teacher in their own school had already advanced far beyond the level of performance to be expected from a disadvantaged class. The director believed that the problems of discipline and interest level confronted by the regular classroom teacher of disadvantaged youth could not be demonstrated in such a situation.

The suggestion was made by a number of the participants that either the demonstration class be eliminated or experience be provided in the regular summer session secondary school. The staff of the institute made a further suggestion—that some of the participants of this year's institute be employed as teachers in a local school for the summer session where they might serve also as demonstration teachers for succeeding institutes. Both enrollees and staff expressed the belief that a six-week program was too short to encompass general learnings, observation, and demonstration experiences.

In order to determine enrollee attitude change, three attitude inventories were administered at the beginning and at the end of the institute. The first measured prejudice and authoritarianism; the second, "intellectual attitudes"; the third, an adaptation of the Semantic Differential scale developed by Osgood, elicited enrollee reactions to six different terms: disadvantaged pupil, school dropout, underachiever, colored child, child, and poor person.

To date, only the data pertaining to the first two inventories have been analyzed. The results indicate no significant difference in authoritarianism between the first and the second administration of the tests. There was, however, a significant increase in "intellectual attitudes" over the six-week period. The students tended to express more positive attitudes toward intellectual pursuits. Since the institute was intellectually oriented, the director believed that this response indicated that the institute had accomplished at least one of its purposes.

The director commented that the most meaningful aspect of the six-week institute was the emotional effect upon the participants and the staff. He pointed to the fact that biases, prejudices (both conscious and unconscious), ignorance, self-motives were all exposed in what might be called group therapy. In his final report he stated,

"We decided to force introspection and apparently we were successful. Coping with disadvantaged children seems to be a function of coping with self rather than a function of techniques."

The director felt that the major lack of the institute program was the absence of a continuing program of supervision and assistance during the school year. Future institutes should make provision for such assistance in the form of observations of participants' classrooms, and weekly seminars, where problems arising from current classroom activities might be discussed and solutions explored and tested.

There have been some follow-up activities. The participants of the Hofstra institute have organized into a continuing group, with plans for intervisitation, meetings, and publication of a monthly bulletin. By these means, they hope to reinforce one another and to further the preparation of future teachers of disadvantaged youth. In two instances participants from the same school system made preparations to implement institute learnings by involving their principals in program reorganization in their schools to accommodate new arrangement of classes. In another case, the program of English and social studies for an entire school district has been revised so that the new foci acquired at the institute may be used as a curriculum base. In still another case, a program called "Talent Search," conducted in one of the local school systems and considered a failure, was to be revitalized with specific suggestions growing out of experiences provided by the summer institute. A scholarship fund, known as SAC (Sponsor a Child), set up at Hofstra as a result of the summer institute, is designed to further the study of disadvantaged youth in art, music, and drama.

The participants suggested a 2-day conference with the staff during the Christmas holidays. The staff agreed to interview principals during the year to determine changes in attitudes and behavior of institute graduates. Two new courses—one for the fall term, the other projected for the spring term of the following year—dealing with the problems of the disadvantaged child, are being introduced at Hofstra in the School of Education. As a result of speeches before school administrators and talks with them, the director has found a receptivity to change which he feels is an encouraging sign for the future.

NDEA SUMMER INSTITUTE FOR PRESCHOOL AND KINDERGARTEN TEACHERS AND SUPERVISORS OF DISADVANTAGED CHILDREN: NEW YORK MEDICAL COLLEGE, INSTITUTE FOR DEVELOPMENTAL STUDIES, NEW YORK, NEW YORK

Studies conducted at the Institute for Developmental Studies of New York Medical College had revealed that the disadvantaged child, already limited in his basic language skills, encounters teachers who have not been trained to deal with his disabilities. Further, these studies reveal that the existing teacher education programs are inadequate in quality and scope, particularly when applied to the unique problems that characterize the depressed inner city within a metropolitan area.

The Institute for Developmental Studies believed that it had amassed knowledge of disadvantaged children which it was able to translate into action through an effective teacher education program. The summer institute which it developed was designed to emphasize learning disabilities in general, covering such areas as learning theory, cognitive development, the sociology of learning, the use of appropriate programming of materials and procedures, and intensive study of psychological and sociological factors affecting disadvantaged preschool and kindergarten children.

These areas were developed in four courses during the summer institute. Socio-Psychological Characteristics of Disadvantaged Children, was a lecture-discussion course designed to give participants greater depth in understanding of the relationships between early environmental conditions and the psychological development of the child. Topics included learning theory, cognition, language, and perception.

Teaching Disadvantaged Young Children dealt with the current Institute of Developmental Studies research and experimentation in techniques, procedures, and practices of educating disadvantaged children, with specific emphasis on preschool disadvantaged children. It covered as topics: cognition, language development, perception, room arrangement, materials of instruction, organizational structure and grouping for learning, articulation with regular school programs, and working with parents of disadvantaged children.

Reading Readiness and the Young Child from Disadvantaged Circumstances was based on lectures, demonstrations, and discussions on recent research into special problems of reading readiness and reading disabilities.

The final course, Materials Development for Disadvantaged Young Children, was concerned with the development of materials using different media. Participants worked on materials most appropriate for their respective school situations. Stress was placed on simple materials that participants themselves could make for use in their classrooms.

According to the director, the content of the program reflected a sequential order of formal class sessions dealing with the problems related to classroom learning. The most important feature of the institute, he related, was the opportunity given each participant to observe classrooms in operation, to participate in them as assistants to the teachers, and to assume a teaching role as well.

Mornings were devoted to this practical teaching experience under the guidance of teachers trained at the Institute for Developmental Studies. In the afternoon, participants engaged in conferences evaluating their practical activities and attended the formal classroom sessions. These sessions permitted coordination of classroom experience with practicum.

Concomitant experience was provided for participants in community agencies. One example was the field work at the Bloomingdale preschool project, which was coordinated by the Social Service Department of the Institute for Developmental Studies. Participants also chose an area of special interest which they pursued as a project. Some participants selected work in the development of materials, such as tapes to increase the attention or listening skills of young children. Others specialized in a case study of a specific child.

Evaluation of the institute was structured through a number of devices. During the month of October a 2-day work conference was planned for participants that centered on successes and problems in implementing some of the ideas gained from the summer institute.

A questionnaire was worked out to be sent to participants at the end of the school year 1965–1966, the responses to which will be compared with data gathered from the same questionnaire given during the institute. Consultative staff help will be available to participants throughout the school year.

This five-week summer institute enrolled 25 participants, 11 of whom were from the Greater New York area and the remaining 14 from widely scattered sections of the country. Eleven of the participants were teachers; 11 were on a supervisory level, and the remaining 3 were a guidance counselor coordinator, an early childhood resource teacher, and a reading coordinator. The average age of participants was 45; the range from 23 to 55. Selection for this institute was difficult, since there were 300 applications and only 25 places available.

The participants reported some of the understandings and techniques they gained from their experiences at the institute. Among these were the need for early intervention in education to insure later achievement, taking the form of special help in language, perceptual, and cognitive skills. They cited the need to adapt teaching techniques to the children's learning styles and to encourage verbalization and interaction among children. They mentioned the importance of developing a positive self-image as a basis for learning, noting also that teacher warmth, sensitivity, and understanding were essential to the learning situation. Special techniques included use of the Language Master, tape recorder, alphabet board, flannel board, and language skills machines to free teachers for work with individual children.

Both staff and enrollees reported that the emphasis of the institute on relating strategies, techniques, and materials to the specific disadvantaged children with whom the participants will be working was a strength of the institute. The tone of the summer institute, as evidenced by the sharing between participants and staff and among participants at different levels (teacher, administrator, other school personnel), and the consequent interaction were seen by staff and participants as enabling the summer institute to have maximal effect.

Participants reported that they might have benefited by more home visits and field trips to other agencies or institutes in the city. However, in the short time allotted to the institute, they felt that on the whole much had been accomplished.

The Aware Team reported the following strengths of the program. The summer institute was geared to a research program, which served to focus constant attention on evaluation. The research also provided a consistent point of view and an identifiable grounding for the procedures demonstrated. The staff was perceived as being well grounded in this theoretical-practical program. They appeared to work well together and were friendly and available to participants. Guest speakers were carefully selected and adequately programmed. Attention was given to new materials and techniques and to their use in programs for disadvantaged children as well as to new uses for common materials.

The Aware Team suggested that the practical experiences of the program could have been made more germane by employing a supervisor to help participants relate these experiences to the purpose of the summer institute. The Team also suggested that a common residence might have afforded greater opportunity for participant interchange and reflection. In this regard the staff noted that some enrollees did not evidence a high degree of involvement in the institute and the staff did not seem to be able to motivate them. More time and personnel for the selection process might have facilitated screening out such poorly motivated teachers, the Aware Team believed.

Another shortcoming of the program might have been remedied, according to the Team, by the provision of more time for participants to work in the laboratory classrooms. However, the Team believed that this recommendation did not apply to administrators, who appeared to need a program of experience more carefully planned to meet their specific requirements.

In summary, the summer institute appeared to the Aware Team to be heavily weighted on the cognitive side. At the time of the Team's visit some of the participants' comments to Team members seemed to suggest that more direct attention to affective learnings would have been valuable. It was reported by the director, however, that although the Aware Team did not see this part of the program, attention was paid throughout the summer institute to the problem of changing or improving attitudes of participants toward disadvantaged children. It is the position of the Institute for Developmental Studies that cognitive and affective learnings are not separate. The director reported that research conducted among the participants would tend to show that some of their attitudes had been positively changed as a result of the institute.

NDEA INSTITUTE FOR SECONDARY SCHOOL TEACHERS AND SUPERVISORS OF DISADVANTAGED YOUTH: THE PENNSYLVANIA STATE UNIVERSITY, UNIVERSITY PARK, PENNSYLVANIA

The Pennsylvania State University, situated amidst small rural communities, offered an extensive language laboratory program for teachers working with rural disadvantaged youth in the fields of English and reading. Through use of graphics, language, and reading laboratories the program stressed the development of competency in new techniques and materials under the supervision of personnel who were experienced in working with disadvantaged youth. The institute offered no practicum experience and only limited observation in local schools. Although the director's plans for a highly sophisticated use of the laboratories never materialized, the institute experience appeared to be successful in terms of attitude changes and high morale among enrollees. The high quality of the staff, their interaction with the participants on an informal basis, and the fact that, both enrollees and staff lived on campus seemed to the Aware Team to be major influences on participant learning.

The enrollee group was small, consisting of 30 classroom teachers, supervisors, and principals chosen on a statewide basis from junior and senior high schools. Teachers of disadvantaged youth from rural areas were given priority and many came from neighboring communities. Preference was given to junior high school teachers in accordance with the finding of research studies that the crucial grade for keeping students in school is Grade 9. The institute was particularly interested in selecting applicants who would be in the position of educating their colleagues to the uses of new materials and methods for working with disadvantaged children. In the view of the director a practicum experience was not particularly useful for these participants, since they had a first-hand knowledge of the problems involved and needed background more than experience. These enrollees sought answers to the problem of helping students with virtually no academic interest or skill in English and reading to discover meaningful content in their disciplines.

The institute program consisted of three courses: Remedial Reading, Linguistics, and Communications, with a laboratory experience as a part of each course. While the development of new techniques and materials was the major concern of these courses, the strength of the program lay in its interdisciplinary approach to English where, according to the director, "content, theory, and application were all one, all mutually supportive."

The institute staff, which worked closely together—sitting in on each other's courses, attending field trips with the enrollees, and participating in weekly colloquia with them—were responsible for integration of the course material. Language was the common dimension of the three courses. The development of skills in reading, speech, and writing was demonstrated to be intrinsic to every new technique presented. The key word here was "communication," the role of the mass media in expanding the contacts of rural disadvantaged youth with their cultural heritage, and the function of the school in utilization of these media.

According to the plan of the institute, language laboratories would be used in connection with the linguistic course for the development of individualized pattern drills by the enrollees. Major revisions of this aspect of the program had to be made when it was discovered that only four of the participants had language laboratories in their schools where master tapes could be used. It soon became apparent to the director that his plan to have enrollees develop four-track pattern drills for programmed learning was completely unrealistic in view of the participants' unfamiliarity with even the simplest tape recorders. It was decided to use the language laboratory only for illustrative purposes during the remainder of the Institute.

The graphics laboratory, used in the remedial reading course, proved to be more practical and manageable than the language laboratory.

Only 2 of the 30 enrollees had had any prior experience with audiovisual equipment. By the end of the course, however, all the participants had learned to run a tape recorder, as well as filmstrip, opaque, overhead, and movie projectors. The graphics laboratory was so equipped that the enrollees could make their own materials for the audiovisual equipment. They learned to design graphics, to Xerox materials, cut and run stencils, and develop slides for use with or without machines. Thus the course work was supplemented by the development of materials the participants would be able to use in their home schools.

The participants also gained familiarity with reading machines, such as tachistoscopes and pacers. With this familiarity came the understanding that these machines are useful only with an individualized approach on the part of the teacher to each pupil and his particular reading problem.

The core of the institute program was the instruction provided by the three staff members in their lectures and demonstrations. As the director pointed out, their selection was based on the criteria of extensive classroom experience with disadvantaged youth and outstanding ability not only in the affective area but also in the cognitive area of teaching. As a group he felt they knew their subjects thoroughly, were highly imaginative and lucid in presentation, and were capable of persuasion via "low key" demonstrations. On this point the Aware Team concurred.

Consultants from the departments of psychology, sociology, and education were invited as speakers during the first week of the institute and at special colloquia. The psychologist and the sociologist focused upon the differences between rural and urban disadvantaged youth and upon some of the principles implied by these differences for classroom teaching. The educational psychologist stressed the importance of the teacher's attitude and its effect on these students. He demonstrated strategies that the participants could use when working with their colleagues in evolving programs in their home school systems. Local administrators of school systems with a high proportion of disadvantaged youth spoke of their approaches to the problem and suggested program modifications they felt would be desirable. On later visits to local schools the participants compared what they had heard from these administrators and what they actually saw in the classroom, often finding a discrepancy between the two.

Institute participants observed in classrooms of three local school districts but were not able to try out any of the newer materials for working with disadvantaged youth. Having had experience with some outstanding teachers at the institute who had demonstrated these techniques and materials, participants found it difficult to tolerate teachers going through the "parts of speech" and "diagramming" rituals with students whom they perceived as trapped in these summer classrooms. Participants were also sensitive to the sarcasm and hate shown toward the students by the teachers being observed. Where well-meaning but poorly trained teachers were working with the disadvantaged, complete boredom set in. Such comments from the enrollees as, "I could see myself doing the same things last year, and I couldn't stand it," or, "If I had been that kid, I would have told the teacher to go to hell," typified the reaction of the enrollees to the observation experience.

A unique type of pre- and post-testing and evaluation was employed at Pennsylvania State University. Enrollees had their teaching techniques with disadvantaged children taped before the start of the institute and again in the fall when they were back in their local school. Comparisons will be made, according to the Withall Social-Climate Index of Classrooms, of differences perceived. In this way positive changes in both approach and technique may be seen and evaluated by the teachers themselves, lending reinforcement to any changes recognized during the institute itself, but which can only be verified in actual classroom process.

The Aware Team found definite evidence of attitude change toward teaching disadvantaged youth in the areas of English and reading which had come about without a practicum or any real involvement in community schools serving disadvantaged children. As one participant expressed it, "I have always felt uncomfortable teaching many things in English—traditional grammar, for instance. And now I can see that I have to modernize my methods and teach something the kids need and can use."

The enrollees claimed that the most significant changes resulting from their institute experience were in their perception of subject matter and in their attitudes toward the disadvantaged. The director noted that alterations in curriculum were not only possible but were actually recommended by the State Department of Education (Curriculum Guide 1965); this fact came as a shock to participants. Evidence of attitudinal change was also revealed in daily logs kept by the participants, and in observations made by the staff. Changes in their teaching techniques were documented by an analysis of sessions of their communications classes, which had been video-taped.

It was generally agreed by staff, enrollees, and Aware Team members that the program should be eight weeks in length and that six weeks was far too short a time in which to accomplish the objectives of the institute. It seemed to the Aware Team that the development of a practicum in the community and school, with the time and materials for testing and development of techniques and methods, would only have strengthened the institute. The director plans to propose an institute for eight weeks next summer in which one full week of teaching will be afforded all participants in a cooperating school system in Huntingdon, Pennsylvania. The director would like to see the eighth week of the institute used for follow-up, where trained observers would be able to evaluate the application of institute content in the participants' classrooms.

The director suggested that some kind of screening device, such as an attitude test, projective test, or observation schedule, be used to avoid selection of participants who seemed opposed to any change whatever. Five of the participants showed evidence of being what the director termed "aginners." It was reported that it made little difference what the topic was—they were "agin" it. He felt that extensive use of language laboratories for use with disadvantaged students would be better handled under a research program than an institute program.

The Aware Team found that while the curriculum library was excellent for general units of work and curriculum guidelines, there was no separate section of materials developed for disadvantaged students. There were materials that offered descriptions of the disadvantaged, along with the usual complement of commentaries, but these were not supplemented by actual lesson plans or unit plans for classroom use.

One of the major objectives of the institute was to help enrollees develop processes and structure for the education of their colleagues in the use of materials and methods for working with the disadvantaged. This objective, at the time of the Aware Team visit, did not seem to be met. Without a team approach in the recruitment of personnel and without direct lines of communication between the University and the participants' school districts, the Team questioned whether the hoped-for changes among the colleagues of the teachers at the institute would come about. However, the director reported, he has post-institute data that show widespread change among the teaching colleagues of institute participants.

The Education Department at the Pennsylvania State University has been interested for some time in starting a program designed to educate teachers of disadvantaged youth. According to the director, the institute did much to catalyze thinking and helped to bring the program closer to reality. The institute showed that a significant number of teachers are interested in such a program, that personnel is available to direct it, and that progress has been made in building a library of significant materials concerning disadvantaged youth and their learning behavior.

What impressed the Aware Team most about the institute program was the outstanding rapport between staff and enrollees and the fact that attitudinal changes appear to have come about without any practicum.

NDEA SUMMER INSTITUTE FOR ELEMENTARY AND SECONDARY SCHOOL TEACHERS OF DISADVANTAGED YOUTH: UNIVERSITY OF PUERTO RICO, RIO PIEDRAS, PUERTO RICO

To the tourist's mind the words Puerto Rico conjure golden beaches and the lively surf of the Caribbean dappled by the gloss of the full moon or the blazing sun. There is, however, the real Puerto Rico, one quite apart from the tourist's daydream. This is an island proud of its progress but still marked by poverty.

An offensive on poverty was mounted in the early forties which has resulted in clear evidence of improvement, but which is still short of its total goal. The efforts to reach this goal have led to a deep concern for large sections of the island's population, which appear to be left out of the general stream of socioeconomic advancement and which seek incorporation into the Commonwealth's progress.

Though the Puerto Rican Department of Instruction has for years taken positive action to combat the terrible effects of poverty and the resultant educational handicaps, the Department believed increased effort was needed. Universities began to meet the challenge. Consultants and organizers of many programs to aid the disadvantaged were prepared in the universities, but it was understood that the University of Puerto Rico had a further role to play.

The leadership of the University reasoned that new endeavors to improve education might effectively center on the classroom teacher. The effectiveness of schools serving the depressed areas may partially be determined by the recruitment and retention of competent and devoted teachers. Because of the present high turnover among teachers and the difficulty in recruiting new teachers, many schools have teachers who need further education. The principal target then became the teacher and her own knowledge and perception of the problems of disadvantaged children. Thus the eight-week Summer Institute for Elementary and Secondary Teachers of Disadvantaged Children and Youth came into being.

This program encompassed teachers, experienced and new, in their orientation and training to provide appropriate methods, curriculum materials, and approaches to functional classroom management. As envisioned, the program investigated the problems of the disadvantaged child in order to improve the efficiency of those teachers who work with such children. Enhanced understanding of the child and the need to increase teacher retention in the depressed area schools were the main foci. The institute accepted classroom teachers only. In this respect it differed from many institutes on the mainland.

The program was geared to the development of a clear concept of the teacher's role in working with disadvantaged children and youth. Special reference was made to the improvement of the youth's self-image and perception of his school environment. Emphasis on the areas of family, labor, and social pathology also covered the role of social agencies in the disadvantaged community. This knowledge was expected to provide the teacher with the information needed to form a realistic basis for the planning and execution of her teaching activities. Each enrollee was expected to be able to speak, read, and write in both English and Spanish. The teachers selected were persons who would be working with disadvantaged youth during the coming school year.

An incident reported by the staff psychologist gives insight into the differing backgrounds participants brought to the institute. During a discussion of home visits, one participant, Mrs. A., made a generalization about disadvantaged families based on her observations of one family she had visited. Another participant, Mrs. B., refused to accept the generality as valid, asserting that Mrs. A. was using her own middle class standards in ascribing to all poor people certain characteristics. Mrs. B., herself from a disadvantaged background, took the position that each family was individual; their only commonality was poverty. She felt that generalizations such as Mrs. A.'s led to stereotypes which precluded understanding and help.

Mrs. A. remarked that Mrs. B. was being hypersensitive because Mrs. A. had been speaking only of one family and had not meant to make a general statement concerning large groups of disadvantaged people. However, she allowed that she should have been specific in her comments and that the fault of stereotyping is one that each person should guard against, including Mrs. B.

The psychologist, by perceptive handling of this situation, helped to bring the conflict to resolution in terms of deeper understanding between the two women. Their sympathies as well as their tempers had been evoked and now a reasoned approach to their roles as teachers and as concerned human beings could be taken.

The majority of the participants reported that they viewed themselves as middle class and that, as such, they needed close contact with the life conditions of the disadvantaged. The institute provided this through the practicum, home visits, and field trips to disadvantaged neighborhoods.

This fact was substantiated in the enrollee interviews with the Aware Team. Enrollees felt that they had gained more insight into what it means to be disadvantaged, and into the effects such a situation might have upon a child. They found themselves more compassionate and tolerant of a child who was, for example, late or absent. The knowledge that such children sometimes have no shoes to wear, or have had little or no sleep, and in some instances lack transportation was no longer merely an intellectual abstraction. The participants reported they could put their knowledge of the children to work in helping to design improved educational experiences for them.

The Aware Team's report of this site visit was not as comprehensive as some other reports have been. The function of this visit was an exploratory one. It was for the purpose of developing guidelines for future visits. A further difficulty was that the classes were conducted in Spanish, and the flow of communication was hindered by interpretation.

The Team reported observing the great sensitivity to the needs of enrollees as shown by the way schedules were changed to provide more time for informal discussions and group conferences. Also noted was the focus on communication: teacher to child, child to teacher.

Another strength was the use of a full-time psychologist on the staff. The ability to bring to the surface the true feelings of enrollees, even to the extent of allowing clashes when necessary, was viewed as an enabling factor.

The attitude of the faculty was reported as an area of strength. Disadvantaged children were not regarded by faculty as a breed apart; this reasoning made possible a real identification of the participant with the disadvantaged child. This identification was further enhanced by home visits, which gave greater understanding of the life conditions that confront the disadvantaged.

The Aware Team reported that although the program had potentiality for impact, the grade span appeared too wide. The inclusion of K through 12 fragmented the design. Teachers of K through 8 and teachers of 9 through 12 seemed to be operating in their own schools under very different conditions. A reason for this might be that the elementary schools have a large number of disadvantaged children but few of these children go on to high school. A narrowing of the span of grade levels was suggested by the Aware Team.

The general tone of the institute seemed to be one of excitement over a real and deep experience, participants and Aware Team related. The cognitive aspects were difficult to assess because of the language barrier. There were some political dissensions; Independents vs. Statehood parties, but these appeared to be handled in a constructive manner. A comment by one enrollee could sum up the effectiveness of the Institute: "Something is happening to me."

NDEA SUMMER INSTITUTE FOR ELEMENTARY TEACHERS OF SPANISH-SPEAKING DISADVANTAGED CHILDREN: UNIVERSITY OF TEXAS, AUSTIN, TEXAS

There are well over a million people of Mexican origin living in Texas today, the majority of them Spanish-speaking. The public educational system has traditionally been designed for the native, English-speaking child and geared to his needs. Under such an instructional program, according to research conducted at the University of Texas, approximately 80 percent of the beginning first graders from a non-English background fail in their initial school experience; they are unable to learn to read. Many of these youngsters are from economically disadvantaged homes that have a high percentage of family illiteracy. Some of these children do not succeed partly because of poor school attendance due to family migration or lack of parental interest. However, the largest single contributing factor, according to the study mentioned above, is the language barrier.

The Texas Summer Institute for Teachers of Spanish-Speaking Disadvantaged Children was designed to provide teachers with the special skills, knowledge, and attitudes needed to increase the probability for academic achievement of these children. The institute program grew out of a first-grade reading research project (U. S. Office of Education No. 2648) with Spanish-speaking children, in which several members of the institute staff had worked together developing new materials and techniques that utilize experiential, conceptual, and linguistic buildups based on "culture fair" science content. Their experiences in this project led them to a realization of the need for a multiple approach in dealing with the psychological, social, and economic factors that affect the learning of these children.

The institute program offered advanced study in new techniques and materials dealing with the language and experiential development of Spanish-speaking children through closely supervised classroom experience, linguistic instruction, and language laboratory practice. An important aspect of the institute program was its focus upon Spanish culture, its folk dances, folk songs, history, and sociological characteristics.

There were 30 enrollees at the institute, 22 teachers and 8 supervisors, both Spanish-American and Anglo-American. The central focus of the institute program was on the supervised practicum experience, which lasted for six of the nine weeks of the institute. The participants were assigned in pairs to teach in the Austin public school preschool English classes, where they worked with the classroom teacher, forming a three-member team. Every morning for one hour the participants worked with the children in intensive language pattern drills. They used a variety of language activities, among them songs, role-playing, and puppetry. Each three-member team together planned each day's instructional program, defining the role of each in relation to the language sessions and to the program as a whole. The teaching team used lesson plans in basic English prepared by the University of Texas staff, and the institute participants made use of new science-mathematics content materials for developing oral language.

The initial week of the institute was used to orient the participants to the cultural and psychological background of the Spanish-speaking child; to the audiolingual techniques for developing oral language abilities; to the new materials involving mathematics-science content; and to activities designed for developing cognitive skills and experiential backgrounds. Demonstrations were given by the institute staff using children enrolled in the preschool program of the Austin public schools. Together participants began practicing the audiolingual techniques they would be using during their supervised student teaching experience. Despite the fact that all the participants except supervisors and principals had taught classes containing a majority of Spanish-speaking pupils, most of the material presented to them during the orientation week was unfamiliar, and they expressed a need for further observation before beginning their practicum experience. Student teaching assignments were delayed for three days so that the enrollees could have additional language-pattern practice.

An important characteristic of this institute was its flexibility in meeting the needs of the participants. The assistant director was in close touch with participant activities at all times so that new participant needs could be identified almost immediately and program modifications made. The director stressed that the institute could not be meaningful unless the problems encountered by the participants from day to day were faced openly and continuously. For example, the staff found that participants were not ready for the theory underlying curriculum building and therefore placed additional emphasis on this aspect of the program.

In addition to the daily one-hour practicum experience, the institute program consisted of a 2-hour lecture course in reading, which included techniques and demonstrations, and a linguistic and language laboratory course. The remaining time was spent in library assignments, preparation of materials, and individual conferences with instructional staff.

The lecture course placed special emphasis on structuring the new techniques into the socioeconomic setting of the Spanish-American child. Extensive use was made of consultants, many of them from the University of Texas, who, in the view of the director, made valuable contributions to the institute program. These specialists remained with the group for long discussion periods following their lectures and were available for further consultation upon request. Several of them had been involved in research projects with Spanish-speaking disadvantaged children. One consultant was engaged in developing the rationale of the science content as a vehicle for developing oral language. Another, who had created interlanguage test materials, was able to discuss with enrollees the problem of creating valid testing instruments for Spanish-speaking school populations and the administration of such tests. An international authority on teaching foreign language in elementary school, who was particularly interested in the language problems of Spanish-speaking Americans, was able to point up some of the theoretical models underlying new language methods and materials.

The language laboratory course was planned to focus upon the reading-writing and speaking-listening problems of the Spanish-speaking school beginner. The aim of the course was the development of teacher understanding of and competence in standard language patterns. Individualized assistance was planned for the participants; Spanish-Americans were to be given the opportunity to improve their own language skills and English-speaking participants were to be given assistance in Spanish. However, these planned activities were only partially realized. Attention was given to new techniques in spelling instruction, handwriting, creative writing, and drama as well as ways of utilizing subject content for language development.

Two field trips were undertaken—the first to a Job Corps Center at Camp Gary, the second to preschool classes and community centers in San Antonio. The purpose of these trips was further to orient participants to the needs of disadvantaged youth and to the possibilities of compensatory education.

Specific provisions for follow-up were planned by the institute. The immediate administrative superior of each participant received a letter from the director reminding the supervisor that one of his teachers had attended an institute for teachers of Spanish-speaking disadvantaged children and stressing the need for lending administrative support to the participant's applications of what he had learned about Spanish-speaking pupils. Three of the participants were subsequently made directors of local Head Start or migrant programs. Participants from Austin were to be visited by a member of the institute staff. Participants in San Antonio, some of whom will be teaching experimental classes in the University of Texas project, will be visited regularly (not less than once every two weeks) by members of the project and institute staff.

The enrollees considered the supervised practicum to be one of the major strengths of the institute. Many had come expecting to find the usual methods courses and were pleased by the lack of formal course work in education. Some said that they would like to have spent more time working with children. The suggestions ranged from teaching two hours a day to permitting participants to operate an entire school for eight weeks.

The participants commented on the excellence of the staff, especially the two supervisors of the practicum. They appreciated the opportunity to improve their own language skills and to learn some Spanish-speaking folklore. They would have liked a continuation of the formal lectures on cultural anthropology and sociology given at the beginning of the institute. The staff agreed with the enrollees on this point.

The Aware Team found the rapport between staff and enrollees unusually strong. They commented on the willingness of the staff to encourage participants to disagree and to provide opportunity for discussion of disagreements. The institute program is unique in the sense that it utilized a "patterned" approach to learning. Participants were encouraged to study the learning principles upon which this approach is based but were not pressured into an unquestioning acceptance of it. When some of the institute participants expressed a different philosophy of learning, the director invited a consultant who was in basic agreement with the dissenters to lead a week-long seminar exploring and demonstrating learning experiences based on the theory of the dissenters.

It was the opinion of the Aware Team that the cognitive aspects of the program were appropriately related to the purposes of the institute and to the needs of the participants. They felt that the institute experience was having an observable impact on most of the participants, which was evident in their oral statements, their attitudes toward the children, and their behavior in the practicum, where they utilized learning principles in exploring new ways to work with children. The participants prepared useful materials to be used as teaching aids. The faculty was particularly pleased with the creativity and skill with which the participants developed new materials for their classroom use.

The director noted that the experience of the staff in working together on research closely related to the institute content had been extremely helpful in planning an effective institute program in a short period of time. He pointed to the advantages of the institute's university setting, not only in the availability of consultants, but in the administrative support given institute operations—arranging for space and equipment and help in obtaining materials and hiring staff for the institute.

There was agreement among staff, enrollees, and Aware Team members that the theory of curriculum building could have been emphasized less or omitted from the institute program. Participants frankly admitted that they were not ready for the instruction in curriculum building at the level at which it was offered. They suggested that the curriculum phase of the institute be left to form the basis of an advanced institute.

The Aware Team would have liked to see the enrollees spend more time with the children and recommended that an additional supervisor be added to the practicum.

The institute had a noticeable psychological effect on the Spanish-speaking enrollees. They stressed, in their interview with the Aware Team, how they themselves had been taught in the past to forsake their Mexican culture. The institute experience was the first time they had been urged to remember that they had roots in Mexico. Their pride in learning about their native culture was expressed repeatedly. Some of the institute experiences had been threatening to them, yet they felt that these experiences should not be changed or omitted from the program. This was the case with the language laboratory, which some of the older members of this group found difficult; however, they saw the need for speech correction if they were to serve as models for primary school children. The Spanish-American enrollees, realizing that they had been cheated of their real heritage, wanted to insure their pupils the right to be proud of being Spanish-American. The institute staff, seeing the impact of this experience on the ego strength of the participants, state that they plan to work more intensively in this direction in future institutes.

NDEA SUMMER INSTITUTE FOR ELEMENTARY AND SECONDARY SCHOOL TEACHERS OF DISADVANTAGED CHILDREN AND YOUTH: WESTERN WASHINGTON STATE COLLEGE, BELLINGHAM, WASHINGTON

The broad range of industrial and agrarian productivity of the state of Washington has drawn men and their families from other parts of the country to work in its factories and upon its farms. With the influx have come problems: those of unskilled manpower, deteriorating housing, low incomes, and educational deprivation. Some members of three groups in particular reflect symptoms of severe disadvantagement.

The members of the first group are not, however, newcomers. They are Washington's longest-time residents. Of the 27,076 Indians in the state, thousands of them find it necessary to leave the reservation each year because of inadequate resources within it. Once off the reservation they tend to concentrate in the larger cities where their income levels are half that of the average Washington resident. Their children, the faculty of Western Washington State College reports, experience a high incidence of failure in the early years of school; 65 percent are reported as having failed one year by the end of second grade.

Migrant labor constitutes the second group. Generally Spanish-speaking, the migrant families follow the crops during the picking season through the Pacific Northwest. Their constant movement and uncertainty of employment produce conditions not conducive for their children obtaining continuity in education.

The third group are unskilled laborers, with an increasing proportion of Negroes, who come looking for steady work and better opportunities. Many find work in the mixed industry and shipping of Seattle and Tacoma. They tend to settle into the inner-city cores.

In designing an institute for teachers of the disadvantaged at Western Washington State College at Bellingham the director stated that school personnel need to acquaint themselves with the backgrounds and problems of the children from these groups. The institute was planned so that teachers could explore remedial techniques that would unlock intellectual potential and would encourage participants to try to evolve a more appropriate curriculum and methodology relating experience to learnings.

Out of the 480 applicants, 50 participants were selected from the elementary and secondary levels who would be working with disadvantaged children in the following school year. The majority of teachers enrolled came from within the state; the remaining 6 were from as far away as South Dakota, two of these Catholic nuns. Eight participants came from Seattle, 6 from Bellingham itself. Where this was possible, teams consisting of teachers, guidance counselors, and a representative from the supervisory staff were admitted from the same school or district. It was believed that upon their return they could put into action plans and programs developed during their institute experience. The director expressed the opinion that a team could attack the low educational level of the disadvantaged more effectively than could an isolated individual. Among the participants there were twice as many men as women. More than half the participants had taught for more than 10 years.

At Western Washington there were two interesting programmatic emphases: the team approach and a week-long camping experience on Orcas Island. Since the team approach meant that the principals and teachers worked together on problems common to their school, it was necessary that rapport between administrative and classroom roles be established. Initially teachers were hesitant in expressing themselves. However, with the focus on a common goal rather than intrastaff evaluation, the selection of supervisors and teachers from the same school was a strength, in the view of both the Aware Team and the institute director. One enrollee reported on this in the following manner, "I gained an awareness of what can be done when the administration, teachers, and finances combine to face a felt need."

A most important and innovative aspect of this institute was that time was scheduled throughout the program for team planning. Projects were developed by the participants, *with* their principals, which they planned to undertake on return to their schools.

The sixth week of the institute was devoted to group camping on Orcas Island in Puget Sound. Participants from the institute, staff, and 50 children camped together in the rustic setting. During this time the participants became "family" for the children, whose ages ranged from 8 to 15. Each participant was assigned one child to work with intensively. The children had been earlier selected by the institute staff in cooperation with community welfare departments and private relief agencies. They came primarily from the Lummi Reservation, with a few from the inner city of Seattle, from Tacoma, and from nearby small towns and rural communities. It had been expected that there would be a number of migrant children in the group. With the failure of the berry crop, however, the adjacent migrant camps were unoccupied, so that no migrant children were available at the time of the institute.

The group of 50 children was quite obviously disadvantaged. Some had only the clothes they arrived in; others needed bedding equipment, and sleeping bags were bought for them. For the teachers living with these children there was the opportunity to become deeply involved in the life style of one child and to respond to affective aspects of a differing subculture. In such close contact implications could more readily be drawn with regard to a child's coping ability when he had suffered discrimination on two counts: from his economic disadvantagement and from his color.

Reactions from the children to this experience were varied. One said, on viewing the number of adults at the camp, "This looks like a teachers' meeting." Some of the children impressed the participants as being defensively hostile and boastful. In a few cases a child would attempt to denigrate the potential meaning of the experience by a retreat from a close relationship with his "family." Knowing that the experience would soon end, how could a child learn to trust? Finding answers to this question and developing strategies for improving the child's self-concept and ego strength were the main tasks for the participants.

From the participants came a mixed response. In the view of many, the camp had provided the most fruitful part of the institute, allowing a close-up of the problem. Responses ranged from, "It was good for the kids but it didn't do the teachers any good," to "It has been enlightening to work with colored children," or "It was hard to work with a child for just a week, to learn about him, see the help he needs, and to be unable to follow up on him and give him some real help." For a number of teachers the lack of organization and structure in the program on the Island was disturbing. "The structure of unstructure" was not comfortably perceived. For another such program it was recommended that teachers work together with children and that more complete profiles of each child be available earlier in the program. In the group interview few wanted to change the one-to-one relationship with the children. Participants stressed that more time with the children would be beneficial and that the camping experience should come *at the end* of a practicum experience with them.

Since the emphasis in the institute was on local educational problems, the participants believed there were too few staff members familiar with the area. Two staff members were from the College faculty, another proved to be more familiar with the problems of the disadvantaged in Harlem, and the fourth, a sociologist, was from the Tobago Island in the West Indies. Seven of the 13 visiting lecturers spoke from personal knowledge of local problems. However, when participants responded during a group interview with the Aware Team, criticism was expressed by a number that there had been too much time given the "experts" via the lecture platform and not enough time devoted to interaction among institute members themselves.

Seminars in the psychological, sociological, and educational implications of the disadvantaged examined the effects of cultural-economic deprivation on youth and children, with a biweekly seminar devoted to a multidisciplinary approach, where institute participants and staff shared in searching out strategies for working with these children. Individual research projects were undertaken by each participant enabling him to make inquiries into a current problem and to devise ways of meeting it that might be relevant to his own school situation.

Enrollees expressed criticism of the cognitive aspects of the program, stating that it was heavily weighted in areas of theoretical content. There seemed to be too many out-of-state speakers. Specificity was lacking in the more comprehensive global approach, and speakers tended to be repetitive, since little time was given to their orientation to the total program. "Less time spent sitting in the classroom" and "Less theory and talk about the problem, more practical experience in teaching these youth" were comments made by participants.

Further difficulties were encountered in the experiential aspects of the program. Minimum emphasis was placed on instructional processes such as small-group discussions, home visits, and field teaching experience. Field trips were taken to Indian reservations, migrant work camps, and the Seattle inner city. Since these trips were taken by small groups, without opportunity for feedback to the total group, vicarious sharing was not possible. The intensive week on Orcas Island in some measure offset these programmatic deficiencies, but enrollees reported some concern for the loss of opportunities to work closely with children in some type of ongoing practicum experience.

"I feel we could be more involved with students, disadvantaged students. This might be in a classroom situation or face to face or whatever, but let's work with the kids," said one participant. "The active work with children, followed by seminar evaluation and discussion with other members of the institute, would have been more valuable than lectures by "experts" unfamiliar with problems in the Northwest," another noted.

The Aware Team suggested that there seemed to be a tendency to disperse the program across too broad a field, as evidenced by the wide grade span of the participants. To involve teachers from first through twelfth grade, submitting three populations of disadvantaged for study and taking participants from both rural and slum schools, seemed to result in a dilution rather than a distillation of content and focus.

It was suggested by the director and recommended as a change by the Aware Team that the grade span of participants be narrowed. In this connection the Aware Team also suggested a reduced number of enrollees; however, the possibility for effective follow-up was seen to be greatly enhanced by the presence of both supervisory and teacher personnel in the same institute.

A further strength reported by the Aware Team was the high calibre of the staff (only 2 of whom were full-time members) and the high level of ability, competence, and experience of the participants themselves. Statements like "Utilize participants more," and "What I had hoped to see was other teachers in action solving these problems," and "I would set up committees of teachers to help me plan," illustrate the participants' ability and willingness to assume a more active responsibility for the program. Enrollee expectations for specific strategies and techniques demonstrated by curriculum experts, as reported in the Aware Team group interview, could only be theoretically, but not practically implemented, since the only experience with children was the week on Orcas Island.

There were two other impactful aspects of the program: (1) the scheduling of institute time for team planning of specific projects to be carried out in the participants' own schools, and (2) the selection of children who were indeed disadvantaged for the experiential component. The latter appeared to be lacking in most programs visited.

In summary, the institute at Western Washington set itself an ambitious task in alerting teachers to current research and approaches to a wide gamut of disadvantagement, and in attempting to change some of the *a priori* attitudes held by many. Pairing teachers and children during the week on Orcas Island provided an interpersonal experience. In the words of one teacher, "We all tend to live in a world of faulty generalizations, looking at the world through cliché-colored glasses." For many participants, this confrontation encouraged them to see the disadvantaged for the first time without those glasses.

Case studies of selected programs

CHAPTER 4

Introduction

Four programs, one sponsored by the Office of Economic Opportunity and three NDEA institutes, have been selected to provide opportunity for more detailed studies in the processes of preparing teachers to work with disadvantaged children and youth. The criteria for selection of programs to be so reported included proper focus of the program, the existence of innovative aspects, and the existence of elements which might profitably be incorporated into future programs.

In these case studies the programs have been written from the report of the Aware Team and the final reports of the program directors. Thus they include the directors' own evaluations of their programs.

NDEA SUMMER INSTITUTE FOR ELEMENTARY SCHOOL TEACHERS OF DISADVANTAGED CHILDREN AND YOUTH (PRESCHOOL THROUGH SIXTH GRADE, INNER-CITY) BALL STATE UNIVERSITY, MUNCIE, INDIANA

The NDEA Institute held at Ball State University in the summer of 1965 was designed precisely to meet the needs of elementary school teachers of disadvantaged children and youth who work in midwestern inner-city schools. Smaller midwestern cities in Indiana, Illinois, Kentucky, Ohio, and Michigan are beginning to face some of the educational problems with which the larger metropolitan centers have been dealing for some time.

Muncie, Indiana, the eighth largest city in the state, is a case in point. In the 1920's and 1930's Muncie was selected as the prototype of the small midwestern American community. Robert and Helen Lynd in MIDDLETOWN and MIDDLETOWN IN TRANSITION minutely described Muncie in terms of population, economics, education, and cultural patterns, and in their second book, studied the changes wrought in the passing of a decade. Since then, Muncie remains somewhat typical in that it reflects the growth and change common in American urban life. For example, in the ten-year period between the 1950 and the 1960 U. S. census, its population increased more than 10,000. Similar growth patterns are found in other midwestern urban communities, which, in part, are becoming larger as the rural populations migrate to the cities in increasing numbers.

The rural-to-urban migrants generally have incomes in the lowest third of the national living scale. They lack readily marketable urban job skills. Their life style differs sharply from that of the city dweller. They may be highly visible as are the Negro and Indian internal migrants, because of skin color; or easily identifiable, as are the Appalachian and "poor whites," because of speech patterns, differences in dress, and folkways. They gravitate to the older cores of the cities because they expect to find low-cost housing there. Their children drift into and out of the inner-city schools.

Some of the teachers in such schools feel that the kind of teaching which was effective with previous school populations is not effective with the children now attending their schools. They point to low achievement on tests, inability to read at grade level, lack of parental concern with education, and high dropout rate as indications that something is wrong. The NDEA institute at Ball State University surveyed some of these teachers about their concerns in teaching children. Here are some responses:

–"Improving the seemingly nonchalant attitudes of parents and the 'so-so' attitudes of students"

–"Understanding the backgrounds of these children so that a better job may be done in the classroom"

–"Reaching the nonreaders and becoming acquainted with suitable materials"

–"Working for better correlation between the curriculum and the children's real life experiences; helping adults and parents understand the learning situation"

–"Better understanding of the Negro child—reacting to his reactions, motivating his desire to learn, developing his sense of responsibility, assisting him to the utmost in learning"

–"Helping children adjust themselves to life in an urban community"

With these comments and other information to work from, an institute was designed to help 29 midwestern teachers improve their understandings and skills in working with the disadvantaged inner-city child. The program was carefully tailored to effect a balance between cognitive and affective learnings for the participants. Learning experiences involved lectures, films, tapes, assigned and suggested reading; introductions to, experiences with, and development of teaching materials; individual and group conferences, field experiences in the disadvantaged community; and intensive teaching experiences with disadvantaged children in a closely supervised practicum setting in inner-city schools. During the eight-week institute, four weeks were spent in residence at Ball State University and in the community of Muncie, four in residence in a YMCA in Indianapolis and in the adjacent community and schools.

One of the features that contributed to the quality of the learning experience was the residential accommodations of the program. Both participants and faculty lived and worked in the same building during the four weeks spent on campus at Ball State University. The institute report describes the facilities:

A very large room was provided on the main floor at Williams Residence Hall for classroom-seminar purposes. The classroom had air-conditioning, making it an ideal setting for this type of institute. The area was large enough to house all participants comfortably and to provide for:

1. Ample space for several round tables (groups of six) to be permanently housed for small group discussions, lectures, and seminars.
2. Ample space for comfortable chairs to be arranged in a circle for large group discussions.
3. Ample space for several large tables to display a great number of educational books and materials, and for use by the participants.
4. Interest centers to stimulate participants' reading and utilization of materials.

In addition, a separate room adjacent to the entranceway of the classroom housed the library of professional books, periodicals, and audiovisual materials. This library and social lounging area had comfortable furniture and was also air-conditioned.

The classroom and library facilities housed audiovisual equipment for use by the staff when needed. This equipment was always available for independent, individual, and/or small-group use by participants.

The residence hall room facilities provided for the participants were located on the second floor of the same building, housing two to each room. The participants were arbitrarily assigned to the rooms as they arrived on campus. This provided opportunity for integrated room arrangements, which proved very beneficial for the participants, as well as serving to reinforce direct and indirect objectives of the institute's program. However, it should be understood that the policy of Ball State University residence halls does not condone segregation during the regular school year.

The hall in which participants were housed provided a large corner lounge with comfortable chairs which enabled the participants to get together informally to have discussion and/or listen to records and tapes of lectures and speakers of national conferences for their review.

With the Institute's library, classroom-seminar, and cafeteria services all located one flight below, the entire arrangement of facilities provided by Ball State University for the institute proved to be most ideal and definitely contributed to the success of the first four weeks of the institute.

Similar, if slightly less comfortable and convenient, facilities were provided for participants and staff at the Fall Creek YMCA in Indianapolis. Nine of the women participants had to be temporarily housed at a nearby YWCA until space became available at the YMCA for them. This caused a temporary disruption in the cohesiveness of the group which was remedied when the nine were reunited with the group in the YMCA.

The residential experience for both participants and institute staff was a planned part of the institute process aimed at building awareness of group dynamics, providing the maximum opportunities for mutual exchange of ideas and information, sharing of experiences, intellectual cross-fertilization, and for some, a first experience in living and working closely with members of a different racial and ethnic background. The Aware Team and the institute staff reported that living and working together for the whole eight weeks exerted a significant influence on the participants' growth.

The following is a sampling of the way participants reported their reactions to this aspect of the institute: "Just studying, feeling, living this problem of teaching disadvantaged children for eight weeks in such an invigorating atmosphere has brought forth untold growth and depths of understanding of which I am becoming conscious only at the present time"; "I enjoyed the freedom and flexibility in the program of the institute that let me explore ideas I had not tried or heard of before"; "The close relationship of participants and the staff brought to light my frailities and my capabilities. Acceptance happened to be the key and unlocked doors to increased understanding of true learning and how it can take place in my own classroom."

The institute was designed so that participants could have four weeks of in-depth experiences in two kinds of midwestern city cores—the smaller community of Muncie and the larger, industrial city of Indianapolis. It was believed that in the smaller community it would be easier for the participants to get perspective on the disadvantaged inner city as a segment of the whole. In the larger city setting, the participants tested self and knowledge about children, homes, schools, and agencies in the disadvantaged areas of the community and explored the problem in a larger context. In both cities, direct experiences in the community and direct teaching experiences with children were planned for the participants, giving opportunity to build a personal collection of observations, teaching experiences, and repertoire of skills. These two placements made possible the comparison of situations and responses.

The field experiences provided for participants in both Muncie and Indianapolis were varied and imaginative, according to the Aware Team Report. In addition to the more usual visits to community agencies, courts, city summer schools and playgrounds, Operation Head Start programs, camps, and day nurseries, participants were assigned to visit a laundromat in a disadvantaged area on a Saturday morning to observe family life, children taking responsibility, and the total milieu. Visits to the homes of children with whom participants were working in the practicum were also arranged. Discussions such as "Guidelines for Community Observation and Visitation," "The Family as a Social Unit," and "Adjustment to New Environment" were conducted by staff with participants. Each field experience was followed up by small-group discussion and in some cases, by written reports. On Sundays participants were encouraged, although not required, to attend services of their own faith in churches in the community of their practicum schools.

The practicum experience was tailored to the expressed needs of the individual participants. Participants were given latitude in their choice of grade level of children with whom they wished to gain experience. One emphasis of the practicum was the intelligent selection of materials with which to help children learn. Participants studied the needs of the children assigned to them in order to identify the existing materials that would be most beneficial. If the participant could not locate suitable materials in the ample collection provided by the institute, he was encouraged to devise original materials with the aid of staff or other participants. Much use was made of tape recorders by participants with practicum children. Cameras, "Initial Teaching Alphabet," primary typewriters, the Chandler projector, and a portable workshop kit were also mentioned by participants as being particularly useful.

Conferences—individual and group—reinforced learnings after practicum sessions. The tone of these, as reported by the Aware Team, was reality-oriented, with both staff and participants relating the practicum experiences to what the participant could reasonably expect to be able to use when he returned to his home classroom. Each participant prepared for presentation to the entire institute group an activity he had developed in the practicum that he was going to use with his own class in September. In this way attention to concrete learnings was emphasized by institute staff.

Another device used to encourage carry-over of the institute experiences to the schools in which the participants were to teach in the fall was reported by the Aware Team. Each participant, after finishing his practicum experience, wrote a letter to himself describing insights gained during the practicum. These letters, stamped and self-addressed to their home schools, were collected and held by the staff, to be mailed in the late fall to the writers.

The participants themselves expressed the values which they had gained from the practicum experience:

–"Realization that each child must be accepted as he is and that each one can make progress through the teacher's genuine interest in him"

–"Increased faith in and respect for individual children and real trust that they will succeed if given opportunities"

–"Greater willingness to give 'that little extra bit' to each child"

–"To listen and not prejudge him"

–"To look at school through his eyes"

–"New outlook and keener sensitivity to the vast possibilities for learning which exist beyond the classroom"

–"Greater confidence in oneself as a teacher"

–"Broader knowledge and understanding of various teaching materials and ideas on method and content"

–"Greater concern for involving parents in school and for closer home-school relationships"

The staff commented on the value of the practicum experience for the participants, particularly noting that the latitude allowed in letting participants help design their own practicum experiences made for most meaningful participation.

One goal of the institute, according to participants and observers, was woven into the very fabric of the institute: to develop awareness of and sensitivity to oneself as a teacher of disadvantaged children. The residential experience, the community participation, the practicum, the lectures, the films, and the reading assignments all contributed to the development of this awareness and sensitivity. An incident told to a member of the Aware Team by the participant to whom it happened illustrates the kinds of growth made possible by the process of the institute.

The participant, a Negro teacher from the South, was invited for dinner to the home of a white child with whom she worked in the practicum. The teacher recounted that at first she made an excuse to the child's parent so that she would not have to accept the invitation. Upon reflection, however, she realized that she had reacted first as a Negro, fearing that problems might arise from the offer which she did not feel prepared to meet. After she had made this self-discovery, a second invitation to the same home was extended, which she accepted, she said, because she was a teacher and as a teacher she had something to offer the child. The dinner proved to be a success. The participant stated that her best learning experience was becoming able to confront her own fears.

Another example of self-acceptance and personal growth was fostered by the supportive relationships developed within the institute. One participant had never been swimming in her life because she had a birthmark that she considered disfiguring and that would be revealed by a bathing suit. However, during residence at the Indianapolis YMCA, staff and participants used the YMCA swimming pool frequently. At one of these swimming parties, the participant not only wore a swimsuit but was taught to swim by other participants.

In response to open-ended questions by staff, the participants identified areas of understanding in which they had achieved growth. Eighty-six percent of the participants said they had improved their ability to listen; 79 percent mentioned an increased ability to sense the feelings of others. Another area mentioned by 79 percent of participants was a better understanding and use of materials in working with disadvantaged children. Other areas frequently mentioned were understanding of community and school and its people, and understanding of children, to get a feeling of their life space.

The 29 participants themselves represented a cross section of midwestern elementary school personnel. There were 21 women and 7 men teachers and one male principal. Eighteen held bachelor's degrees, 11 had completed their master's degrees. All 29 enrolled in the institute for graduate credit. The median age range was 34 to 35. Four had been teaching from one to three years; 5 from four to five years; 7 from six to ten years; and 12 from 11 to 15 years. Fifteen were married, 14 were single.

In reporting on the schools from which they came, 14 teachers said they taught in schools with enrollments from 100 to 499; 13 teachers taught in schools with enrollments from 500 to 999; and 2 teachers taught in schools with enrollments from 1,500 to 1,999. All teachers served in schools where a majority of the children were considered disadvantaged.

In their home school systems, one teacher taught in a system with 1,000 to 1,499 children enrolled, 2 taught in a system with 2,000 to 3,999 children enrolled; and 26 reported their systems enrolled 4,000 or more children. The median-size city in which their school system was located had a population of 70,000 to 99,999.

Applicants to the institute were required to meet the usual qualifications for NDEA institutes, in addition to other standards required of participants in a program designed for elementary, midwestern inner-city teachers of disadvantaged children and youth. The director discussed in detail the questions the Admissions Committee asked about each applicant to the institute. Because, in the opinion of staff and the Aware Team, these criteria were extremely helpful in selecting applicants best able to use the experiences of the institute for improving the quality of their teaching in disadvantaged schools, the questions are quoted here from the final report of the institute:

1. Can he profit from attendance at the institute? Has he taken relevant background courses in his own educational training on the elementary school level? Was he merely a person who has specialized on a secondary program and has made some attempt to teach on the elementary level?
2. Will he be able to multiply himself? Is he in a position to benefit from the experience of the institute? Will he be able to influence other teachers? Does his principal or supervisor and/or superintendent have confidence in him, and will they gain by his experience of the institute?
3. Does he have a genuine interest in this field and is his professional background adequate? Can he profit from his experience? To what degree has he attempted to train himself and to keep informed through inservice workshops, seminars, or personal reading? Does he indicate a mature concept of the needs, and desire to seek improvement of self in working with and understanding children of the culturally disadvantaged?
4. Does he come from an area where the need is great? Are many of the students in his classes from a disadvantaged environment? What proportions of such students are there in his schools, his community?
5. Does the final selection represent a fair geographical distribution of the opportunity to secure training, and to provide uniqueness of experience relevant to the objectives of the institute? Would good cross-fertilization of background and experience be provided for in the institute and its participants?

Through this process, in which the total institute staff was actively involved, 30 original candidates and 19 alternates were selected. Five of the original candidates withdrew their applications for personal reasons and were replaced by four of the alternates (because of the lateness of one candidate in withdrawing, it was not possible to replace him). In all, 465 inquiries were received about the institute; 443 application sets were distributed to those persons inquiring; 222 completed applications were returned. The 19 alternates were considered to be of the first rank, equal in qualifications to the 30 original candidates. Application sets were completed by applicants in 34 of the 48 continental states.

The staff of the institute included a director, 2 full-time staff members, 3 half-time staff members, one graduate assistant, and one full-time secretary. The director assisted in the practicum experiences of one group of participants as well as directing the institute. One staff member served as assistant director, taught the course, Education of the Inner-City Child, and supervised a group of participants in the practicum. The 2 part-time staff members shared the coordination of the practicum experience. The Aware Team reported that the staff individually and collectively contributed uniquely to the overall quality of the institute. One set the tone of the institute and with great skill, according to the view of the Aware Team, guided the developing process that made sensitivity training possible. Another's major contribution was the presentation of curriculum and materials in useful and meaningful ways. A third provided insights from another discipline. This man frankly admitted his lack of first-hand experiences with disadvantaged children and entered, with the participants, into the practicum experiences in order to remedy this deficiency. The participants reported that he even arranged to take practicum students fishing with him so that he could get to know them better. Another provided knowledge in child study research instruments and a strong emphasis on the importance for the teacher of understanding and accepting each child as a unique individual. Another staff member, on leave from the inner-city public schools, used his first-hand knowledge of that city and its school personnel and students for the benefit of the participants.

The staff as a whole expressed a willingness to conduct personal follow-up on the institute, even though this activity was not a part of the institute proposal and in consequence no funds were available for extended follow-up. In addition, the staff, partly because of the warm relationships established with the participants in the residential and working experience, offered to make themselves available to participants during the academic year for phone and mail consultation on problems that might arise.

Follow-up attempts that were a part of the institute proposal involved contact with each participant to ascertain what impact the institute had on his in-classroom behavior. Administrators and supervisors will be surveyed to obtain their reactions to changes in participants affecting their own classrooms, schools, and community. In this connection one member of the institute staff intends doing a doctoral project on the institute and its impact on the participants while in session and afterwards. A part of his study will require making visits to the participants in the classroom.

The participants themselves tried to predict what kind of thing they will do differently as a result of the institute when they return to their own schools in September. Some of their projections, which will be followed up, are quoted here:

1. *Build up each child's self-image*—"Establish a personal relationship with each child" · "Know each child first of all" · "Talk less. Listen more" · "Recognize each pupil as a unique person worthy of accomplishments on his own" · "Focus more attention on the child rather than on subject matter alone" · "Find time with each child to make him feel that he has communicated with me each day" · "Make each child feel he is important" · "See that each child goes home at the end of the day liking himself a little better"
2. *Provide a permissive, meaningful classroom atmosphere for good personal growth and learning to take place*—"Provide opportunities for free exchange of ideas and opinions" · "Encourage children to ask questions, to be inquisitive" · "Arouse curiosity through interest centers in the room, independent activities, live animals"
3. *Individualized instruction*—"Use the textbook less" · "Provide independent activities according to each child's needs and interests" · "Use flexible grouping so that instruction is more often done in small groups or with individuals" · "Develop listening skills through use of a tape recorder and storytelling or reading sessions" · "Be a model listener myself"
4. *Foster and nurture creativity*—"Provide a climate for creativity" · "Provide a variety of opportunities for creative work in the language arts, science, math, social studies—in all curriculum areas" · "Reward creative behavior" · "Be respectful of unusual questions and ideas" · "Occasionally have children do something for 'practice' without threat of evaluation"

5. *Involve parents in school-community activities*—"Organize a home room PTA" · "Invite parents to visit classrooms and observe children at work" · "Hold parent conferences in school, at teacher's homes as early as possible or before start of school year" · "Improve methods of reporting to parents"
6. *Establish good relationships with the administration and the faculty*—"Confer with principal for permission to try out new ways that may work with disadvantaged children" · "Seek cooperation of the administration to expand field trips program of the school" · "Take an active part in arranging assemblies using resource persons from the community" · "Convey messages received from the institute through meaningful bulletin boards in faculty lounge, informal conversations, and setting the example in your classroom"
7. *Make effective use of community resources*—"Establish referral communication with community agencies" · "Publicize importance of coordinating school and community services" · "Invite resource persons, particularly successful Negroes from all walks of life in the community" · "Know more of the community through various contacts with individuals and small groups"

In studying the overall impact of the institute as reflected by participants, staff, and the Aware Team, the consensus was that in planning, program process, selection of staff and participants, tone, balance between cognitive and affective aspects, and meeting the needs of the participants, little was left to be desired. All three groups did make suggestions or recommendations about changes that might be made in planning similar future institutes. The most frequently mentioned change concerned scheduling. A day's program normally started at 7:30 a.m. and ended at 9:00 p.m., with breaks for lunch and dinner. The staff reported that, in spite of the heavily scheduled day, program content remained flexible and the atmosphere permissive. The participants concurred, although they thought some evening lectures could have been omitted. Within the schedule, time was allowed for reading, informal discussion, and reflection. The staff indicated that perhaps some time devoted to field experiences might well have been applied to further practicum experiences. All agreed that the totality of the residential experience intensified impact and made the institute most meaningful.

Both staff and the Aware Team believed that the institute made real progress toward fulfilling its objectives. The participants gave concrete evidence of this in response to three questions: What was the most significant thing that happened to you during this institute? What was the second most significant thing that happened to you during this institute? What was the third most significant thing that happened to you during this institute? In the process of this study the answers to these open-end questions were categorized and it was discovered that they corresponded to stated objectives of the institute to a remarkable degree.

The first objective was "to develop awareness of and sensitivity to oneself as a teacher of disadvantaged children"; 28 percent of the participants reported that the development of such awareness and sensitivity was the most important thing that had happened to them. The second objective was "to help each participant develop respect for children of disadvantaged areas in their struggle for growth and learning"; 60 percent of the participants reported that they believed they had increased their respect for children in this manner and that this was the most important thing that had happened to them in the institute; 12 percent responded that they had become aware of the unique kinds of problems faced by children and school of the inner city.

Things seen as the second most important in the institute were reported by participants as: the opportunity to acquire specialized psychological and sociological insights into the problems and educational needs of disadvantaged children and youth (38 percent of participants); the increase of teaching skill in actual learning-teaching situations in an inner-city school (31 percent of participants); the opportunity to become acquainted with a variety of materials and ideas about method and content that improves one's ability to work most effectively with the particular children in one's own room (31 percent of participants). These three experiences corresponded directly with the objectives numbered four, six, and seven, respectively, in the institute proposal.

The responses reported as third in importance to the participants during the institute were: development of teachers' sensitivity to disadvantaged children, and sufficient understanding about ways of working with them that they will have increased faith in the educability of the children and genuine hope for the improvement of their learning opportunities (24 percent of participant response); and involvement of teachers in careful study of the inner-city community and development of the ability to "read" such a community more effectively (52 percent of participant response). These areas corresponded to objectives numbered five and nine, respectively, in the institute proposal.

Twenty-nine percent of participants listed another area as the third most important to them in the institute. This response did not specifically match any objective listed in the proposal: "Growth in being a better listener, and a keener observer as a result of individual teaching, dynamics of institute, and community field experiences."

If one criterion for measuring the effectiveness of an institute is that it satisfactorily achieved its stated objectives both in the eyes of those involved and in the perception of outside observers, it would seem reasonable to suggest that the NDEA summer institute at Ball State University might be studied as a useful model for an institute for elementary school teachers of the inner-city disadvantaged child.

INSTITUTE FOR TRAINING ASSISTANTS IN PRESCHOOL AND DAY CARE CENTERS FOR UNDERPRIVILEDGED CHILDREN IN ANTIPOVERTY TARGET AREAS IN BOSTON: GARLAND JUNIOR COLLEGE, BOSTON, MASSACHUSETTS

Efforts to meet the rapidly increasing need for preschool centers for disadvantaged children in the Boston area appeared to be blocked by an inadequate supply of qualified teachers. Garland Junior College believed that this situation called for a thorough review of the whole teaching structure in preschool and day care activities. Its preliminary investigations indicated that effective work with disadvantaged children required the preparation and placement of subprofessionals in order to maintain or even increase the ratio of concerned adults to children in the classroom, and at the same time expand the number of children in day care centers.

To implement this concept Garland Junior College proposed to the Office of Economic Opportunity a summer program to prepare high school graduates and college freshmen as teacher-aides. It was further proposed that the candidates be selected from a wide spectrum of economic environments so that interaction in a multiclass situation could be fostered through a residential program. A research component was incorporated, the purpose of which was to discover whether the impact of a residential experience (working, learning, and living together) would provide participants opportunity for interaction without jeopardizing the quality of instruction.

A Project Aware Team visited this program at Garland Junior College during the summer of 1965. Of all the educational institutions sponsoring programs or institutes visited by the Aware Team, Garland was the only one which permitted Project Aware to review a proposal for a 1966 summer program. This case study will attempt to describe the 1965 summer program and then to contrast it with the planned program for 1966 so that conclusions may be drawn about how one institution developed changes in the light of previous experience.

The 1965 program was a new departure for Garland Junior College, which is viewed by some as a small private junior college for middle and upper class girls, an image reflected from several community sources. The staff of the institute was aware that this impression was prevalent in the community but described it as no longer valid. They believed this summer institute was one way of dispelling the false impression that Garland still catered primarily to upper class students.

A factor motivating development of the program was Garland's desire to use faculty and staff capabilities as well as the residence houses during the summer. A combination of events and personalities at Garland led some faculty members to design a teacher-aide training program related to its Child Study Department. Boston's private community planning agency, Action for Boston Community Development (ABCD), joined Garland in requesting funds.

Institute participants were housed in a residence hall of the College, where a man and wife who were also advisers acted as house parents. The students lived in rooms suitable for one to four students. The group ate together in the residence house dining room.

The candidates selected to participate in this program were 25 young women—high school seniors, high school graduates, or college freshmen. Fifteen of this group were described by staff as coming from a lower class background and 10 from a middle or upper class background. Nine of the disadvantaged were Negro and 5 of the middle and upper class participants were Garland students. The selection criterion outlined in the plan of operation was to have an evenly balanced group for the purposes of (1) developing interaction and (2) pairing the advantaged with the disadvantaged for research data.

During an informal poll of half the total group of participants, responses to questions concerning parents' occupations ranged from professional and managerial to clerical and blue collar occupations, with only a few semiskilled or unskilled occcupations represented. These responses raise the question whether all 15 participants described by staff as disadvantaged were in fact economically deprived. The entire group appeared to aspire to upward mobility. Most of the young women in the so-called disadvantaged group, as well as those in the advantaged group, saw the program as a step toward some other career, i.e., clinical psychology, social work, or teaching, and not as a goal in itself.

An important feature of the program was the residential experience with emphasis on living, studying, and working together in an atmosphere of open communication and candor. The staff role in this process was to help participants use the realities of the experience for optimum growth. The Office of Economic Opportunity did not underwrite the residential part of the program, so that private funds were sought for this purpose. The inadequacy of funds made it necessary for trainees who could afford to pay their own residence fees to do so.

As participants talked together, they discovered that some of them had been required to pay residence fees and others had not. Exploration of the topic among trainees led to their discovery that they had been selected from different socioeconomic groups. Those from disadvantaged areas of the city resented what they perceived as implicit labeling. The ensuing discussion was heated and in the end valuable.

The curriculum appeared to encompass a substantial, though brief, preschool teacher education program to teach participants how to assume the functions of active teacher-aides. The content was twofold: (1) child development and learning theory and (2) practical preparation in the use of materials, and methods of preschool teaching (arts, music, rhythms, songs, and games). Orientation was given through lectures on the ways, means, and reasons for establishing a preschool or nursery; and on the teacher's relationship to students, parents, and the community. Emphasis was placed on understanding the play and learning functions of various kinds of toys, games, and activities. Additionally, class experiences were structured so that each participant could play various roles, among them the role of the teacher, followed by an evaluation of her performance by the group and a repeat performance based on the evaluation.

An incident that occurred during the role-playing sessions indicates the kinds of perceptions which the trainees were formulating. A number of participants had role-played preschool children exhibiting aggression, hostility, fear, and withdrawal. The discussions that followed were concerned with various psychological aspects of behavior.

Then a young woman went to the front of the class and portrayed a child just waking up from his mid-morning nap, moving around the room in a clumsy, uncomfortable manner. The class was speculating upon the psychological factors that might have caused the child to behave in this way. The role-player pointed out that the child she was portraying had put her shoes on opposite feet (right on left and left on right) and was merely physically uncomfortable, a warning to explore physical concerns before assuming that a pathological situation exists.

There was curriculum emphasis upon general self-improvement which featured a remedial reading course for all participants, geared to develop better reading and better study habits. Extensive library facilities were available to the participants, and the librarian kept records of each student's extra reading. Art and music were also available—for the personal growth of participants and as a part of their work with children. Cultural programs and trips around the Boston area were planned for all students.

The trainees were divided into two mixed groups for teaching in a day care center, alternating with study in the classroom. At the beginning of the program the participants were perceived as aides, in the sense of providing mechanical help in the classroom. However, this assignment caused dissatisfaction among the students. The professional team of the institute and day care center staff members explored the roles of teacher and teacher-aide. This resulted in a change of role for the participants, who became more active teaching assistants.

Although the scope of the curriculum permitted the participant to function as an assistant to a preschool or day care center teacher, one requirement in the local Boston system for the position of teacher assistant is 2 years of college. There are a few employment opportunities available in the year-round day care centers operated by the Associated Day Care Centers of Boston, a privately financed organization. However, the possibility of employment for the more successful participants as teacher assistants is in doubt because of the high requirements for these positions. ABCD is attempting to get the current requirements for teacher assistant changed so that graduates of the institute may qualify.

The 14-member institute staff was headed by a director. Faculty comprised 4 course instructors; a supervisor of student teaching who acted as liaison for communication between the preschool center and the institute; six master teachers in preschool classrooms; and 2 remedial reading and study skills instructors. They were from the faculties of Garland Junior College, Harvard University, Brandeis University, and the Quincy, Massachusetts, public schools.

The director of the program placed a strong emphasis on informal and continuing communication among staff as well as between staff and student, and among students. This mode, initiated with the intensive application interview, extended throughout the program. Regular house meetings were held to deal with problems of living together. The resident houseparents acted as confidential counselors. They led "bull sessions" on topics ranging from literature to sex education.

The director, a trained psychologist, and other staff were available for student counseling, both at the personal level and for career planning. The staff reported that even the most reserved trainees began to participate more freely as rapport was established. There appeared to be extensive interaction among participants transcending class and racial lines. In particular, participants responded to Negro trainees who expressed themselves well.

A research component, originally called for in the institute proposal, was not adequately funded by the Office of Economic Opportunity.

This research was viewed by the College as a central part of the program. Significant data had been gathered through completion of various standard tests (Wechsler Adult Intelligence Scale and Allport-Vernon-Lindzey Study of Values, Third Edition), through interviews with all candidates as part of the selection procedure, and through records kept by staff and participants. Tape recordings were also made of every session of the institute but the College could not proceed with the follow-up evaluation and assessment of effects, strengths, and weaknesses of the program, nor could faculty find answers to some questions they believe need investigation, without these funds for evaluation. Answers to such questions as "Will this program perform an important function for the participants?" and "What aspects of the program had the greatest impact?" might help determine the validity of the program and could help the faculty of the College plan for future work in this area with greater insight.

The College undertook, as part of the institute process, to make a documentary motion picture showing the goals of the institute and the experiences of the participants and staff as they lived it. This film was foreseen as being of use to others in planning institutes, as a recruiting device for potential trainees, and as an instrument for indoctrinating participants of other institutes in the institute process. The tape recordings of the daily meetings and work experiences of the participants already mentioned were to serve a double purpose—as commentary for the film and as data for evaluation.*

The impact of the Garland Junior College institute has been demonstrated. Because the staff learned early in the institute that the trainees were anxious to become full-fledged assistants to the teachers, not merely physical helpers, they were able to organize the program to provide participants a broad and meaningful experience. A preliminary report, "Garland Junior College Summer Institute—A Résumé," indicates that all participants seeking positions as teacher-aides in nursery schools have been placed except one. Others have undertaken further training on the college level, while still others have been helped to select a career.

* OEO funds were finally made available for both the evaluation and the film.

The participants' free expression of their desire to assume more responsibilities significantly demonstrates the openness of communication that prevailed. This openness encouraged interaction that developed positive relationships and simplified problems (such as the confrontation over differences in residence fees) as they arose.

The institute director has received letters from other educational institutions requesting information on the institute process used. The findings of the institute also provided one source for "A Model Institute for Administrators, Teachers, and Teacher-Aides" written by the staff of Project Aware for the Office of Economic Opportunity.

In summary, this program made a definite contribution to the development of the emerging paraprofessions of teacher-aides and teacher assistants.

The proposed program for the summer of 1966 differs in two main respects from the program described here. In addition to expanding the institute for the training of young women as teacher-aides, a new component has been added: a two-week leadership institute for 25 administrators, leaders, and teachers to conduct or to work with ongoing teacher-aide programs at appropriate levels. It is designed to enable them to accelerate attainment of early childhood educational goals for all disadvantaged children on a year-round basis.

This leadership institute would demonstrate, through direct experience of a laboratory type, the methods, curriculum, personnel, and administrative procedures that may be followed in implementing other programs in early childhood education.

Recruitment for this phase of the program would be concerned with bringing in teams from a school or district, consisting of one administrator and two or three teachers, who would be asked to recommend high school graduates from their own community to be enrolled in the teacher-aide section of the program.

To provide opportunity for orientation, the leadership institute would start on the Monday preceding the Thursday opening of the teacher-aide institute. This would enable the leadership group to take maximum advantage of the opportunity to observe the opening phases of the teacher-aide institute. The leadership program is divided into four phases:

1) Indoctrination. (On the whole, both administrators and teachers will be working together here.)
2) Review of admissions procedures and observation of the opening stages of the teacher-aide institute.
3) Practicum and panels (field trips and seminars).
4) Final evaluation by staff and the leadership group.

Aside from the leadership institute, which is a major innovation in the proposed 1966 program, there are various internal differences in the new program for teacher-aides. The total number of participants in this phase of the program has been raised from 25 to 50. Selection of candidates will be proportioned as follows: 40 percent will be college freshmen, and 60 percent high school graduates from disadvantaged backgrounds. The increase in size of the participant body necessitates an increase in faculty size and the expansion of residence facilities from one house to two.

A problem encountered in the 1965 summer institute is to be avoided by charging all participants residential fees which can be paid out of their stipends. The residential experience will also be more intensively studied as part of the evaluation of the 1966 institute. The evaluation component of the previous year's program has been amplified to include not only this further evaluation of the residential experience, but also the use of testing instruments to predict the candidates' potential for operating effectively within the institute experience and to measure their success in applying institute learnings after they have accepted teacher-aide positions.

The Aware Team believes that the new proposal reflects the efforts of Garland Junior Collge to evaluate realistically the experiences of one summer and to use these evaluations as a foundation on which to develop a more comprehensive program for the future.

NDEA SUMMER INSTITUTE FOR TEACHERS OF DISADVANTAGED CHILDREN AND YOUTH: TUFTS UNIVERSITY, MEDFORD, MASSACHUSETTS

It may be reasonably assumed that no institute conducted during the summer of 1965 was totally free from problems, tensions, and conflicts of some kind. These occur as part of the process of change and growth, processes that are central to the concept of institutes for preparing teachers to work more effectively with disadvantaged children and youth. The Tufts University institute was designed with the recognition that conflict is inevitable and that, with skill on the part of the staff, such conflict could be channeled productively. The director of the program states that it is not yet certain that the institute accomplished this goal—all the evidence is not yet in. However, the attempt was made and the process of the institute encourages close examination.

This institute was created to serve 60 teachers working with disadvantaged children and youth in public schools in the Boston area. The institute proposal described the target group of participants in this manner:

> Many of these teachers are not, for example, "middle class" in the sense that is often used in describing teachers of disadvantaged youth. They are not necessarily teachers who move around a great deal; often they have been teaching in the same school for a good many years. They are often not themselves the products of a public educational system. They are, in short, a rather special kind of teacher requiring a rather special kind of in-service assistance.

For such teachers the Tufts summer institute offered three kinds of learning experience: (1) substantive review of the findings on socioeconomic and psychological background of the pupils and their families, with particular reference to their educational implications; (2) methods-materials practicum with children and youth (preschool through Grade 9) who come from disadvantaged homes and who were enrolled in a summer school program under private and public auspices; and (3) a sensitivity training program.

The substantive review of the socioeconomic and psychological background of these children was based on the findings of the sociologist, psychologist, social worker, educator, and others. The following topics were explored, with special reference to the educational needs and learning handicaps of the students who attend schools in disadvantaged areas: factors in urban life that affect learning and teaching; cognition and perception; language growth and development (class status, values, motivation); development of self-concept; school as a social system; school as an ego-supporting institution; teacher-administrator factors relating to potency for change; the role of the school as a cooperative community agency. These topics were studied in the daily one-hour lecture and the small-group discussions.

The materials and methods practicum consisted of class-room, laboratory, and field work with the disadvantaged child and his family. This section represented the major integrating experience for the participants. The special needs of the disadvantaged student were studied and analyzed. Attempts were made to plan and implement differentiated programs, to experiment with a wide variety of new materials and methods, and to develop new teacher-made materials. Home visits and parent conferences were held, and contacts were made and maintained with youth-serving agencies and organizations within the neighborhood and the wider community. These activities were discussed in the daily morning practicum and a one-hour afternoon seminar.

Laboratory assignments for teachers in Grades 4 through 6 were made within the experimental Boston Elementary Summer School. Teachers in Grades 7 through 9 took their practicum in the regular Boston Summer School Program. Preschool teachers took their practicum in the Head Start Program and in the laboratory school of the Department of Child Development, Tufts University. Teachers working in Grades 1 through 3 were placed in playgrounds operated by the Park and Recreation Department and in a camp center on Thompson Island conducted under the auspices of the Salvation Army Boy's Club. The freedom prevailing in the playgrounds and the Thompson Island camp and the new materials and methods available to the experimental Boston Elementary Summer School made these the richest of all the practicum experiences.

The third process for learning was sensitivity training. It has been hypothesized that child-teacher and parent-teacher relationships are of major importance in assisting the disadvantaged child to learn. How a teacher feels about himself and about different and sometimes difficult children and parents can help or hinder the learning process. These feelings are more likely to be influential factors when there is a wide variation in value systems between the teacher's personal and professional world and the world of the children he teaches. Self-acceptance and acceptance of others are closely interrelated and can set limits on the teacher's effectiveness.

A full week of sensitivity training was provided to help participants to see themselves, to learn how to see others, and to discuss how they themselves are seen by others. At the same time, insights and skills in dynamics of group behavior were explored. Included within the sensitivity training was a concentrated experience in the training group (T-group). Four separate T-groups were established. Each participant took part in an agendaless group. Participants met together for 20 hours. They studied group dynamics by examining their individual and group behavior as it evolved in the T-group. This phase of sensitivity training focused on self-awareness and the concept of change. In addition to twice-a-day T-group sessions, skill-building lectures and sessions were conducted. The sessions drew on the educational experiences of participants in their urban-centered practicum work. This intensive week of sensitivity training took place during the seventh week of the institute.

From the very first week of the institute the staff recognized that conflicts were developing. This was implicit in the sociometry of the group.

The largest segment of participants (48) came from the inner-city schools of one community, Boston. They were carefully selected so that a number of administrators, including principals and vice-principals, would come from schools with the heaviest Negro enrollment. Among the participants were about a dozen Negro teachers; in addition, 4 of the supervisory teaching staff were also Negroes. The remainder of the 60 participants (12) came from the rim cities of the metropolitan area, including Somerville, Cambridge, Medford, and Quincy. Groupings were quickly formed. The director reported that they continued to present some problems to the staff throughout the seven weeks of the institute. In his opinion it could not be said that the 60 participants were ever actually welded into one integrated group. A number of factors worked against this integration.

First, there was the group of Boston teachers versus the non-Boston group. The 48 Boston teachers dominated the scene, in the perception of the staff, and some of the non-Boston members described themselves as feeling like outsiders. They complained that the staff focused exclusively on the Boston school system in working with participants.

The director stated that, from his own observation and from conversations with institute staff and members of the Boston public school administration, it was evident that a steady, systematic feedback was maintained from the institute to the school administration offices in Boston. He further reported that to him some of the feedback reports seemed to have a negative tone that was also much in evidence at general institute discussions in both the practicum seminars and the substantive reviews.

This problem became more acute as the institute continued and was observed by members of the Aware Team. The Team commented on the skill of the institute staff in dealing with the problem and noted that a segment of the Boston teachers did have positive attitudes toward the institute. These persons were younger teachers from the Boston system, who appeared to be eager for help, amenable to suggestion, and less defensive in protecting the *status quo.*

Another grouping within the institute was the Negro participants. Although this group presented an opportunity for white and Negro participants to work and discuss in close contact with one another, the two groups experienced difficulties in communicating with each other at the outset. The director's impression was that the groups became more polarized as the institute neared its close. Some open resentment toward the Negro institute instructors on the part of a few participants was noted.

Another dichotomy was observed by staff from the seating positions habitually assumed by participants. Men and women chose to sit in groups of their own sex. A number of visiting lecturers commented on this fact to the participants and staff attempted to make remedial rearrangements, but the division continued.

The usual grade groupings were also apparent, in part due to the fact that groups met according to grade level in the practicum. The staff attempted to break up these groupings for the substantive discussion and to rotate staff leadership among the various sessions.

The staff, the director, and the Aware Team separately suggested that the group dynamics of the institute might have benefited had the sensitivity training been scheduled early in the institute rather than in the seventh week. This affective portion of the institute program provided, in addition to the T-group sessions, an hour-long skill session each afternoon, with participants meeting in two groups of 30 each. Two staff members conducted each group. The skill sessions consisted of role-playing; one-way and two-way communication exercises; discussions of the role of conflict; and intergroup competition exercises.

The staff had noted that initially in the sensitivity training a significant number of participants had strong negative feelings about the institute. The question of whether the institute "had spent too much time on the Negro problem" was especially charged with feeling. A number of Boston teachers stated that they felt they were under attack at the institute and were not interested in changing under pressure.

Since the participants had been together for six weeks, much time was spent in discussing the institute, although they did not all know one another. They evidenced reluctance, however, to look at their own T-groups or to become concerned about their own participation. The theme of race relations also appeared in the T-groups.

Because of the "agendaless" nature of the T-groups, an overwhelming amount of anxiety seemed to be generated among the participants at the start, the staff reported. Hostility felt toward the trainers was often projected onto other staff members and the institute in general. A number of participants threatened to leave the groups. The predictable conflict between members desiring structure and those opposing it was observed by the trainers.

All four T-group trainers reported that they found it necessary to be supportive, direct, and active. One of the problems was to keep anxiety to manageable levels rather than allow it to immobilize the groups. Generally staff agreed that the experience of self-introspection and awareness was a new dimension for the majority of participants and a highly threatening endeavor. Nevertheless, the training staff felt that numerous small gains were achieved by the participants, both as groups and as individuals.

Increased awareness of group interaction and factors contributing to group "fight or flight" was shown by participants, and patterns of individual dominance were pointed out to some members by others in the group. Also many of the silent group members became dissatisfied with their own failure to participate and increased their efforts to contribute, the staff noted.

There was general agreement that, although the week of sensitivity training did not accomplish miracles, it did help to integrate and dramatize some of the content and attitudinal change advanced in the first six weeks of the program. The director and the staff recommended not only moving the sensitivity training to an early week in the schedule of the institute but possibly extending its duration to two weeks in order to insure greater effectiveness of this technique.

Another area of experiential learning concerned the practicum. This was structured according to the grade level groupings of preschool, primary grades, middle grades, and junior high school. Of the four groups, two provided the richest learning experience for the participants, in their own perception as well as that of the staff. These were the program for the primary grades, which consisted of reading and study groups at city playgrounds and on Thompson Island in Boston Harbor and the Grades 4 through 6 Boston Elementary Summer Program. The primary grades program was an informal, unstructured program to which the participants responded with imagination. The middle-grades program was experimental in nature—with small classes, new methods, and skilled teachers to meet the remediation and enrichment needs of disadvantaged children. Field trips were made, special lectures and demonstrations given, and laboratory activities conducted, as well as supervised observation of and work with children.

The participants in the practicum groups reported on some of the things they will try to do differently in September when they return to their own schools. They "promised" to have patience, understanding, and faith in their students' ability to learn. They plan to use audiovisual aids more frequently and to design lessons that will allow the children to use their own styles of learning and their own strengths.

Some of the staff feared that the lack of communication and the traditions of the Boston school system might inhibit organized dissemination and use of the principles and methods, techniques and materials developed at the institute. However, some participants informed the staff that they planned to confer with their principals in the hope of speaking to the staff at the preschool meetings held in their buildings. Others planned to use informal contacts with other teachers in sharing the philosophy, objectives, and methods that can help children succeed.

It was suggested by staff and the Aware Team that one factor that permitted the primary and middle-grades practicums to achieve greater success than the others was that there was more freedom to plan and innovate within these two programs. The other practicum groups had to work in traditional classrooms with little opportunity for innovation or for selection of classroom teachers. Participants were obliged to accept a lesser degree of participation in the classroom than had originally been envisioned. In general they agreed that greater learning took place in the practicum seminars than in the practicum classrooms with the children, because of these limiting factors.

The staff, on the other hand, believed that these participants were unable to get the maximum benefit from the practicum experience partly because they were constantly seeking some blueprint, some master plan, or magic formula that would work in every situation with any given group of children. Despite the insistence of the staff that there is no such thing, the participants seemed to be sitting back and waiting for it miraculously to appear. The associate director also noted that this group of patricipants seemed to be extremely dependent on structured situations which, he stated, retarded the development and use of their own abilities.

The cognitive aspects of the program were presented by various methods. The total staff was employed as a team in presenting a substantive review of the psychosocial and socioeconomic background of the disadvantaged child, with particular reference to the Negro community. Available to the institute were the resources of the Lincoln Filene Center at Tufts University, which has been a pioneer in educational programs and educational research, particularly that concerned with American race relations and the impact of the Negro self-image on learning. Great reliance was placed on the use of audiovisual aids, particularly films, to stimulate discussion and fix learning. Some participants reported that they considered the films extremely valuable and that they should have replaced the speakers. Others suggested that fewer films should have been used.

According to the director, effective use was made of authorities (Thomas Pettigrew, Kenneth Clark, Martin Deutsch, Frank Riessman, and others). Many of these speakers were used in two sessions on a half, full-day, or 2-day basis.

Some participants reacted to this aspect of the institute as being "too heavily loaded with Negro propaganda," and one staff member, in a minority report, suggested that "at times the institute deteriorated into a seminar on civil rights." However, the majority of staff and participants agreed that this part of the program was of great value.

The Aware Team reported that in an interview with 12 participants there seemed to be complete agreement as to the value of the lectures but little agreement as to their meaning. An example was the reaction of two participants to Frank Riessman's lecture. A white participant insisted that Riessman had said, "Don't try to be a social worker. Be a teacher. Teach." In support of her contention that there was too much emphasis on attitudinal change, a Negro participant heatedly declared that the other participant was quoting out of context. Both enrollees agreed that they had enjoyed Riessman enormously, but his words meant different things to each of them.

The ultimate effect of these three parts of the institute would never be known had not there been definite provision for an evaluation component in the institute proposal. The results of this evaluation are not yet available, since it was designed to be carried out over a period of time, beginning in the seventh week institute and continued in the "eighth week." This was to be a broken week, consisting of five Saturday meetings, extended from October through April. This final "week" has several purposes exclusive of evaluation—to provide opportunity for feedback reports on innovations that worked or did not work, on problems solved or not solved, and to discuss the knowledge, understandings, and proficiencies developed during the seven-week summer session.

The Alfred P. Sloan School of Management, Massachusetts Institute of Technology, cooperated with the director in setting up an objective plan for appraisal of selected outcomes that was carried on by a doctoral candidate at the School of Management. The uniqueness of this feature of the institute, in the perception of the Aware Team, lies within the intelligence and scope of its design. Because of this it is being reported here in careful detail.

"Evaluation," according to Herbert Hyman, "refers to the procedures of fact-finding about the results of planned social action, which in turn move the spiral of planning ever upward." The major problem in this process, as Hyman points out, is "to provide objective, systematic, and comprehensive evidence on the degree to which the program achieves its intended objectives plus the degree to which it produces other unanticipated consequences." The plan for the evaluation of the Tufts University institute was developed in the framework of this definition, starting with an examination of the objectives.

The formal objectives of the institute are eleven in number but they have in common the changing of attitudes toward disadvantaged children and youth. In order to evaluate the program it was necessary to determine that these objectives were subject to measurement, for each objective had to be translated into operational goals.

A person's attitude toward a social object is said to be comprised of three components: affective, cognitive, and action tendency. The institute objectives were perceived by the evaluation staff as lending themselves neatly to categorization within this conceptual framework. The three major goals of the program were stated in the following terms:

1. *Affective*—to develop positive feelings toward and respect for disadvantaged youth and their families, to enhance the teachers' self-acceptance and acceptance of others.
2. *Cognitive*—to increase understanding in a wide variety of areas related to the problem of teaching disadvantaged youth.
3. *Action tendency*—skill and practice in the application of a wide variety of new tools and techniques, strongly implying a need to develop behavioral flexibility.

This separation does not imply that these components are completely independent. Much empirical work has shown that to a certain extent they are related, and that experimentally inducing changes in one component leads to changes in the others. According to the evaluation staff, the institute's objectives, as well as the tripartite structure of the program, suggest that the above conceptualization is relevant. The operational objectives of the evaluation program were therefore developed in this three-part framework.

In the affective section the two major areas of concern deal with the participants' *acceptance of self* and *acceptance of others.* Much theoretical and empirical work, particularly in the area of client-centered psychotherapy, suggests that only the person who truly accepts himself can truly accept others. To measure this the Dorris-Levenson-Hanfmann Sentence Completion Tests (SCT), a semiprojective instrument, were used. Also the Harding and Schuman Reactions Questionnaire was employed to measure the individual's empathy or sympathetic identification with the "underdog."

In the cognitive area one of the elements of interest was identified as the degree to which the institute had been successful in increasing the individual's intellectual understanding of the problems associated with teaching disadvantaged youth. The evaluation staff believed that more important than what the individual learned was the impact, if any, of these intellectual pursuits on the nature of his thinking.

It was proposed to use an instrument that measures an individual's level of commitment to a norm of rationality. Rational thinking is characterized by a persistent attempt to secure information, to correct misinformation, to be logical in deduction, to be cautious in inference, to make appropriate differentiations and qualifications. Irrationality can be characterized by hasty judgment or prejudgment, overgeneralization, and thinking in stereotype, among other things. The Harding and Schuman scale of rationality of thinking with respect to various ethnic groups yields significant data. Four types of people are identifiable: rationalists, prorationalists, antirationalists, and confused. An interesting group are the prorationalists, who exhibit an irrational bias in favor of a particular ethnic group, or what Allport calls "love prejudice." It was assumed by the evaluation staff that the objectives of the institute did not support such an orientation. However, they considered it very important to determine whether or to what degree this reaction might represent an unanticipated consequence of the overall program.

In the action-tendency area, gathering objective data at best represents an exceedingly difficult and time-consuming problem, the evaluation staff reported. However, since the ultimate effectiveness of the institute rests upon the increased ability of the participant to deal with the problems of teaching disadvantaged children and youth in his own school, systems of measurement for this factor had to be found.

The evaluators decided that the objectives of the institute did not seem to have as a primary concern specific types of action or behavior. The program was not meant to provide a set formula for participants, even though it became clear in the summer session that some participants thought so. The evaluation staff identified the outcomes the institute was designed to bring about as an improvement of diagnostic ability and the development of an enhanced repertoire of behavioral skills, a sense of behavioral flexibility. Increased social sensitivity was seen as a necessary condition but not sufficient in itself to improve teaching ability. Even with increased sensitivity the participant lacking the behavioral flexibility to respond differentially to the wide variety of needs and demands of disadvantaged children and youth would appear to have come only halfway.

An approach to measuring effectiveness in this area comes from a substantial body of work done by Fred Fiedler on leadership style and group performance. Utilizing an instrument comparable to Osgood's Semantic Differential, Fiedler has found that the most effective leaders, across a wide variety of groups, tend to be those who distinguish most markedly between "best liked and least liked" coworkers. This instrument can be viewed as measuring an individual's level of diagnostic or behavioral flexibility.

Many other variables could be expected to condition a participant's reaction or response to the institute program and not all could be measured. The two which seemed worthy of investigation to the evaluation staff were the participant's level of psychological anomy and his particular pattern of interpersonal values. Psychological anomy is a multifaceted concept, the core of which is a feeling of moral emptiness. It is closely related to a number of personality variables known to impair learning, communication, and interpersonal interaction. A very brief but highly reliable and valid scale developed by McClosky and Schaar was employed to measure this variable. The Gordon Survey of Interpersonal Values was used to tap individual values in the areas of support, conformity, recognition, independence, benevolence, and leadership.

The selected battery of instruments required between 60 to 80 minutes to complete. The first battery was given to the total group of participants at the beginning of the institute, prior to any extensive orientation. At the end of the sixth week (directly preceding the sensitivity training week) one-half of the total participant group chosen on a random-sample basis completed the entire battery for the second time. At the end of the week of sensitivity training, the remaining half of the participants took the battery for the second time. Splitting the group enabled the evaluation staff to examine the differential effect of the sensitivity training experience over and above the impact of the first six weeks of the Institute program.

It was also planned to readminister the battery at the end of the follow-up sessions (the "eighth" week of the Institute). Other data were being gathered from participants at two points in time: before the end of the 1965 school year (pre-institute) and sometime in the middle of the 1966 fall term (post-institute). It was suggested by the director and the Aware Team that the report of the findings of such an extensive evaluation process may be extremely valuable in assessing the effectiveness of this particular program and in planning for future institutes.

The Aware Team reported that their observations of the institute raised questions about the number and selection of participants. As noted, there were 60 participants, all chosen from the Boston area, 35 male and 25 female; the median age range was 35 through 39 years; 42 were married, 18 single; 25 held bachelor's degrees; 34 master's degrees, and one participant had more than a master's degree. The majority taught in schools with enrollments ranging from 500 to 999 children. Participants had from one to 20 years of teaching experience, the mean being 5 years.

One question of the Aware Team concerned the number of participants in relation to the sociometry of the institute. It was observed that there is a greater tendency to form small groupings in a large institute than in a small one, where more intimate communication among participants is readily effected. The selection of participants exclusively from the Boston area was mentioned as a possibly divisive factor. The reported feelings of some participants that the institute was "slanted" toward the teachers from the Boston city system might have been obviated had participants been chosen from other cities in the Northeast or from other sections of the country.

The staff was reported by the Aware Team as being outstanding Besides the director and associate director there were 5 members of the teaching staff, and 4 members of the sensitivity training staff, plus one evaluator; 3 staff members were recruited from the faculty of Tufts University, 4 from the local school systems, and 4 from Boston University. The evaluator was from the Massachusetts Institute of Technology. The appointment of a substantial number of Negroes to the staff was perceived by the Aware Team as approaching the issue of race in a most direct and positive manner.

The staff gave every evidence to the Aware Team of being highly involved in the institute and aware of the total program and process. The ferment apparent among the participants was viewed by the staff as evidence that the institute was an intensely moving experience, and while staff members did not all agree that the total experience was completely positive, they reported individual signs of change.

The Aware Team asked if there were any ways in which staff members saw the institute experience as differing from other teacher education. They responded that it differed in two areas: (1) the understandings gained by teachers about the self-concept of most disadvantaged children and the ego strengths needed by the teacher to deal with the varied behavior that is environmentally conditioned; and (2) the direct experience with the life conditions of disadvantaged children.

The institute was housed in the Lincoln Filene Center for Citizenship and Public Affairs on the Tufts University campus. The choice of this location took into account the availability of the staff and resources of the Center as well as the area in which the Center has been working during the past few years. That area is American race relations and more specifically the impact of the self-image of the Negro on schools and civic education, which contributed to the total impact of the institute experience on the participants. Directly opposite the Lincoln Filene Center was the University library, the resources of which were at the disposal of the participants. The institute also had the resources of the Eliot-Pearson Department of Child Study, including a laboratory preschool equipped with observational facilities, during the summer session. This facility, the primary setting on Thompson Island, and the less ideal classroom in the Boston city schools, formed the practicum settings. Because the participants lived in the local area, residential facilities on campus were not necessary.

The Aware Team reported their assessment of the major strengths of this institute to be the head-on approach to prejudice by the appointment of Negro supervisors, the high quality of the staff, the brilliance of the design of the institute, the establishment of a beginning flow of communication between the Boston school system and the University, the excellent provisions for follow-up and evaluation throughout the year, and, perhaps most important, the increased faith in children's potential evidenced by many participants. Such strengths may possibly counterbalance the *sturm und drang* of the summer session.

NDEA INSTITUTE FOR TEACHERS OF DISADVANTAGED YOUTH: DOMINICAN COLLEGE, RACINE, WISCONSIN

Members of a local community rarely hear about two offices of the federal government combining their forces to make possible a program to benefit their own neighborhood. In an article in the February 27, 1965, *Racine Journal Times*, the citizens of Racine read about such a venture in the improvement of education for the disadvantaged children of their area and their teachers:

> The primary purpose of this summer's program is to train teachers in the special skills needed to meet the needs and problems of the disadvantaged child. To do so, this line-up of resources has been mobilized: the federal government has made one grant through the U. S. Office of Education under the National Defense Education Act which will set up a nine-week institute of training for 45 elementary teachers. Dominican College will administer the institute. A second federal grant from the Office of Economic Opportunity will finance special summer schools for disadvantaged chil-

dren. These schools will serve, in effect, as laboratories for the teachers, who will attend academic lectures and seminars at Dominican part of the time, and go out to apply their developing skills in the schools the rest of the time. The summer schools will be operated by the Racine Unified School District and parochial schools. . . . In this program there is something for everyone involved: the child himself, the teachers, and the community; and it is an example of well-planned coordination of community and federal resources.

As the article indicates, coordination was begun at the federal level. Integral to the design of the program was cooperation between the local public school system and the local parochial school system. The plans for the program delved further into the possibilities of integrating the local community into the institute. Community leadership outside the College served on the faculty: the associate director was a supervisor in the Racine public schools, a staff member was executive director of the Racine United Community Services, and a staff consultant was from the staff of the Racine County mental health clinic. Local industry cooperated: a local publishing foundation provided consultants for the preschool practicum who benefited by gathering ideas for the preparation of publications for teachers of the disadvantaged; the Johnson Foundation donated its retreat house for use by participants on three occasions; the public library, museum, zoo, telephone company, and local industries cooperated in developing learning experiences for the teachers and children in the practicum. Finally, the entire community in less direct, but nevertheless effective ways, showed continuing concern and interest in the entire program.

The institute which so captured the imagination of the Racine community was focused on the laboratory experience, the practicum.

The greatest and most unique aspect, giving the most profound strength to the institute, was the six weeks of supervised field work wherein the participants were given opportunities to 'test out' the various concepts, theories, ideas learned, read about, or shared during the first two weeks.

This statement from the director's final report bears out observations of the Aware Team and the participants that the practicum was the heart of the institute. However, before beginning this experience, the participants studied in an intensive two-week workshop on campus, meeting daily from 8:30 in the morning until 3:30 in the afternoon. The day began with a general session, followed by small-group meetings for working intensively on problems of common interest. The scope of the content area ranged from the philosophical and psychological nature of man through sociological and anthropological knowledge relevant to change of attitudes toward the disadvantaged children, to preschool education of disadvantaged children, language arts for the disadvantaged, and literature. Guest lecturers as well as staff contributed to these general sessions, and a series of films concerning disadvantaged children and intergroup relations was shown. The small groups were set up, according to grade level, in four divisions: preschool, Grades 1 and 2, Grades 3 and 4, and Grades 5 and 6. Later in the institute, participants indicated that they wished to restructure their groups according to their interests, rather than the grades they taught. This rearrangement was expedited.

The six-week practicum followed the two weeks of intensive preparation. As a condition of their acceptance at the institute, the participants contracted to teach in the OEO Community Action Program (CAP) summer schools held both in Racine public schools and in parochial schools. Twelve participants taught at three parochial schools; 33 participants at eight public schools. The classes of these teachers were kept small, up to 15 children, and they were held only in the mornings.

Every schoolday afternoon and occasionally on Saturdays the participants reassembled on campus for continued study and supervision by staff. Individual and group conferences on practicum experiences were held at that time.

The multifaceted experimentation encouraged by the institute characterized the practicum. It provided opportunities for the participants to work in a variety of ways in a supportive, nonthreatening environment. Here they had the opportunity without some of the pressures they might have felt in their own classrooms during the school year to explore the effectiveness of different ways of working with disadvantaged children and youth. As one participant remarked, "Never before had I had an opportunity to find out how children can learn without being a slave to the tyranny of the curriculum."

In this practicum participants could pose questions and seek answers—individually through their direct work with children and collectively as they studied in the afternoon with other participants and staff, who were also involved in the same process—some of the questions they asked themselves, "Are the Montessori materials effective?" "What happens if you have a classroom made up solely of boys (or girls)?" "What happens in a classroom in which many of the children are related?"

In one school the first through third grades were held together in primary, ungraded classrooms, while the fourth through sixth grades were organized departmentally. In the latter framework one teacher's specialization was that of providing exciting and creative experiences for the children.

Another unique feature of the practicum was the inclusion in the OEO-CAP summer schools of teachers who were not participants in the institute. The presence of these teachers provided opportunities for participants and institute staff to test learnings against other professionals in the same classroom situations who were not being exposed to the institute process. Participants reported that they became more aware of changes that were taking place within them as a result of the institute by contrasting their views and classroom behavior with those of their nonparticipant colleagues.

The ninth, final week of the institute was devoted to an evaluation of the experience by participants and institute staff. This was a culminating activity supplementing weekly evaluations held during the course of the institute.

Attitude testing that had been administered before the institute started was repeated in this last week. The following table demonstrates some attitude shifts from June to August on the part of 45 participants.

Interviewers' Ratings of Participants' Involvement Regarding Race Relations (Adapted from Melvin Tumin's Attitudinal Check)

Rating	*Number in June*	*Number in August*
Very distant	0	0
Distant	6	2
Neutral	16	10
Involved	18	23
Very involved	5	8
Did not complete second phase	0	2

The battery of tests included three others that reflected comparable shifts in the area measured.

Over the five-day period of the final week the participants answered a series of essay questions in which they evaluated the institute experience and reported ways in which they intended to change their own behavior. A few of their remarks are illustrative:

–"See children as persons and respect the dignity of each."

– "Teach the child, transcend the curriculum."

– "Now that I've learned to appreciate his (the disadvantaged child's) dialect, I will help him and let him appreciate it too."

– "Give the children, through field trips, experiences they have not had before."

– "The most important aim for me is to permit the children to acquire competence, success."

– "I must know myself and then be willing to change. This summer has made it possible for me to change my attitudes and goals in teaching. I must continue to grow as a person and permit my students to do the same."

– "As Faulkner's hero said in *Intruder in the Dust* (a movie participants had viewed at the institute), I hope I'm not 'too cluttered' and full of notions to really *listen* to the children."

The director reported that many of the participants seemed to recognize the importance of the home-school relationship. They plan to encourage interaction and revitalize parent-teacher conferences. Many indicated that they are eager to devise and use new materials to help each child build a better self-concept.

It will not be possible, the staff stated, to know how many of these plans are put into effect by the participants returning to their own schools until the school year advances. Follow-up on institute learnings was to be accomplished through articles contributed by participants to the Racine Inner-City Council's organ of communication, *Focus*. And finally, all participants planned to meet on Teacher's Institute Day sponsored by Racine Unified District #1—the theme of the discussion, to be "Teaching the Disadvantaged Child—A Reevaluation."

All the participants in the institute (45) had been teaching in the local schools and all except one, who was moving to New Mexico, planned to continue teaching disadvantaged children in Racine. Their median age range was 30 to 34. There were 17 male and 28 female participants. Twenty-two were single and 23 married. All participants had completed their bachelor's degree; 9 had completed their master's degree. Twenty-three participants taught in schools with enrollments of 100 to 499; 33 participants taught in public schools, and the 12 teachers in parochial schools were nuns. Twenty participants had 5 years or less of teaching experience; 13 had from 6 to 10 years, and 12 had over 10 years. Nineteen taught in schools with enrollments of from 500 to 999; 2 taught in schools with enrollments over 1,500, and one in a school with enrollment of less than 100.

In the belief of the director and staff, the concentration of local participants allowed maximum fusion of information and attitudes gained during the course of the institute. The faculty unanimously agreed that there was the maximum possibility for carry-over when two or more persons from a school staff are involved in the institute experience.

Both the staff and the director suggested that the institute might have been strengthened had there been more Negro participants. However, it was not possible to make selections on this basis.

Some participants suggested that there was more emphasis on race relations than on disadvantagement in the institute. One stated that she was willing to learn how to teach the disadvantaged but she did not wish to hear so many lectures on race relations. Another said, "I would not like to see the only people mentioned as being disadvantaged as being just Negroes. Too much time was spent equating Negro with disadvantaged. There are others." Still another participant suggested more time could have been spent discussing the problems of Indian, migrant, and Spanish-speaking disadvantaged children. Another gave the opinion that housing, jobs, and employment are not related to education of the disadvantaged *per se* and therefore have no place in the content of the institute.

Given such a divergence of background information, attitudes, and education among participants, the Aware Team observed that the program was particularly well designed to meet their specific needs at that moment in time. Other strengths of the institute were perceived by the Aware Team as being correlation of content with laboratory experiences by all paricipants; the dedication of staff to the task of improving teachers' attitudes toward disadvantaged children; the excellent campus facilities for the instructional program, including library and teaching materials; and the strong support for the total concept of working with disadvantaged children on the part of the College administration and faculty. In support of this last observation the Team reported that the president of the College and the dean were strongly committed to having an effective institute and were willing to provide all necessary resources for the achievement of this goal.

The institute was seen by the Aware Team as well organized and well presented. The Team made special mention of the emphasis on Negro history and culture and the emphasis on psychological and sociological aspects of disadvantaged children as being appropriate. The affective aspects of the institute, particularly the practicum, the Aware Team believed, were outstanding. More difficult to substantiate objectively, but apparent to the Team, was the tone of the institute, where the atmosphere was one of hard work and sincere interest. The Team also commented on the high professional standards originated by the staff and reflected in the actions of the participants.

One possible change proposed by the visiting Team was that participant learning and interaction might be stimulated by the acceptance of participants outside the immediate locality. On the other hand, staff stated that for maximum impact of the institute, the selection of local teachers only was important. There was general agreement that the inclusion of parochial school teachers, the nuns, along with public school teachers helped cut through many of the prejudices and preconceived notions that had existed in both groups. This was evident in large- and small-group discussions and in the close relationships that formed between individuals from both groups.

There seems to be consensus, not only among those involved in the institute and among members of the Aware Team, but also from community sources (and an observer from the Office of Education concurred) that the NDEA summer institute at Dominican College, together with the OEO-CAP laboratory schools, made possible positive changes in the educational opportunities of Racine's disadvantaged children. Teachers in 12 public and parochial schools will be approaching at least some aspects of their work with these children differently. Forty-five teachers work with approximately 1,350 children, nearly that many families will be indirectly or directly involved representing an estimated 5,550 persons. The community cannot help but become aware of a phenomenon that affects so many of its members, and perhaps will take pride in the cooperation it provided to help the project succeed.

The institutional approach as perceived by administrators

CHAPTER 5

Analysis of replies to written questionnaires on institutional approach

To discover how the preparation of school personnel to work with disadvantaged children and youth is incorporated into preservice and in-service programs, questionnaires were sent to deans of colleges of teacher education, chairmen of departments of education in institutions of higher learning, and superintendents of selected school systems throughout the country.

The population for the colleges and universities consisted of the member institutions of the American Association of Colleges for Teacher Education. The population for school systems comprised those in localities with a population of 100,000 or more, school systems recommended by state superintendents of instruction in reply to an inquiry from Project Aware about possible respondents, and school systems in communities judged by the National Association of Intergroup Relations Officials as having a high proportion of disadvantaged persons in their population.

There were 1,050 questionnaires[1] sent to deans, department chairmen, and superintendents of schools in July, 1965, with a follow-up letter sent in October of the same year. There was a 35 percent return from colleges and universities and a 54 percent return from school systems.

A large proportion of the replies could not be processed, since many respondents described programs such as Head Start projects, which were designed to serve the disadvantaged directly rather than to prepare school personnel to work with disadvantaged children and youth. Many deans, department chairmen, and superintendents of

[1] See Appendix D for letter of transmittal, Appendix E for questionnaires for school systems (Form A), and Appendix F for questionnaires for colleges and universities (another version of Form A).

schools sent materials descriptive of their various approaches to the problem of disadvantaged groups in their communities in lieu of completed questionnaires, so that the actual response was greater than the number of questionnaires returned.

School systems and institutions of higher learning were also asked to return a more comprehensive questionnaire for each of the programs specifically designed to prepare school personnel for working with disadvantaged children and youth. Form A covered the total approach, while Form B[2] covered specific programs. Copies of Form B were also sent to the 61 summer institutes for teachers of disadvantaged children and youth operating under Title XI of the National Defense Education Act and to 15 teacher education programs financed under the Economic Opportunity Act. There was a 100 percent response from the NDEA institutes and a 67 percent response from the OEO programs,[3] many of which had not started operation when the forms were sent out. Reports on specific programs are contained in Chapter 6.

The total mailing consisted of 1,127 questionnaires sent to institutions of higher learning, school systems, NDEA summer institutes, and OEO programs. There were 503 questionnaires returned, of which 294 were Form A's, describing the total approach of school systems or institutions of higher learning; 209 were Form B's, describing specific programs for the prepartion of school personnel to work with the disadvantaged. There was an overall response of 45 per cent. However, many respondents replied to both Forms A and B, indicating that they not only integrated teacher education for work with the disadvantaged into their total curriculum but had also developed specific programs for this purpose alone. In fact, several schools and colleges reported numerous specific programs of this nature and one school system as many as 27. Therefore, the number of questionnaires returned cannot be equated with the number of institutions reporting. The response of 503 questionnaires represents rather the extent of program activities—institutional or specific—reported.

[2] See Appendix G for the questionnaire regarding specific programs (Form B).

[3] In addition to the 10 questionnaires returned by directors of OEO-financed teacher education programs, 7 directors reported OEO as the main source of funds secured through local community action agencies.

In this chapter the institutional approach by school systems and by institutions of higher learning will be analyzed.

School Systems

There were 101 school systems reporting from 29 states and the District of Columbia. Some replies were received from each of the nine regions into which the country was divided for purposes of this study (see Table 1).

Forty-three school systems reported specific programs, while 56 stated that this type of education was incorporated into their in-service training as a whole. Thirty-one school systems reported plans for programs of this type in 1965-1966 and 23 reported such plans for 1966-1967. Only 6 of the 101 school systems reported that they saw no need for such education. In their general statements the school systems reported that 90 specific programs were in operation. Actually, 89 specific programs were spelled out in the four-page questionnaire known as Form B,[4] which are analyzed in Chapter 6.

The way in which the school systems incorporated preparation of school personnel for work with the disadvantaged into the total curriculum was described in 44 of the questionnaires. There were 79 comments as to specific methods of incorporating this type of teacher education into the entire system.

Among the 18 items listed in Table 2 as "other" were inter- and intra-school visitations, demonstration lessons, tutorial centers, encouragement of teachers to attend conferences on teaching the disadvantaged, counseling, and special projects.

Some verbatim reports from respondents reveal the variety of approaches used by school systems and add a note of reality to this description of activities.

We object to a general program for the disadvantaged because the term is too vague. Instead we have in-service programs related to better understanding of the emotionally disturbed, the slow learner, the Negro, the new urban dweller, and migrant children. Our school attendance runs over 95

[4] See Appendix G.

TABLE 1 – Total Approach of School Systems to Teacher Education for Work with the Disadvantaged, Arranged by Regions

	New England	*Middle Atlantic*	*South Atlantic*	*East North Central*	*East South Central*	*West North Central*	*West South Central*	*Mountain*	*Pacific*	*Total*
Conducted special programs for teachers of disadvantaged	2	11	6	7	2	4	3	2	6	43
Incorporated such teacher education into whole system	3	14	8	15	2	2	3	4	5	56
Has plans for such programs in 1965–1966	2	6	5	5	1	1	1	2	8	31
Has plans for such programs in 1966–1967	1	5	3	4	2	1	1	2	4	23
Sees no need for such teacher education	0	2	0	2	0	0	0	2	0	6

TABLE 2 – How 44 School Systems Incorporated Teacher Education for Work with the Disadvantaged into Their Total Curriculum

	Number of Comments
As part of in-service courses and programs for teachers, counselors, and administrative staff	21
In curriculum bulletins, committees, etc.	11
Through speakers, films, discussion	9
Included in in-service workshops	9
Included in the orientation of new teachers	6
By adding additional, special personnel	5
Other	18
TOTAL	79

percent even in winter. Attendance in the suburbs does not equal that in the center of the city.

We distributed a one-page information sheet to all elementary teachers each week with practical suggestions for working with the disadvantaged. The director of Pupil Personnel Services holds monthly meetings with helping teachers, speech correctionists, school social workers, and school psychologists, at which time problems and methods of working with disadvantaged children are discussed.

The problem of teaching the disadvantaged is regularly discussed in our subject and grade level curriculum councils.

Attention is given to providing for individual differences, thereby helping to meet the needs of the deprived, within regular in-service and orientation programs. We have developed an internship program and much of the student teaching is conducted in schools where the children are predominantly deprived.

During the past year 28 projects related to the teaching and understanding of the disadvantaged child were developed.

In 95 schools last year teams of teachers were involved in curriculum modification and program development for primary-age disadvantaged children.

A committee was organized to review instructional materials now used to determine whether they accurately describe the contribution of the Negro in the country's development.

We have, among many activities, conducted active research in the classroom to improve language facilities for 'poorly languaged' children in the inner-city schools; used reading specialists to provide diagnostic, remedial motivations and enrich experiences of teachers; put individual pupils on a flexible schedule; developed team teaching; worked with preschool parent organizations in the inner-city schools; and paired school staff from disadvantaged and more advantaged areas in six 2-hour staff sessions devoted to the problems of children in the inner-city schools.

City-wide curriculum study committees, special education teacher committees, counselor discussion groups, special services groups, and administrators place the needs of our disadvantaged pupils high on the agenda of priority topics. Changes in text books, courses of study, and teacher and counselor attitudes are some of the many results of meeting this problem head on.

Colleges and Universities

There were 193 colleges and universities reporting from 46 states. Replies came from each of the nine regions. For purposes of brevity the respondents will be referred to as *colleges* rather than as institutions of higher learning—the term covering both colleges and universities (see Table 3).

Sixty-five colleges reported that they conducted specific programs for this purpose while 122 stated that teaching teachers to work with the disadvantaged was incorporated into the entire curriculum. Forty-six colleges reported plans for this type of program in 1965-1966, and 51 colleges had such plans for 1966-1967. Only 12 colleges (6 percent) stated that they saw no need for preparing school personnel to work with the disadvantaged. It is significant that only 6 percent of both school systems and colleges took this position. However, 26 colleges returned questionnaires which were completely blank with the exception of the name of the institution. Some of these blanks were returned from every region. Others replied, but their comments were not germane to this study, so they were not processed.

Those who reported incorporating this type of teacher education into the total curriculum stressed courses as a means of so doing, particularly in psychology, social anthropology, and methods. Of the 77 references to courses, 21 were related to special courses on teaching teachers to work with the disadvantaged.

Actual quotations from the replies lend specificity to the outline of activities:

TABLE 3 – Total Approach of Colleges and Universities to Teacher Education for the Disadvantaged, Arranged by Regions

	New England	*Middle Atlantic*	*South Atlantic*	*East North Central*	*East South Central*	*West North Central*	*West South Central*	*Mountain*	*Pacific*	*Total*
Conducted special programs for teachers of disadvantaged	3	14	5	13	7	6	5	4	8	65
Incorporated such teacher education into whole system	6	17	16	25	11	20	11	5	11	122
Has plans for such programs in 1965–1966	4	10	4	6	8	3	4	2	5	46
Has plans for such programs in 1966–1967	1	5	10	11	5	6	7	3	4	51
Sees no need for such teacher education	1	0	2	2	1	4	2	0	0	12

As an outgrowth of a course in education psychology, approximately 50 students were involved in a tutoring program in a low-income housing project. Each student worked two hours a week for seven weeks.

We offer a special minor in Indian education, including experience in living and teaching among Indians.

Such courses as "Education across Cultures in the Southwest" and "Teaching English as a Second Language" are specifically directed toward the teaching of disadvantaged students. "Early Childhood Education" is becoming more concerned with teacher education for work with the disadvantaged in response to statewide needs for teacher training for OEO-sponsored preacademic classes which have not been in existence before.

The report on our tutorial program for lower class urban children includes such items as: description of the life space of the child or adolescent, list of developmental tasks, analysis of self, description of child's value system, statement regarding child's overall adjustment, and analysis of incentives used to motivate child to learn.

All facets, undergraduate and graduate, of our teacher education programs have an urban orientation, with particular emphasis on teaching the disadvantaged. In cooperation with the Board of Education we use the schools in disadvantaged areas as centers of experimentation, research, and training. We operate a curriculum development center for preparation of and experimentation with materials which focus on the urban scene, for use in teacher education.

We try to have each of the students who is preparing to teach do some preprofessional work in social agencies for children in deprived areas.

All beginning students are required to conduct a school-community study

TABLE 4 – How 122 Colleges and Universities Incorporated Teacher Education for Work with the Disadvantaged into Their Total Curriculum

	Number of Comments
Course work	77
Student teaching in special service schools	36
Field trips and school visitations	19
Special projects	14
Seminars and workshops	13
Tutorial programs	10
Community services	6
Special programs, films, lectures	4
Other	6
TOTAL	185

and a high percentage of these studies are done in deprived areas. Many departments also require that at least one of the students' two teaching experiences be in a deprived neighborhood.

Two "feasibility studies" have been completed. One dealt with sending student teachers to work with classes in the inner city and in a detention home. The other was concerned with conducting educational course work in an inner-city cooperative educational center. Both have been completed and the procedures developed in the former have become a part of the regular program.

Teachers in training have an opportunity to observe group interaction sessions and listen to interplay of opinions among disadvantaged 14- and 15-year-olds in a program to rehabilitate delinquent youth. This experience has been evaluated by many students as the most revealing of their current semester.

The college has conducted a five-year value-sharing study for student teachers in slum area schools.

Our student teachers experience relationships with children in social situations such as an orphanage or a neighborhood center. However, we need to do a lot more to help our teachers become competent for work in the inner city.

There is too much emphasis on problems. There should be more emphasis on solutions.

At present, teacher education for work with the disadvantaged is done in an incidental way. We are at the stage of formulating tentative plans for a program in this area.

Our "Social Foundations" course deals with these problems, as do the basic methods courses. We see no need for a full-time program in our institution as yet.

Our student teachers are placed according to their interest. If they are concerned with this area, they are placed, if possible, in one of the Special Service Schools.

We see some real danger in separating this type of preparation from the broader stream of good teacher education, in order to ride the crest of a wave of popular and political interest.

We do a poor job in teaching teachers to work with the disadvantaged. The only emphasis this type of teacher receives is in the general discussion of individual differences, individualizing instruction, and motivation of students.

Teachers and administrators have had mass meetings for the last *two years* on the disadvantaged. *Now* we are attempting to stop giving more background and are going to give them specific techniques . . . the Do's and Don'ts of a disadvantaged area.

The range of attitudes expressed by the respondents in both schools and colleges is illustrated by the following contrasting statements: "At times, I suppose, they (our teachers) are subjected to the type of community you describe," and "We believe all will be better teachers for understanding the problems related to teaching children with vast differences in experiential background."

Specific programs as perceived by their directors

CHAPTER 6

Further analysis of replies to questionnaires: programs for teachers of the disadvantaged

There were 209 questionnaires returned by directors of programs specifically designed to prepare school personnel for working with disadvantaged children and youth. This four-page questionnaire[1] (referred to in Chapter 5 as Form B) presented checklist questions under the following major headings: (1) Rationale for the Program, (2) Organizational Data, (3) Instructional Content, (4) Instructional Process, and (5) Evaluation and Follow-up. On the last page, space was left for program evaluation by the administrators. These open-ended questions dealt with (1) Main Strengths of the Program, (2) Suggested Changes, (3) Reasons for Changes, and (4) Kinds of Assistance Needed to Improve Program.

The replies were analyzed in terms of simple frequencies and percents. Responses were divided for purposes of comparison into three main categories:

	Number of replies (N)
NDEA institutes	61
School systems	89
Colleges and universities	59

There were two categories of respondents whose "N" was deemed too small to warrant their treatment separately: OEO teacher education programs and programs jointly sponsored by a college and a school system. Only 10 of the 15 OEO teacher-training programs submitted questionnaires. These are categorized under schools or colleges, respectively, depending upon the sponsorship. Seven programs reported that OEO was partially responsible for the financing, while

[1] See Appendix G.

21 programs reported the use of federal funds other than OEO or NDEA funds.

An analysis of the 10 OEO questionnaires revealed close correlation with the responses from NDEA directors except for more emphasis on practical application to the classroom rather than theoretical program components. This discrepancy may well have been due to the fact that some OEO programs were focused on the preparation of teacher-aides.

In the 25 programs jointly sponsored by colleges and school systems, chief responsibility appeared to rest with either one or the other of the sponsoring institutions as evidenced by the title of the director, the letter of transmittal, the extent of financial commitment, or other indices of prime responsibility. Like the OEO programs, these replies were categorized as either school-sponsored or college-sponsored programs, depending upon where the chief responsibility appeared to lie.

The total enrollment figures give dramatic evidence of the scope of the programs, nationwide. More than 23,000 school faculty, staff, student teachers, and teacher-aides were reported as participating in specific programs, with 9 percent of the 209 respondents not reporting. The high enrollment was due in large measure to the enormous in-service programs conducted in some of the larger cities. New York City reported thousands of teachers and administrators as participants in their ongoing in-service program, which was geared primarily to the teaching of disadvantaged children and youth.

The geographical distribution is indicated on the accompanying maps.

Rationale for Program

FOCUS: The focus of the program, in terms of the type of disadvantaged groups served, was primarily on Negroes in the inner cities, in all three populations (urban, 86 percent; Negroes, 78 percent). The college programs were more evenly divided between urban and rural settings than were the other groups (42 percent rural). The colleges also placed relatively higher emphasis on education for teach-

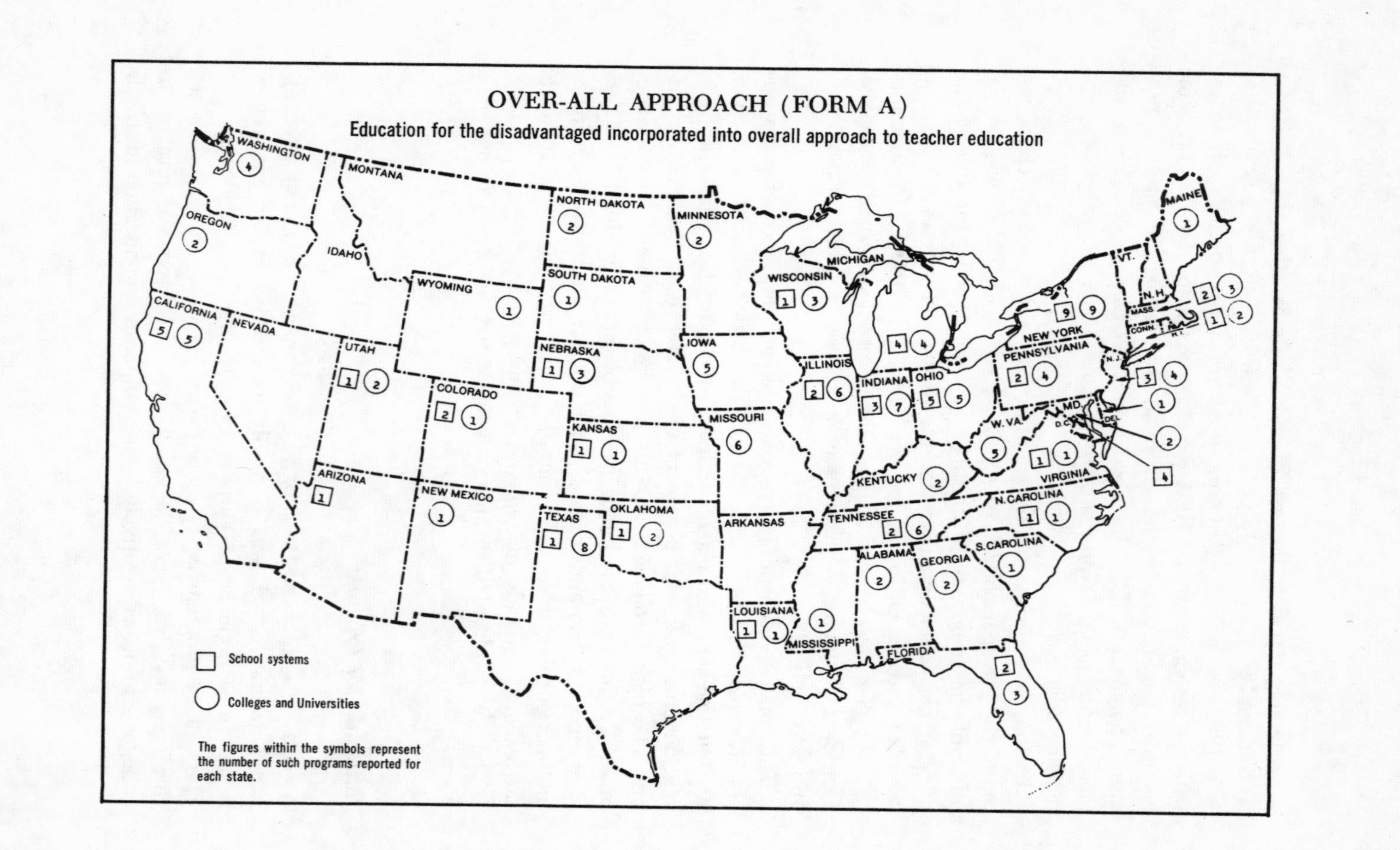
OVER-ALL APPROACH (FORM A)
Education for the disadvantaged incorporated into overall approach to teacher education
WASHINGTON
MONTANA
NORTH DAKOTA
MINNESOTA
OREGON
IDAHO
WYOMING
SOUTH DAKOTA
WISCONSIN
MICHIGAN
CALIFORNIA
NEVADA
UTAH
NEBRASKA
IOWA
ILLINOIS
INDIANA
OHIO
COLORADO
KANSAS
MISSOURI
ARIZONA
NEW MEXICO
TEXAS
OKLAHOMA
ARKANSAS
KENTUCKY
TENNESSEE
LOUISIANA
MISSISSIPPI
ALABAMA
GEORGIA
FLORIDA
S. CAROLINA
N. CAROLINA
VIRGINIA
W. VA.
MD.
D.C.
DEL.
N.J.
PENNSYLVANIA
NEW YORK
VT.
N.H.
MASS.
CONN.
R.I.
MAINE
School systems
Colleges and Universities
The figures within the symbols represent the number of such programs reported for each state.

SPECIFIC PROGRAMS (FORM B)

Programs designed specifically to prepare school personnel for work with disadvantaged children and youth

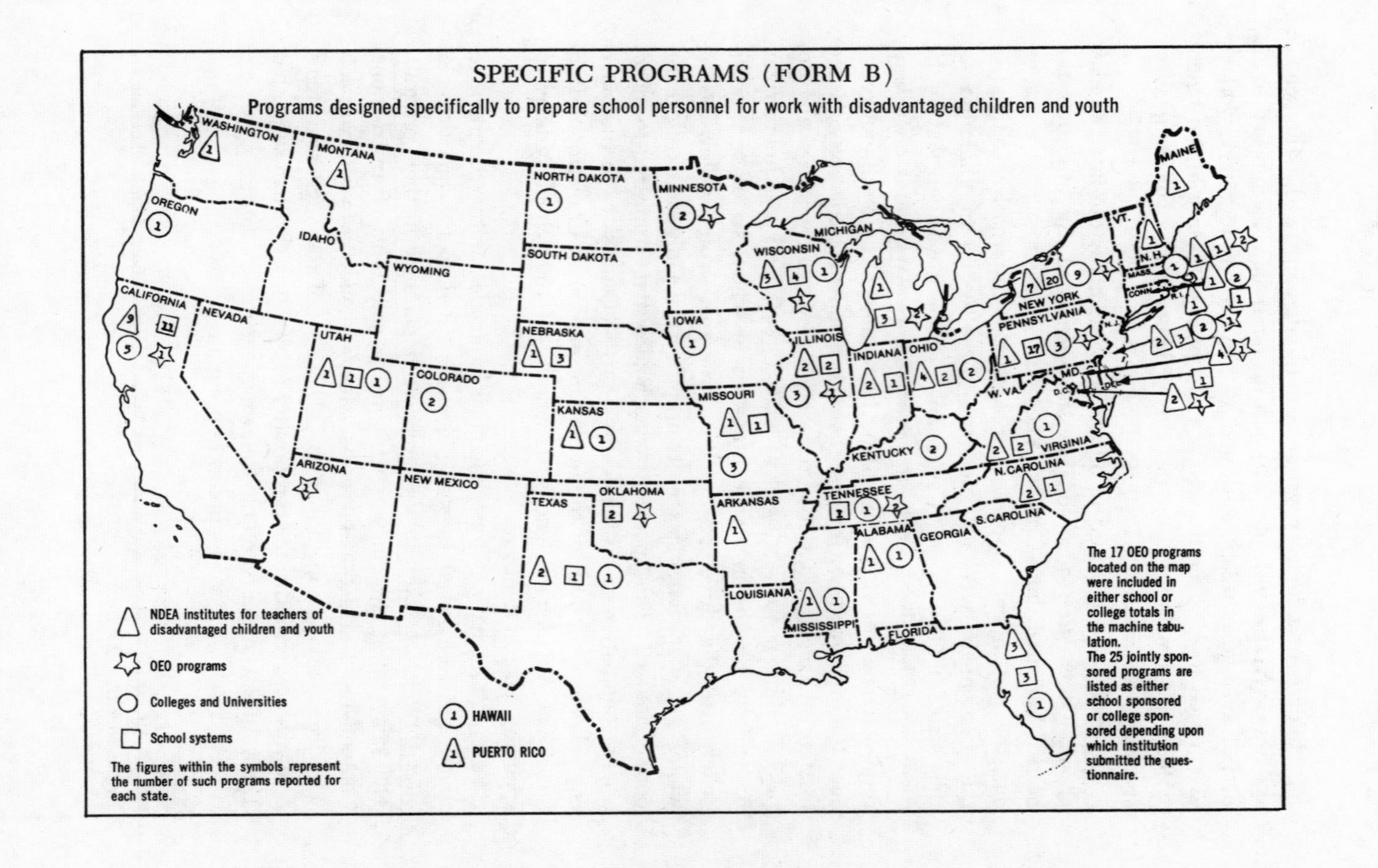

ing children of migratory workers and Indians than did the school systems or NDEA institutes (20 percent for Indians as opposed to an overall average of 12 percent, and 17 percent for migratory workers as opposed to an overall average of 10 percent). Only in the school systems did a majority of the programs (53 percent) focus on Spanish-speaking Americans.

Approximately one-third of all the respondents wrote in statements about "Other groups served" in the section of the questionnaire headed Various Ethnic Groups. When write-in comments were numerous, the respondents apparently believed the alternatives offered in the questionnaire were not adequate. In the section on ethnic groups, they wrote in "low-income Caucasians," which, it was believed by the researchers, had been covered in the first two questions on urban/rural communities characterized by low family income without reference to ethnic factors. However, many respondents apparently wished to state specifically that they were concerned with economically deprived white people, as well as with those of other ethnic origin, particularly for the in-service programs in school systems. Approximately half the directors of school programs wrote in "low-income whites" as a special focus of their programs. Only one college reported similarly. This specificity by school systems appeared to reflect a large population of economically deprived Caucasians in the inner-city schools as a result of the in-migrant movement to metropoli from areas like Appalachia. The vast majority of the school systems responding were in the larger cities.

PURPOSE: As part of reporting their rationale for the program, respondents were asked to rate objectives listed in the questionnaire on a three-point scale[2] of their relative importance in their program. The same rating system was used in the categories of Instructional Content and Instructional Process. Most respondents were extremely selective in giving top ratings to only a few of the suggested items. A few, however, indicated top priority to almost every item suggested. The ratings were based on the following legend:

1–applies to program

[2] The relative importance was indicated by single-checking, double-checking, or triple-checking the item.

2–important in program
3–key item in program

In view of the different interpretations of the scale, both "important in program" and "key item in program" ratings had significance (i.e., double-checked and triple-checked). Also important was the number of blanks (no answer) left for any given item, since these revealed the areas of least concern to respondents.

Two-thirds of the NDEA directors stated that "Attitudinal and behavioral change of enrollees" was a key purpose for their program; slightly more than half checked "Understanding the culture and life conditions of various disadvantaged groups" as having priority among their objectives; while half of them rated "Development and improvement of instructional skills, techniques, materials" as a key purpose.

For schools and colleges, approximately one-third of the directors checked these three purposes as key items. However, there were relatively few blanks for any of these items in any of the groups (less than 15 percent in all cases.) Therefore, although the intensity of interest varied, there was wide acceptance of these purposes. Only "Research" drew a majority of blanks (no answer) in all populations, with relatively fewer blanks (no answer) for the colleges (54 percent).

"Curriculum development and revision" was checked as a key item by only 7 percent of the NDEA directors and by 12 percent of all respondents. However, only 29 percent of respondents failed to check this item at all, revealing that the objective was included in most programs, although de-emphasized.

When asked to specify a purpose for their program other than those listed in the questionnaire, 19 percent of the NDEA directors, 17 percent of the directors of school programs, and 19 percent of the directors of college programs wrote in comments. "Development of skills in parent education" was reported as a program objective by one NDEA director, while a school system responded in a similar vein, specifying "parent-community involvement" as a purpose. Two school systems reported that their programs were aimed at "increasing the holding power of teachers" and "giving teachers support as they face new situations." This would seem to indicate an area of increasing concern with the high turnover rate among teachers in the inner-city schools and the inadequate preparation of teachers for the realities of working in disadvantaged areas.

The majority of write-in comments on Purposes actually related to Instructional Content or Instructional Process. The additional entries had already been placed by the researchers under what they deemed to be appropriate categories in the questionnaire, but some respondents repeated them under Purposes because of their programmatic emphasis. An example is the listing of "Assessment of instruments for language ability" as a key objective, and the checking of "Testing existing materials" under Content, by two school systems.

Organizational Data

LENGTH AND TIME OF PROGRAM: The number of hours enrollees worked per week followed a bell-shaped curve for the overall average, ranging from less than 10 hours a week to 50 and over, with the greatest concentration from 20 to 49 hours per week. The NDEA institutes were unique in the high frequency of responses falling in the range of 30 to 49 hours per week. The responses from school systems and colleges, on the other hand, were more evenly spread over the whole range.

Relatively few special programs ran more than nine weeks. Only one out of every five directors estimated the duration in terms of months rather than weeks.

All the NDEA institutes were held in the summer of 1965; approximately one-third of the school programs and more than half the college programs were operative at that time.

Approximately half the schools and colleges indicated that this was an ongoing program of several years' duration. Approximately 40 percent of both school and college programs reported a starting date within the last five years, which reveals how this type of teacher education has increased in the last few years.

NUMBER AND TYPE OF ENROLLEES: The enrollment figures varied among the three groups: 80 percent of the NDEA institutes had from 30 to 70 enrollees, with only one institute over 70, while 39 percent of the schools and 28 percent of the colleges reported an enrollment over 70.

The total enrollment reported was 23,109, with only 9 percent of the respondents failing to answer the question on enrollment. Extrapolation of this figure provides an estimated 25,395 as the revised total.

TABLE 5 – Number and Type of Personnel Enrolled in Programs Reporting

Type	*Number*	*Percent*
Teachers	15,073	73
Administrators	2,157	10
Counselors, social workers, and psychologists	604	3
Other school personnel	2,993	14
TOTALS:	20,827	100

The "Other school personnel" referred to in Table 5 comprises instructional supervisors, curriculum coordinators, community coordinators, special service teachers (such as home visitors) school nurses, and teaching principals.[3] For the NDEA institutes the proportion of teachers is higher than for the other groups (87 percent as opposed to 73 percent). This discrepancy was undoubtedly due to the fact that funds were available under Title XI of the National Defense Education Act specifically for teacher education. The proportion of administrators for NDEA institutes was only slightly smaller than the overall average (9 percent as opposed to 10 percent), but the proportion of counselors, psychologists, social workers, and other school personnel was considerably smaller for NDEA than the average (4 percent as opposed to 17 percent).

An important implication of the relatively small proportion of administrators in all three respondent groups is that it provides an empirical base for the enrollees' frequent comment that follow-up in their own schools would be impeded by failure to involve administrators in the program, and by the consequent apathy, lack of understanding, or outright opposition of the decision-makers within their respective schools. This fear was frequently expressed in group interviews with enrollees and in their written comments, not only regarding principals and central office administrative staff, but also regarding instructional supervisors in their own schools.

A skit prepared by one of the enrollees in an NDEA institute of

[3] Some respondents classified these as administrators.

how he envisioned his reception upon his return to his own school vividly illustrates this fear. In the skit, each time the teacher attempted to report his institute experience to his principal and to suggest some innovations for the school, the principal would counter with sarcasm or show indifference. The mock interview ended with the principal's request for a report that was obviously destined for the files.

Three additional types of enrollees were reported in the write-in comments: student teachers, assistant teachers, and teacher-aides, which added significantly to the choices in the questionnaire.

CRITERIA FOR SELECTION OF ENROLLEES: The NDEA institutes gave less weight to academic record as a criterion for enrollee selection than to such qualifications as "Experience with the disadvantaged," "Appointment to work with the disadvantaged," "Apparent commitment to goals of program," and "Superior's recommendation"—all of which were checked by more than 80 percent of the NDEA directors. Colleges gave high priority to "Commitment," while schools stressed "Appointment to work with the disadvantaged," "Commitment" and "Superior's recommendation." More than a third of all three groups listed other criteria that did not reveal any particular pattern.

Other criteria for eligibility were reported in the write-in comments by 14 school systems but by only 4 NDEA institutes and colleges. There was wide variance in these additional criteria, which ranged from such entries as "Minimum of three years' experience" and "Assignment to work in desegregated schools[4] in the fall of 1966," to "Demonstrated potential for changing others." Geographic limitations were indicated as criteria by some respondents. Five programs (four in colleges and one in a school system) stated as their principal criterion that the enrollees must be volunteers, an indication of the increasing interest in developing adjunctive staff from a new source of multiskilled personnel. Three directors reported that preference was given to teams from the same school—a practice lauded by enrollees, directors, and Aware Teams alike in other sections of this report.

SELECTION PROCEDURES: Application forms and references were the principal procedures used in selecting enrollees for the NDEA insti-

[4] In southern cities, where school systems had just been desegregated.

tutes, while nearly half the directors reported using essays as a method of evaluating applicants. Only 17 percent used interviews. The colleges also stressed application forms, but not one of the items suggested in the questionnaire was checked by a majority of the school systems. In both schools and colleges, approximately one-third of the respondents reported other methods.

Write-in comments by school systems noted such considerations as: "expressions of interest by teachers" and "observation of applicants teaching a class." Four college programs utilized testing as another selection procedure.

FULL-TIME PROFESSIONAL STAFF: The full-time staff for the 209 programs was reported as 1,952, with 76 percent of programs reporting. Extrapolation of this figure provides an estimated total of 2,569. Dividing this figure into the extrapolated total enrollment of 25,395 yields an estimated ratio of 1:10, as a very rough approximation of full-time staff to enrollees.

The school systems accounted for 70 percent of the full-time staff members reported: 1,371 out of 1,952. The scope of the school programs in the larger cities was extremely broad.

CREDIT FOR COMPLETION OF PROGRAM: In NDEA institutes and colleges, credit was given for completion of the program in almost every instance (NDEA 93 percent, colleges 80 percent). However, the NDEA institutes reported a larger proportion of graduate students than did the colleges and universities. A frequent write-in comment from the NDEA programs was: "All participants have a bachelor's degree; many already have their master's."

In the school systems less than a third of the programs reported giving credit. Of these, the major portion (27 percent) reported granting credit toward a salary increment. However, only 10 percent of the school systems granted credit toward a degree.

FINANCING: The total expenditures reported—with only 68 percent of the 209 programs reporting—was $19,544,463. Extrapolation of this figure provides an estimated combined budget of $28,742,000. Dividing this figure by the extrapolated enrollment total of 25,395, a very rough approximation of the per capita cost is computed—$1,131. Since the programs varied in length from one week to more than 20 months, the per-capita cost was further obscured. The NDEA institute estimate of $100 per week per participant is perhaps a more accurate figure (see Appendix J).

TRAINING FOR AUXILIARY PERSONNEL: Relatively few of the NDEA institutes or college programs incorporated training of subprofessionals to work with the disadvantaged as part of the institute (9 percent and 17 percent respectively). However, a substantial proportion of the school programs included such training (42 percent). This reveals the gap between the operational needs at the school level and the development of training resources to meet these needs. As the paraprofession of teacher-aides demonstrates its practical values, both educational and economic, the response of teacher educators may be accelerated.

Of the 37 school systems reporting that they trained teacher-aides, 24 expanded this statement, giving data on the function, type of trainees, and/or methods of training. Among training methods mentioned were pre-service orientation, in-service training by supervisory personnel, and training by enrollees in some programs for teachers of disadvantaged youth. A few school systems indicated that the in-service training was conducted under the guidance of the school principal. One school system reported that such topics as attitudes, channels of authority, and knowledge of the community were covered in the orientation for such training.

The types of trainees comprised high school and college students, parents, volunteers, and dropouts.

The functions of trainees were varied and many of them, such as "listening" aides, offered new concepts of the teacher-aide role. The functions reported ranged from simple clerical tasks to assisting the teacher in the classroom. The clerical tasks involved use of duplicating equipment, posting notices on bulletin boards, taking attendance, and the like. The next step up this new career ladder was the preparation of art materials, assistance in audiovisual equipment routines, and library assistance. The final step, reported or inferred by several respondents, was assisting the teacher in the classroom and working with individual children under the teacher's supervision. A two-year course in child development was offered by one junior college to enable graduates to assist teachers in nursery schools for the mentally retarded or socially maladjusted.

COOPERATION WITH OEO PROGRAMS: The wide variance and high frequency of write-in comments in reply to this question reflect the broad scope of the involvement of educational leadership in the programs financed by OEO.

NDEA institutes reported most frequently on cooperating with Head Start programs: 10 sent participants for regular observations, 8 organized sporadic field visits, and 4 provided consultative services. NDEA institutes also worked closely with local Job Corps, Neighborhood Youth Corps, and other Community Action Programs (CAP), such as parent education preschool classes and special enrichment programs in local summer schools. The following direct quotations give more specificity to the cooperation of NDEA institutes.

We worked in special summer classes for disadvantaged youth, conducted by schools and financed by OEO. Thirty-three participants taught as many classes, out of the 60 classes financed under CAP.

The institute cooperated with a demonstration field project for 60 disadvantaged youths who received remedial and compensatory work before going into teacher education for work with the disadvantaged.

The institute established four reading centers in connection with the local CAP.

Teachers enrolled in the institute are required to contact their local Economic Opportunity programs and develop plans for cooperative action next year.

The school in-service programs reported OEO cooperation which was similar in kind but greater in extent: 32 schools cooperated with Head Start programs; 32 with Neighborhood Youth Corps, 13 with the Job Corps; and 13 with other Community Action Programs such as a migrant education program, a public health program, a program for parents in a neighborhood planning corporation, and a literacy program; while 3 cooperated with VISTA.

For the most part, the colleges and universities provided trained personnel for teaching, consultative services, testing services, and teacher education, rather than direct participation in the OEO programs. One college reported that it had trained as many as 251 teachers for Head Start work during the summer, while two colleges supplied work-study students as teacher-aides in OEO programs, where they worked 15 hours a week.

Instructional Content

In the section, "Understanding Disadvantaged Children and Youth," nine content areas were suggested and all but one appeared to be covered with varying degrees of intensity in the curricula. "No answers" were minimal: 10 percent or less in most instances, except for the item "Life conditions of economically deprived the world over," which evoked response from only 30 percent of the programs. Only 1 percent of the school programs gave it top priority in program emphasis—that is, triple-checked it, meaning that this was considered a "key item."

The terms *single-checked, double-checked,* and *triple-checked* will be used frequently to indicate the relative program emphasis given each item on a three-point scale. These terms are more precise than the characterization of each gradation in the scale (i.e., single-checked, "applies to program"; double-checked, "important in program"; triple-checked, "key item in program").

Only for the NDEA institutes was any of the items in this category triple-checked by the majority of respondents. These key items are shown in Table 6.

TABLE 6 – Triple-Checked Items in Study Questionnaire under Category "Understanding the Disadvantaged"

Suggested Content Area	*Percent of NDEA directors who triple-checked item (N = 61)*
How accepting or rejecting attitudes of teachers, often at unconscious level, may affect motivation and learning of children and youth	71
How environmental conditioning may affect:	
Communication skills	66
Self-image	58
Culture and tradition of disadvantaged groups with which majority of the enrollees will be working	55

N = number of NDEA programs.

Three other items were triple-checked by the majority of NDEA directors but were given top priority by less than 30 percent of the other groups. These items fell under other content areas but each had a powerful component of understanding (see Table 7).

TABLE 7 – Triple-Checked Items in Questionnaire with a Component of Understanding, but Not So Categorized

Suggested Content Area	*Percent of NDEA directors who triple-checked item (N = 61)*
The need for understanding self as essential to understanding and relating to others	57
Emphasis upon discovery by children through experiments and problem solving as opposed to being told	56
Attention to individual growth patterns	53

It is striking that not one of the items triple-checked by a majority of the NDEA directors fell into the categories of Instructional Techniques, Instructional Materials, or Special Subject Matter Enrollees Are Being Prepared To Teach. The difference in emphasis upon basic understandings and the practical application of these understandings to the classroom is revealed more clearly when the scores for "important items" (double-checked) and "key items" (triple-checked) are combined. Chart 1 indicates whether any importance was attached to the suggested content area, without differentiating the degree of stress.

The questions start with areas of theoretical content and become more specific in terms of preparation for classroom performance as they progress. Chart 1 presents in graphic form the fact that the more specific the items in terms of actual teaching behavior, the less frequently these items were double-checked or triple-checked to indicate programmatic emphasis.

The actual combined scores for "key items" (triple-checked) and "important items" (double-checked) for Instructional Content are presented in Appendix L. Outstanding is the response by NDEA directors to two of the content areas in the checklist, both of which

CHART 1 – *Relative Emphasis on Areas of Instructional Content*

% of respondents who judged items important	*N* 61	*S* 89	*C* 59	*A* 209
A. *Understanding Disadvantaged Children and Youth*				
1a. Culture and traditions of the disadvantaged				
1b. Culture and traditions of those with whom enrollees work				
2a. Life conditions of the poor the world over				
2b. Life conditions of those with whom enrollees work				
3a. How environment may affect hopes and expectations				
3b. How environment may affect self-image				
3c. How environment may affect communication skills				
3d. How environment may affect behavior patterns				
4. How teachers' attitudes affect learning				
B. *Situational Factors of Concern to Teachers*				
1. Family life				
2. Peer groups				
3. Social stratification				
4. Community organization				
5. School community relations				
6. Group process				
7. Analysis of social conflict				
8. Youth in an era of technological change				
C. *Professional Competence of Teachers*				
1. Need for self-understanding to relate to others				
2. Need for ego strength to deal with aggression				
3. Self insights into satisfactions from teaching				
D. *Conceptual Framework (Teaching Strategies)*				
1. The interests-and-needs approach				
2. The evolving curriculum day by day				
3. Strategies for developing democratic values				

4. Strategies for bringing about behavior changes
5. Use of symbolism in instructional materials
6. The "discovery approach"
7. Attention to individual growth patterns
8. Concept that every teacher is a counselor

E. Instructional Techniques (Specific Methods)

1. Team teaching
2. Teacher-pupil planning and evaluation
3. Establishing the work climate
4. Field trips
5. Project-centered learning
6. Committee activity and special assignments
7. Discussion techniques
8. Programmed teaching
9. Role playing
10. Structured and dramatic presentations
11. Films, television, and other media

F. Instructional Materials (Testing and Development)

1. Testing existing materials
2. Developing new materials

G. Subject Matter Enrollees Will Teach

1. Reading
2. English as a foreign language
3. Modern foreign languages
4. Social studies
5. Science
6. Mathematics
7. Geography
8. Educational media

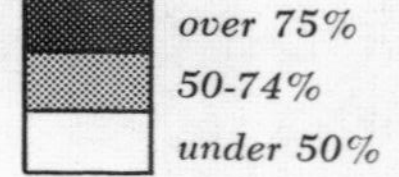

over 75%
50-74%
under 50%

N = NDEA institutes; S = school systems; C = colleges & universities; A = overall average

were emphasized in the programs of over 90 percent of the NDEA summer institutes (Table 8).

TABLE 8 – Items in Questionnaire Either Double- or Triple-Checked by 90 Percent of NDEA Institute Directors

Suggested Content Area	*Percent of NDEA directors who double- or triple-checked items (N = 61)*
How environmental conditioning may affect communication skills	98
How accepting or rejecting attitudes of teachers, often at unconscious level, may affect motivation and learning of children and youth	94

The 10 OEO teacher education projects tended to follow the same general pattern as the NDEA institutes, while both the school and the college programs fell far below in frequency of response. Not one of the suggested content areas was deemed important in the two last mentioned populations by 75 percent or more of the directors. This discrepancy may be evidence of the sense of direction in the NDEA institutes imparted by the conceptual framework of the guidelines prepared by the U. S. Office of Education. Another contributing factor might be that the intensity of the experience in a summer institute provided opportunity for greater concentration on important content areas than the more diffuse approach of the preservice and in-service programs conducted in school systems and institutions of higher learning.

However, even in the NDEA institutes, with their careful preplanning and intense concentration on stated goals, the hierarchy of values indicated for Instructional Content was inconsistent with the expressed intent of the respondents. *Both* "improvement of instructional skills, techniques and materials" *and* "understanding the culture and life conditions of disadvantaged groups" had been triple-checked by more than half the NDEA directors as key objectives for their programs. However, when they were asked how they planned to undergird these two basic purposes through instructional content, the response regarding implementation of the former (improvement of skills, techniques, and materials) was meager, while the response to the latter was overwhelming.

A number of causal factors may have been operative. First, the time pressures of a six- to eight-week program were intense. Second, many directors held firmly to the philosophy that teachers who have the necessary insights and empathy will find a way to translate these insights into their day-to-day operation, in terms of their own teaching styles without outside assistance. Additionally, it may well be assumed that the discrepancy between intent and implementation stemmed in large measure from the vast range of resources provided by the disciplines of anthropology, sociology, and psychology through the media of lectures, literature, and research (a conceptual framework for teaching the disadvantaged that is readily available) and the minimal resources as yet developed for specific teaching strategies, practices, and materials that directly pertain to work with the disadvantaged.

In summary, although the majority of the respondents saw the facilitation of teaching behavior as a major goal in preparing school personnel to work with the disadvantaged, when they were asked how they planned to implement this goal in terms of content, the response fell far below the halfway mark. This discrepancy seems to point to the need for greater conceptualization, experimentation, research, and development of materials in the area of practical classroom performances by teachers of the disadvantaged.

The percent of write-in comments that was checked as either "key items" or "important items" for Instructional Content was relatively low, ranging from 4 to 6 percent for the various categories. It therefore appears that the inadequacy of suggested alternatives in the questionnaire was not a limiting factor in the response to Instructional Content.[5]

Although relatively infrequent, some of the write-in comments in these areas had idiosyncratic significance. The category Understanding Disadvantaged Children and Youth elicited some interesting write-ins:

[5] See Appendix L for complete scores.

- relationship between measured IQ and real ability
- techniques and resources in human relations
- need for inclusion in "mainstream"
- urban ecology, psychology of speech, thought and language
- understanding of concept "culture"
- vocational development
- offering recreational and dramatic experiences to understand why and how disadvantaged children express themselves

Several NDEA directors wrote in "special problems relating to civil rights, desegregation" as an important content area under Situational Factors. "Information about social agencies working with the disadvantaged" was also mentioned, and one NDEA director listed "problems faced by enrollee in effecting change in the local schools" as an item of import among situational factors covered in the institute's content.

Under the heading, Professional Competence of Teachers, additional content areas mentioned were: "analysis of the teaching process," "sophistication re: testing," "educational diagnosis," "understanding class structure," and "ability to relate to the culture level of a particular child." "The need for professionalization of the teacher role" and "adaptable role models" were mentioned as key items, as was "the role of the teacher as an agent-for-change among her colleagues."

Also imaginative were enlargements upon the items listed in the questionnaire under Conceptual Framework. Inductive as well as analytical thinking was mentioned—for example, "teaching methods which emphasize individuality and informality and which aim to enhance teacher-child relationship" was the write-in comment of one director of an OEO program for training teacher-aides.

Additional Instructional Techniques reported were "ungraded classes," "small, flexible grouping," "tutoring," and "use of the Montessori approach."

Many of these teaching strategies, such as those listed for checking in the questionnaire, were valuable for the learning-teaching process in general but were seen as extraordinarily important in working with disadvantaged children and youth.

The write-in for Instructional Materials gave specificity in terms of the application of materials to work with disadvantaged children, citing such illustrative materials as:

- picture files to develop pride in racial and ethnic heritage
- educational improvement brochure
- multiculture readers
- manipulative materials

Under the category of Subject Matter Enrollees Are Being Prepared to Teach, the most frequent write-in was "language arts." In all three populations, the enrichment and development of English, both written and oral, were stressed. Also mentioned were physical education, fine arts, music, English literature, and Negro history.

Major Content Areas other than those suggested in the questionnaire included The Role of the Subprofessional in the School, Career Development, and The Impact of the Urban Community on Education. Most frequently mentioned were areas related to the behavioral sciences.

Instructional Process

Nineteen specific procedures were listed in the questionnaire, to be checked, double-checked, or triple-checked in terms of relative program emphasis. Only 2 items were triple-checked by the majority of NDEA directors. None was triple-checked by the other populations (Table 9).

TABLE 9 – Procedures Judged as Key Items in Programs by NDEA Directors

Item	*Percent of respondents who triple-checked items*
Small group discussion	54
Lectures by Program faculty	53

There were 13 of the 19 listed procedures to which one or more of the populations responded by leaving over 50 percent blank, indicating no activity in this area—a much lower response than in Instructional Content. However, only 16 percent reported procedures other than those listed, of which only 4 percent were triple-checked (key items). Hence the lack of response was not due to inadequacy of the alternatives suggested. Most frequent among the additional items written in were: "demonstration teaching" and "laboratory-clinic."

All 13 items that drew more than 50 percent blanks were so rated by school systems, but only 4 of them were so rated by NDEA institutes and 7 by colleges. The procedures that most of the respondents did not use in their programs are presented below, in descending order of frequency in relation to school systems (Table 10).

TABLE 10 – Procedures Listed in Questionnaire Which Drew 50 Percent or More Blanks in School Systems

	Percent of Answers Left Blank			
Item	*NDEA* (*N* = *61*)	*Schools* (*N* = *89*)	*Colleges* (*N* = *59*)	*Total group* (*N* = *209*)
Scheduled study time	61	75	73	75
T-groups for self-awareness	72	79	78	77
Free time for socializing and recreation	19	76	54	54
Preparation of papers	22	76	42	51
Preparation of daily log	64	76	66	70
Practicum (closely supervised teaching or counseling)	43	74	46	58
Field experience in teaching	35	73	47	55
Field experience with involvement in community affairs	42	66	49	55
Group counseling sessions	47	63	56	57
Research	59	63	51	58
Case studies	28	59	39	47
Home visits	40	57	59	53
Reports of reading	29	52	34	40

N = number of programs reporting.

Analysis of the combined scores for the items that were double checked or triple checked reveals that the procedures most frequently employed by all populations were: "Discussion" (both small group and general) and "Lectures by Program faculty." Only for the NDEA institutes were four other items judged important by the majority of the directors: "Field trips for observation of the community," "Field experience in teaching," "Practicum," and "Individual conferences." The 10 OEO programs also stressed field experience and individual conferences.

It is apparent from Table 11 that while the intensive summer programs placed more emphasis on experiential learning and individual work with the participants, these approaches were utilized to some degree by all populations. It is significant that the only procedure deemed important in the majority of the school in-service programs was "Small-group discussion," which may have been selected because of the limited time available.

Chart 2, arranged in descending order of frequency based on replies from NDEA Institutes, presents the relative emphases in more graphic form.

TABLE 11 – Relative Importance of Procedures to Respondents

Procedures as Listed in Questionnaire	*Percent of respondents who double-checked or triple-checked items*			
	NDEA (N = 61)	*Schools (N = 89)*	*Colleges (N = 59)*	*Total group (N = 209)*
Lectures by visitors	76	23	44	45
Lectures by Program faculty	80	29	54	51
General discussion	73	45	63	58
Small group discussion	87	57	68	68
Group counseling sessions	25	19	10	18
T-group for self-awareness	18	6	10	11
Field trips for observation of community	65	26	41	41
Field experience with involvement in community	45	16	27	27
Field experience in teaching	52	12	36	31
Practicum (closely supervised teaching and/or counseling)	52	19	44	35
Home visits	44	22	17	26
Case studies	35	17	17	22
Research	18	10	20	16
Reports of reading	40	18	22	26
Preparation of papers	41	9	29	24
Preparation of daily log	22	7	15	13
Individual conferences	50	25	49	39
Scheduled study time	17	1	7	7
Free time for socializing and recreation	35	1	15	15
Other	8	1	12	6

CHART 2 — Relative Emphasis on Specific Procedures in Instructional Process in Replies to Questionnaires. Order listed in descending frequency as reported by NDEA Institutes.

	N = 61 *NDEA*	*N = 89* *School*	*N = 59* *College*	*N = 209* *Overall Average*
Small group discussion	75% and over	50% to 74%	50% to 74%	50% to 74%
Lectures by program faculty	75% and over	under 50%	50% to 74%	50% to 74%
Lectures by visitors	75% and over	under 50%	under 50%	under 50%
General discussion	50% to 74%	under 50%	50% to 74%	50% to 74%
Field trips for observation in community	50% to 74%	under 50%	under 50%	under 50%
Field practice in teaching	50% to 74%	under 50%	under 50%	under 50%
Practicum (closely supervised teaching and/or counseling)	50% to 74%	under 50%	under 50%	under 50%
Individual conferences	50% to 74%	under 50%	under 50%	under 50%
Field trips with involvement in community	under 50%	under 50%	under 50%	under 50%
Home visits	under 50%	under 50%	under 50%	under 50%
Preparation of papers	under 50%	under 50%	under 50%	under 50%
Reports of reading	under 50%	under 50%	under 50%	under 50%
Free time for socializing and recreation	under 50%	under 50%	under 50%	under 50%
Case studies	under 50%	under 50%	under 50%	under 50%
Group counseling sessions	under 50%	under 50%	under 50%	under 50%
Preparation of daily log	under 50%	under 50%	under 50%	under 50%
T-groups for self-awareness	under 50%	under 50%	under 50%	under 50%
Research	under 50%	under 50%	under 50%	under 50%
Scheduled study time	under 50%	under 50%	under 50%	under 50%
Other	under 50%	under 50%	under 50%	under 50%

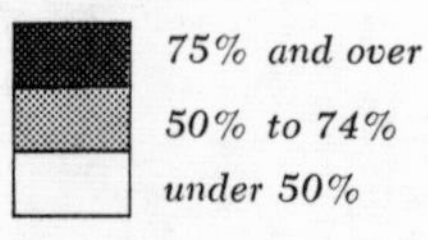

75% and over

50% to 74%

under 50%

The write-in comments for Instructional Process dealt largely with techniques that would facilitate communication and interaction among staff and enrollees.

Methods of Program Evaluation Used

FEEDBACK FROM ENROLLEES DURING PROGRAM

There was overwhelming response to the importance of feedback in the development of program, with positive scores ranging from 82 percent for school programs to 94 percent for NDEA institutes, and an overall average of 87 percent. Both written feedback and discussion were utilized by the vast majority, and in most cases faculty was present at these discussions.

There was a tremendous response to the request for specificity as to what, in fact, was changed as a result of feedback. In almost every instance some specific change was made. The most frequently mentioned change concerned scheduling, which included both pace and hourly schedule. Many respondents reported changes in program, field work, and assignments. A few stated that there was a change in focus and in total approach. In some instances new staff was added—for example, the addition of school personnel to a staff consisting entirely of professors of education, or the addition of staff resulting in an integrated faculty. Changes in overall planning, administration, budget, and enrollee selection were also mentioned. Improvement in staff-enrollee relations and in school-parent-community relations was attributed to feedback by school systems. In addition, increased integration of cognitive and affective aspects of the program as a result of feedback was reported.

EVALUATION BY PROFESSIONAL STAFF

Staff evaluation was seen as important to program development by more directors than was feedback. It was deemed important by as many as 99 percent of the NDEA directors. The emphasis was on staff meetings rather than written evaluation by staff. The specific changes resulting from staff evaluation were similar in kind but not as numerous as changes reported in response to enrollee feedback.

PLAN FOR FOLLOW-UP WITH ENROLLEES AFTER PROGRAM

Approximately two-thirds of the directors in all three populations reported plans for follow-up by personal contact. However, there was a decided difference between NDEA institutes and the other programs with respect to follow-up through letters or questionnaires. Seventy-seven percent of the NDEA directors planned to use this method, while less than half of the colleges and only one-third of the school systems had such plans. On the other hand, class visitations were planned by more than half the school systems and only an approximate one-third of the other populations. Group reunions did not receive a positive response from the majority of any of the three groups—the highest percentage scored by NDEA directors (46 percent).

Other plans for follow-up were reported as:

- bulletin or newsletter by participants
- chain letters
- diaries or logs kept by participants upon return to school
- meetings with administrators
- seminars of participants with their colleagues (nonparticipant)
- released time for workshops and conferences
- pre- and post-testing including the use of classroom tapes
- formation of a permanent organization for participants
- intervisitation
- use of participants for in-service training faculty in their schools
- neighborhood meetings
- conferences with institute director during the year
- annual weekend retreat
- more advanced courses to be taken by participants
- evaluation by principals, supervisors
- permanent school-college council

There was high consensus (over two-thirds for all groups) that follow-up was important for future program development. The relatively high proportion of write-in comments, ranging from 10 percent in school programs to 20 percent for college programs, attests to the variation in approach.

Evaluation of Programs by Administrators

REPLIES TO OPEN-ENDED QUESTIONS

The imaginative quality of many programs is evident in the diversity and originality of the responses to the open-ended questions.

There were two evaluative questions regarding strengths and weaknesses of the programs as perceived by directors. Weaknesses were indicated by the changes the directors stated they would like to make if they were starting again.

There were also two questions dealing with the optimum situation, if time, money, and staff were available. One of these concerned the optimum method of evaluation, which did not seem to be adequately developed in most programs. The other dealt with kinds and sources of assistance needed to improve their programs. The answers to the question on the optimum situation were, in effect, recommendations, so they are reported in Chapter 8 on Recommendations.

MAIN STRENGTHS OF PROGRAMS

The strengths are presented first in broad categories and then in more detail, with the percents figured on the basis of category totals (see Table 12). In every case the items are presented in descending order, based on frequency of response from NDEA directors. The percents for thè other populations were not arranged quantitatively but rather to conform to the NDEA scores. N equals the number of comments, *not* the number of respondents. It is apparent from Table 12 that "Understandings gained" is rated higher than "Improvement of teacher behavior" by approximately 4 to 1 in the Strengths perceived by NDEA directors, approximately 3 to 1 by directors of school programs, and approximately 2 to 1 by directors of college programs.

TABLE 12–Strengths of Programs as Perceived by Their Directors

	Percent of comments as related to each area of strength			
	NDEA (N = 287)	Schools (N = 265)	Colleges (N = 138)	Total group (N = 699)
Understandings gained by enrollees	37	47	39	41
Process employed	28	19	26	24
Preplanning	21	14	17	15
Improvement of enrollees' teaching strategies/methods/ use of materials	9	17	15	13
Operation of program	5	3	3	3

N = number of comments.

When percents are computed within each category, some significant differences become evident. Within each area of strength, the variance is one of kind, not merely of degree, as can be seen from the following analysis, category by category, of strengths perceived by directors (Table 13).

TABLE 13 – Understandings Gained by Enrollees through Participation in Programs

	Percent of comments regarding each specific strength*			
	NDEA (N = 107)	Schools (N = 125)	Colleges (N = 53)	Total group (N = 285)
Better understanding of community/home/parents	30	21	17	24
Understanding values/culture/ life conditions of the disadvantaged	26	25	38	28
Self-understanding by enrollees/ increased commitment	21	33	32	28
Attitudinal change of enrollees toward disadvantaged children	12	21	13	16
Understanding the need for balance of theory and practice	11	—	—	4

* Percents are based on category, *not* total number of comments, and are arranged in descending order of frequency, in relation to NDEA institutes.

The relative importance of relationships with home and parents given in the NDEA institutes as opposed to the other populations is evident in the hierarchy of Understandings Gained.

TABLE 14 – Process Employed by Directors in Programs

	Percent of comments as related to each area of strength			
	NDEA (*N* = *79*)	*Schools* (*N* = *50*)	*Colleges* (*N* = *36*)	*Total group* (*N* = *165*)
Practicum/field experience in teaching	36	24	53	36
Discussion in small groups	16	30	22	22
Demonstration by/observation of master teachers	15	6	—	9
Qualities of instruction: unity, diversity, flexibility/interesting assignments	14	—	—	7
Lectures	11	10	19	13
Social activities	5	—	—	2
Case studies	3	—	—	1
Improved guidance/supervision	—	30	6	10

Both NDEA institutes and colleges rated "practicum" as highest among the procedures employed (see Table 14). Colleges entered this component of process most frequently. The school directors, on the other hand, believed that "Discussion in small groups" was one of the most effective processes used. In a school system, which is in and of itself a kind of practicum for experiment with new ideas and strategies, field experience in teaching was not required. The fact that "Improved guidance and supervision" received the same top rating in school systems as "Discussion in small groups" may indicate a belief on the part of directors that the crucial aspect of the practicum —sensitive, creative supervision—was being fostered within the school situation itself. The absence of any reference to improved supervision in the NDEA institutes may be related to the low proportion of administrators among enrollees.

A comparison of the responses to the checklist of possible procedures and the program strengths in the evaluation by NDEA is revealing. "Practicum" was the sixth item in order of importance in the checklist for program emphasis,[6] while it had the highest score as the main strength of the program. It would appear that even in cases where lectures, discussions, and field trips to community were deemed more important in the planning, the experiential learnings in the practicum proved to be the principal strength, as the program developed. The same comparison is observable for the college programs in lesser degree. The practicum placed fourth in programmatic emphasis and first in perceived strengths, in the minds of the directors of college programs.

TABLE 15 – Preplanning for Program by Sponsoring Institution

	Percent of comments as related to each area of strength			
	NDEA (*N* = *61*)	*Schools* (*N* = *38*)	*Colleges* (*N* = *21*)	*Total group* (*N* = *120*)
Selection of staff	36	16	19	27
Selection of enrollees	28	50	38	37
Planning/focus/goals	15	—	—	7
Facilities	13	5	10	10
Compensation for enrollees	—	3	—	1
Other	8	26	33	18

To most NDEA directors the selection of staff of high calibre was the major strength, while wise selection of participants was the key to strong programming in the other two populations (Table 15). A possible explanation of this discrepancy is that the school systems and colleges used existing staff, who for the most part were presumed to be highly competent, so that the participants constituted the unique and all-important factor for them, while the NDEA institutes started *de novo,* hence the quality of professional staff was a major consideration.

Both "Teaching strategies" and "Use of instructional materials" stood out among the NDEA directors' perception of program strengths in this area (see Table 16). For the directors of school programs, however, "Curriculum development" was seen as the major strength in

[6] See Table 11, preceding.

TABLE 16 – Improvement of Enrollees' Knowledge and Use of Teaching Strategies/Methods/Materials after Participation in Program

	Percent of comments as related to each area of strength			
	NDEA (*N* = *27*)	*Schools* (*N* = *46*)	*Colleges* (*N* = *24*)	*Total group* (*N* = *107*)
Teaching strategies such as clinical diagnosis of pupils' needs/use of inductive approach	33	2	37	18
Use of instructional resources/materials	33	30	17	4
Curriculum development	19	46	29	31
Teaching of communication skills	15	22	17	18

terms of practical application of insights to teaching performance. For the colleges, too, "Curriculum development" was de-emphasized both in the planning and in the evaluation of program strengths by NDEA directors.

TABLE 17 – Operation of Program by Directors

	Percent of comments as related to each area of strength			
	NDEA (*N* = *13*)	*Schools* (*N* = *6*)	*Colleges* (*N* = *4*)	*Total group* (*N* = *23*)
Staff-enrollee relationships	85	—	—	48
Evaluation/follow-up	15	50	25	26
Organization/administration	—	50	75	26

A clear difference among the three populations is discernible in this category, although the small number of comments minimizes significance of the findings. To NDEA directors, "Staff-enrollee relationships" was a major strength; to directors of school in-service programs, "Evaluation/follow-up" and "Organization/administration" appeared of equal strength; while 4 directors of college programs saw "Organization/administration" as the main programmatic strength.

ILLUSTRATIVE QUOTES ON STRENGTHS

For illustration, three complete replies to the question on Strengths are quoted below: one from an NDEA director; one from the director of a teacher-intern program, which was sponsored by a university with the close cooperation of the local school system; and one from the director of an OEO-financed program for training teacher-aides.

QUESTION: *What do you see as the main strengths of your program?*

REPLY 1: *From the director of an NDEA institute*

- The depth of the content rather than the *scope*. Sound theoretical background establishing emphasis on differentiation and specificity. Developing a theme or content through lecture, trip, movie, demonstration.
- The reality of the work done by enrollees in the field teaching experience (Practicum). The design of the Field Supervision made this possible; also the training and experience of the supervisors, who were competent and theoretically oriented preschool teachers, were right for these enrollees. Such supervisors could enable the enrollees to *do*.
- The integrating process which in many ways was built in.
- The timing of lectures by outside consultants—the enrollees were ready for and could immediately consider or *use* their contributions.
- The intensity of involvement which built steadily.
- The use students made of the reading room, and the journal reading material made available.
- The daily written statements and questions of the participants, which were really *used* by supervisors.
- The honesty of the "real-dealing" with *real* problems in demonstration centers, considering *real* problems of participants, and allowing enrollees to analyze the performance of our own staff in demonstrations.
- The positive interaction in the total program including direct work with children and involvement of the principals, of directors, and of supervisors, with the enrollees in joint planning and action.

REPLY 2: *From the director of a teacher-intern program sponsored by a university in cooperation with a school system*

(1) Selection of very capable enrollees, with strong liberal arts background and above average scholastic ability.

(2) Realistic division of responsibility, i.e., (a) assuming half a teaching load in a school throughout the year, for which they earned as they learned; (b) assuming half a load of academic program, for which they could earn a master's degree in education in one calendar year.

(3) Summer orientation before assuming teaching responsibilities referred to in (2) above.

(4) Cooperation between the university and the school district.

REPLY 3: *From the director of an Indian teacher-aide training program*

- One of the main strengths of this program was the inclusion of a demonstration classroom of 25 four- and five-year-old Indian children. This enabled each student to have observation and participation experience in the kindergarten with Indian children.
- These sessions have formed the basis for development of understandings about children's growth, individual differences, management of children, content of the curriculum and organization of the classroom.
- Within all of this, these students have maintained a focus on their role as an aide to the classroom teacher.
- The participants were provided with cultural information that was very necessary in order to understand the preschool Indian child. The aides were shown the value and purposes of education. The either-or concept of an Indian having to choose between being an Indian or an American was discussed. Usually all the advantages of being an Indian were presented. We then studied quite deeply the concept of and-or and decided one could be an Indian *and* an American. So now the aide can become a bridge between education and the community. For only as the people are involved in the education of their children can hope be found for them. The people must determine their own destiny.
- We believe a strength of this program was the opportunity for the aides to have instruction and actual practice in the use of audiovisual equipment and the preparation of instructional materials.

PROGRAM CHANGES SUGGESTED BY DIRECTORS

As in the treatment of the replies about major program strengths, the replies to the question on Changes (see Table 18) are presented in broad categories, first to indicate the areas of greatest concern, and then in more detail, category by category, to demonstrate the components within each major grouping that were mentioned most frequently by directors in each of the three populations. N equals the number of comments, *not* the number of respondents.

TABLE 18 – Areas of Program Change Suggested by Directors

Areas of Change	*Percent of comments related to each area of change*			
	NDEA (*N* = *215*)	*Schools* (*N* = *163*)	*Colleges* (*N* = *72*)	*Total group* (*N* = *450*)
Process	39	19	29	30
Content	27	27	25	27
Preplanning	24	38	29	30
Operation of Program	10	16	17	13

SUGGESTED CHANGES IN PROCESS: A comparison of the process components which were commented upon most frequently under Strengths and under Suggested Changes is revealing. Under Strengths, the procedure most frequently cited by both NDEA and college directors was "Practicum, field experience in teaching." Under Suggested Changes (see Table 19), the procedure cited most frequently by all three populations was "Include or expand field teaching experience and educational contacts with children." It is significant that the highest score (68 percent) for this procedure fell to the school programs, which had the lowest score for "Practicum" under Strengths (only 24 percent). Hence, the lack of intensively supervised field teaching experience appeared to be recognized by directors of in-service programs in the school systems as a detriment to the effectiveness of the entire learning process.

The scores are arranged in descending order in relation to NDEA directors, with the exception of any statement that negates a statement immediately preceding it.

SUGGESTED CHANGES IN CONTENT: There were two areas of emphasis which were of concern to all three populations: "emphasis on teaching strategies, methods and materials," i.e., the practical application of new insights to teaching behavior; and "emphasis on social and behavioral sciences," i.e., the theoretical approach to understanding the needs of disadvantaged children and youth. There was wide variance of opinion as to which of these two content areas should be

TABLE 19 – Changes in Program Process Suggested by Directors

	Percent of comments regarding each specific change			
	NDEA (*N* = *83*)	*Schools* (*N* = *31*)	*Colleges* (*N* = *21*)	*Total group* (*N* = *135*)
Include or expand field teaching experience and educational contacts with children	45	68	43	50
Provide more and better teaching of group dynamics and use small group discussions more extensively and effectively	23	10	33	22
Schedule more free time for independent study, informal sharing, and socializing instead of so many formal reading and written assignments	17	6	3	12
Place less emphasis on socializing	2	—	—	1
Schedule fewer lectures	6	—	5	4
Have more and better lectures	1	10	5	4
Provide more demonstrations by master teachers	4	6	9	5
Schedule more field trips	1	—	5	1
Schedule fewer field trips	1	—	—	1

stressed in specific programs in order to achieve an equilibrium of these essential components in a balanced curriculum. It can be assumed that the contradictions of opinion revealed in Table 20 depend in part upon differences in basic philosophy, in part upon the degree to which the current emphasis on instructional content in each individual program had proved effective.

SUGGESTED CHANGES IN PREPLANNING: The NDEA directors were, for the most part, satisfied with their professional staff. In fact, "selection of staff" received the top score under Preplanning as a main strength of their programs. Hence, "improve the selection of enrollees" appeared to them to be a more important change than "improve the selection of staff" (see Table 21). The directors of college programs also stressed "improve selection of staff," but the directors of in-service programs in school systems reversed the order—their high score was for "improve selection of enrollees." There was difference of opinion

TABLE 20 – Changes in Program Content Suggested by Directors

	Percent of comments regarding each specific change			
	NDEA (*N* = *59*)	*Schools* (*N* = *44*)	*Colleges* (*N* = *18*)	*Total group* (*N* = *121*)
Place more emphasis on teaching strategies, methods and materials for practical application of new insights to teaching behavior	51	68	33	54
Negative of prior statement	3	—	—	2
Develop relevant concepts from social and behavioral sciences more effectively	44	32	61	42
Negative of prior statement	2	—	6	2

regarding the length of NDEA institutes, while several school and college program directors desired stipends for their students similar to those provided under NDEA.

TABLE 21 – Changes in Program Preplanning Suggested by Directors

	Percent of comments related to each specific change			
	NDEA (*N* = *52*)	*Schools* (*N* = *62*)	*Colleges* (*N* = *21*)	*Total group* (*N* = *135*)
Improve selection of enrollees	29	14	33	23
Improve selection of staff	25	37	14	29
Improve planning and focus/ clarify goals	15	18	19	17
Increase duration of program	15	10	14	12
Decrease duration of program	2	—	—	1
Improve facilities	10	3	10	7
Provide stipends for enrollees	—	16	5	8
Other	4	2	5	3

SUGGESTED CHANGES IN OPERATION OF PROGRAM: "Place more emphasis on evaluation and follow-up" was the overwhelming need of directors in all three populations, as they assessed operation of their programs. "Overheavy scheduling" appeared to be something of a problem for both NDEA directors and school programs, while "Increase effectiveness of organization and administration" received some attention in school and college programs.

TABLE 22 – Changes in Operation of Program Suggested by Directors

	Percent of comments regarding each specific change			
	NDEA (*N* = *21*)	*Schools* (*N* = *26*)	*Colleges* (*N* = *12*)	*Total group* (*N* = *59*)
Place more emphasis on evaluation and follow-up	71	54	75	64
Improve scheduling/reduce overheavy schedule	14	15	—	12
Improve staff-enrollee relations	10	12	8	10
Increase effectiveness of administration and organization	5	19	17	14

ILLUSTRATIVE QUOTES ON CHANGES

In order to present a well-rounded picture of how three directors viewed their programs, verbatim quotes are given below, drawn from the same sources as the Strengths quoted above:

QUESTION: *"What, if anything, would you add, omit, or change if you were starting again?"*

REPLY 1: *From the director* of an NDEA institute*

- Add a member to the staff who had been deeply related to the social science of family life, who could integrate the experience of the field visits to health and social agencies throughout the summer (rather than having various people perform this function for different field visits).
- Schedule at least two sessions with certain consultants, such as Dr. Hess or Dr. Malone, when their contribution supplemented or deepened the themes of the Institute.
- Provide better scheduling of time for the integrating seminars, which were planned as discussion of personal reactions.
- Prepare the demonstration field experiences in advance.
- Present more prepared teacher training materials of *special* significance for the particular institute, such as: observational schedules, short tapes, and films.

* The same director whose comments are quoted under Strengths.

- Schedule earlier informal and social opportunities.
- If possible provide some residence time—even if only long weekends —at the beginning, middle, and end of the six-week period.
- Provide more depth of experience in the parent-community work planned for enrollees.
- *I would make these changes because:*
- Training materials *sharpen the theory* and point up to participants their own needs to develop specificity.
- Since the time is brief, the *demonstration field placement has to flash new images;* otherwise the verbal theory is not adequately concretized to get shifts.
- The better prepared the demonstration center, the more room for *well*-supervised participation that is genuinely functional.
- The timing of the field work conferences at the field training centers and of the colloquia, often involving visiting or part-time faculty, were set. When anything was squeezed, the integrating seminar was shortened.
- This institute did not conquer the element of timing that the College has been concerned with in four summer institutes. Certain aspects of the program were improved, especially the field work supervision. The fact that there was no residential time necessitated allowing for a longer lunch hour and reading time in the middle of the day. However, with commuting and very limited dinner and evening time, the afternoon was shortened. With the improved plan for supervision of field work which evolved this summer, it might be possible to plan better use of the four mornings a week devoted to field work.

ADDITIONAL COMMENT

- I would like to submit a plea for different staffing than is indicated in the guidelines. This might vary with each institute, but in any case would demand different budgeting. I would recommend:
- The director, if the one to represent the institute at regional and national level, should be concerned primarily with teaching, supervising, consulting, group leading, and conceptualizing.
- There should be an increased administrative team of staff which would be given status with the participants. Their duties would be financial matters, correspondence, administering of pre- and post-evaluation, recording, report writing, public relations, planning residential and other cultural and social events, planning field trips or community participation, collection of materials and audiovisual aids, helping participants with personal emergencies, implementing the changes in pro-

gram that flexibility and the idea of an evolving program demand. This staff should be working in advance of the Institute.

– Laboratory staff as well as field supervisors and counselors should be added (we had to list these as assistant instructors this year).

REPLY 2: *Changes suggested by the director* of a Teacher Intern Program sponsored by a university with the cooperation of the local school system.*

– Develop even greater coordination with the school administration.

– Strengthen the summer orientation.

– Strengthen the weekly seminars.

– Organize some comprehensive seminars on the urban educational setting.

– *I would make such changes because:*

– In a large school system, communication often breaks down. Red tape affects job placement. Hence coordination is essential.

– The summer orientation should include greater opportunity for supervised classroom experience before the interns start teaching in the Fall on their own.

– The present extremely informal structure of the weekly seminars might profit by more systematic direction.

– The current separate courses in education reduce the time available to interns for electives in their major field, and also tend to be too theoretical. Seminars on urban education would be relevant to the interests of the interns and would have practical application to their specific goals.

REPLY 3: *By the director† of a program for training teacher aides to work on Indian reservations*

Change: There should be more opportunity for each aide to assist in the classroom.
Why: This proved a most productive experience.
Change: All aides should receive financial compensation (stipends, or on some payroll) for their participation.
Why: Money for personal needs poses such a problem for these participants.
Change: I would reduce the length of the program from eight weeks to five or six weeks.

* The same director whose comments are quoted under Strengths.
† The same director whose comments are quoted under Strengths.

Why: Many aides are married women and are the mainstay of their families.
Change: I would locate the program closer to the reservations where the aides live.
Why: So that the enrollees could return home for weekends.
Change: I would allot more of the budget to recreations; cultural activities; visits to museums, theaters and movies.
Why: This aspect of the program proved to be extremely important to the enrollees.

The programs as perceived by the participants

CHAPTER 7

In 33 of the 35 NDEA institutes visited by Aware Teams, 6,074 brief written comments were submitted by 1,054 participants in response to two standard questions:

– What understandings and techniques have you gained thus far?

– What changes would you make if you were planning such a program?*

Analysis of the participants' reactions in this chapter focuses on NDEA institutes alone because the NDEA institutes, planned in accordance with specific guidelines from the U. S. Office of Education, appeared relatively homogeneous in format and direction, and also because the proportion of institutes covered (more than 50 percent of those in operation) is quantitatively significant.

Procedures Used in Data Collection

One of the arrangements agreed upon by directors with respect to Aware Team visits was that the Team would be allowed time for a group interview with all or a sample of the participants—wherever possible without the presence of institute faculty or staff. In some instances the sample was a random selection, in others it was stratified to represent different factors, personal and vocational, among the participants. The written responses were requested at the outset of these group interviews with participants, before either the Team in-

* See Appendix H for guidelines for Aware Team visits.

terviewer or the first respondents could affect the quality of the reactions.

The brief time span of 10 minutes in which to reply to both questions was necessitated in part by the exigencies of the situation. Only an hour was assigned for the whole group interview in most instances and a considerable period of interaction was desired. The time limit was also imposed, in part, in an effort to secure, insofar as possible, free association of ideas rather than a strategic, carefully thought out, "public relations" type of response. It was also believed that the more strongly held views were those most likely to be recorded within a limited period.

However, the 10-minute requirement tended to increase the replies to the first question and decrease the subsequent responses, thus affecting to some degree reliability of the data. One further limitation to the reliability of the data was that the institutes visited had been operating for various lengths of time when the site visits were made. However, no visit was made until after a given institute had been in operation for at least two weeks.

Despite these limitations, the total number (N) of 6,074 comments (nearly 6 per person) was substantial enough to warrant the assumptions that (1) many of the variables such as the period of duration would cancel themselves out, and (2) the central tendencies revealed by the data would be worthy of serious consideration.

The categories and subcategories under which the replies are grouped grew out of the data, themselves. No categories were suggested to the respondents, except that both understandings and techniques were included in the first question. The rationale for the use of these two words was to assess the relative priority given each by the volume and nature of the responses to such global and all-encompassing terms.

Products Related to Purposes

There is a circular relationship between the purposes and the outcomes of an institute. The purposes and the plans for their instructional implementation affect the product, while the product, in turn, both tests and modifies the purposes, as planned. To understand the reactions of participants it is necessary to know what they were reacting to, in terms of the intent of the directors.

In Chapter 6 a salient finding was that the majority of the directors included both "Understanding the life conditions of disadvantaged groups" *and* "Development of instructional skills, techniques, and materials" among their key objectives. However, when the directors were asked to specify how they planned to implement these objectives through instructional content, a discrepancy appeared. There was overwhelming response to suggested items under the first category (Understandings) and meagre response to suggested items under the second category (Instructional Skills, Techniques, and Materials).

Not one of the techniques or materials listed in the questionnaire was checked as a key item under Instructional Content by the majority of the 33 directors of NDEA institutes in which written reactions of participants were obtained—the criterion group on which this chapter is focused.

In essence, then, the directors reported a balanced intent, including the twin goals of (1) deepening insights and (2) developing new teaching skills, but there was imbalance with respect to the curricular undergirding of these two purposes. It was posited in the previous chapter that this apparent discrepancy between expressed intent and plans for the implementation of intent was due, in large part to the inadequacy of the educational resources that are directly related to the teaching of disadvantaged children and youth. The paucity of such resources is in sharp contrast to the richness of expertise, literature, and audiovisual materials that can be brought to bear on the social and behavioral aspects of the problem.

The crucial test of the purposes and their implementation lies, however, not in the perceptions of the directors but in the product—namely, the participants' perceptions of what they have gained by the experience, and what, if anything, they would like to see changed. The reactions of more than a thousand participants in more than half the NDEA institutes have therefore been analyzed as an index of the degree to which basic goals have been realized and for possible improvements in future planning and process.

REPLIES TO QUESTION 1: "Understandings and Techniques Gained"

Of the 6,074 comments (approximately six per person) 3,731 (61 percent) were made in reply to the first question, which indicated positive gain from the experience, while 2,343 (39 percent) expressed somewhat negative reactions in terms of needed changes. Taking into consideration the limitations on the validity of the data imposed by the brief time span allowed for the replies (which tended to decrease the quantity of response to the second of the two questions), the massive response on the positive rather than on the negative side gives statistical support for the purely subjective analysis of the pervasive tone of the institutes reported by the Aware Teams. The overwhelming consensus of the Team members was that a sense of absorbed earnestness, of zeal, of fervency, appeared to prevail in a majority of the institutes. One of the participants expressed it: "I feel rededicated to my task. I am excited about my school year 1965-1966."

Within the responses to Question 1, comments about understandings gained were more than twice as numerous as comments about techniques gained. This disproportionate response would seem to indicate that where instructional content was readily available (as in the case of understandings), the institute program appeared to have a definite impact upon the participants, but in the area where instructional content was not as readily available or had been given low priority in program planning (i.e., techniques), the impact was relatively unimpressive. Chart 3 expresses quantitatively the flow of purpose, content, and outcomes.

The ratio of understandings to techniques may also reflect the theory, espoused by many directors, that if a teacher has the desire to reach the disadvantaged, he will find the way in terms of his own teaching style and of the local situation. Directors with such an orientation stressed the *why* and minimized the *how* of teaching disadvantaged children and youth. Still another possible causal factor for the emphasis on understandings rather than on teaching behavior may have been the short duration of the institutes, which required focus on objectives alone—and the directors opted for understandings when they felt forced to choose.

CHART 3 — Flow Chart of Content and Outcomes Related to Purposes in NDEA Institutes.

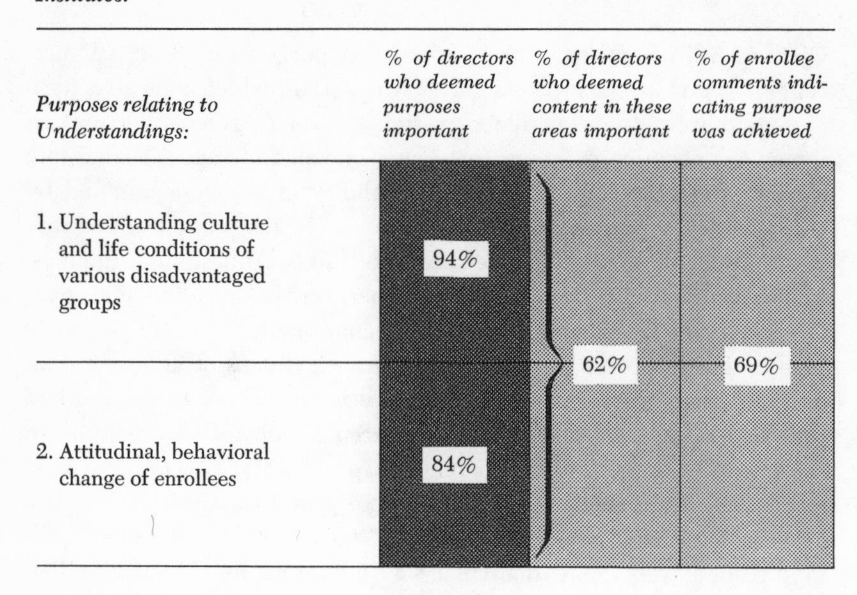

Purposes related to Techniques:

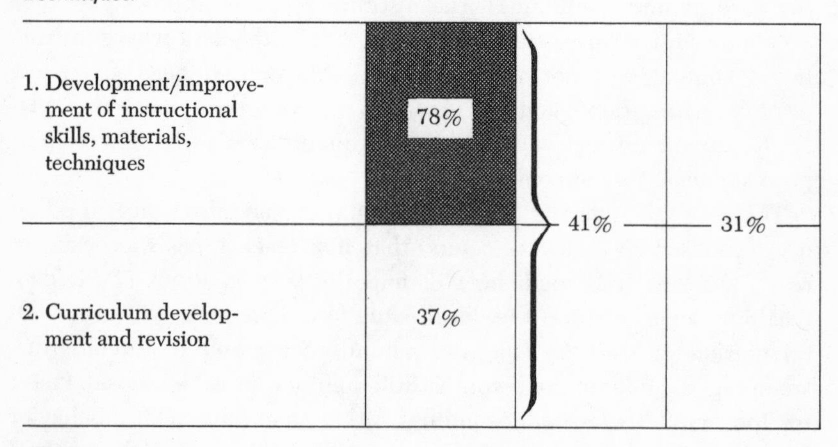

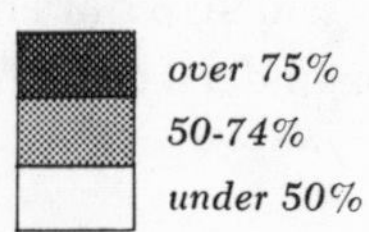

The preponderantly positive reaction of the participants to the programs is clearly revealed in the analysis of the replies to Question 1, "What understandings and techniques have you gained thus far?" (See Table 23.)

TABLE 23–Comments in Reply to Question 1

	Number (N = 3,731)	*Percent*
Understandings gained	2,572	69
No understandings gained	5	—
Techniques gained	1,146	31
No techniques gained	8	—

An analysis of the subitems in each category reveals an emphasis upon theoretical understandings (developmental and situational factors) rather than upon understanding teacher behavior and its effect upon the disadvantaged child. (See Table 24.)

TABLE 24–Understandings Gained by Enrollees through Participation in Program

	Number (N = 2,572)	*Percent*
Developmental or affective aspects of understanding individual child	956	37
Understanding values, history, culture, life conditions, and special problems of disadvantaged children and youth	879	34
Understanding teacher behavior and its effect upon the disadvantaged child	460	18
Understanding school-community relations as they affect the disadvantaged	277	11

In the category of techniques, too, the emphasis is more on the theoretical—that is, on basic strategies as opposed to adaptation of the curriculum to the needs and interests of disadvantaged children and youth. Table 25 reveals this emphasis upon theoretical understandings as opposed to the application of such understandings to teaching behavior.

TABLE 25 – Techniques Gained by Enrollees through Participation in Program

	Number (N = 1,146)	Percent
Instructional strategies and methods which are helpful in working with the disadvantaged	330	29
Importance of and methods for teaching communication skills	245	21
Permissive classroom management, which will elicit maximum response from the disadvantaged	213	19
Negative of prior statement, i.e., more control and structure	2	—
Development and use of instructional materials	141	12
Adaptation of curriculum to needs and interests of disadvantaged child	124	11
Schoolwide strategies, planning, and organization	91	8

Understandings Amplified

Analysis of the frequency distribution of the kinds of understandings reported by participants requires an amplification and interpretation of each of the broad categories of response.

DEVELOPMENTAL, AFFECTIVE ASPECTS OF UNDERSTANDING

Nearly 1,000 comments were grouped under the heading "Developmental or affective aspects of understanding the disadvantaged child." The most frequent comments stressed:

Acceptance and respect of the child as an individual.

The value of recognizing his own level of interest, outlook, and learning achievements, and meeting him on those terms.

Belief in every child's potential.

Understanding the effect of the emotional needs of the disadvantaged child upon his behavior.

Understanding the importance of the child's self-concept in the learning process.

Understanding the need to enrich and use the child's own experiences and provide him with an opportunity for early success experiences.

Understanding of the role of school in the life of the disadvantaged child and the necessity for guidance in the school situation to compensate for or supplement familial influences in the child's development.

To sum up, the emphasis here is upon *the individual child.* This kind of understanding is the cornerstone upon which other teaching strategies are built. That this was the overwhelming response of the participants—the *sine qua non* of working with the disadvantaged—speaks strongly for effective implementation of the basic concepts undergirding the institutes.

I realize more fully that the child himself is the focus of our curriculum—a realization which has meaning for all education but is of paramount importance in working with the disadvantaged.

If we, as teachers, will accept that with which the child comes to us and build on it, we will have taken a giant step.

UNDERSTANDING THE CULTURE OF THE DISADVANTAGED

Almost as frequent as the comments on understanding the individual child's behavior were those on understanding his environment in sociological terms, that is, "understanding the values, history, culture, life conditions and special problems of disadvantaged children and youth." There were nearly 900 comments on this topic—among the most frequent, those calling for:

Definition and identification of environmentally disadvantaged children and youth.

Understanding the need for changing misconceptions regarding the meaning of *disadvantage.*

Appreciation of and respect for differences in values, history, and cultures of various ethnic and socioeconomic groups.

Understanding the life conditions, economic status, and extent of integration among various disadvantaged groups.

Understanding the magnitude of the national problem of poverty and its probable future escalation.

Thus the multifaceted view of sociological factors in the situation, which was given high priority in the planning, seemed to be reflected in the participants' reactions. The following direct quotes give something of the feeling tone of the responses.

I have taught for 15 years in a disadvantaged area but I am shocked that I knew so little about the background of my pupils. I walked to and from school without ever really seeing the neighborhood.

I see now that most economically deprived parents love their children but the strain of survival is so great that it leaves little time to devote to them.

This word "disadvantaged" had many new meanings to me. I see that a child can be disadvantaged in any one of a number of ways and not in other ways.

I have learned that working with the disadvantaged child is not all tears.

RESPONSES REGARDING TEACHER BEHAVIOR

The new insights noted above are primarily theoretical. Another cluster of responses has practical application to the teacher himself in day-to-day classroom experience. The omnibus designation was "Understanding teacher behavior and its effect upon the disadvantaged child." The most frequent comments reveal that the first look was inward:

Increased self awareness.

Understanding the teacher's role in establishing teacher-pupil interaction and rapport.

Understanding the personal qualities essential in the effective teacher such as empathy, patience, and consistency.

Later these insights about the teacher as a person and the teacher in his professional role were built upon in terms of specific strategies. Here, the comments are more conceptual:

I begin to be aware of some of my personal strengths and weaknesses as a teacher.

I have learned to distinguish between the poor learner and the slow learner —an important milestone in my development as a teacher.

I have taught for several years in the same situation in which my practicum places me. I find that in my present role as an institute participant, I feel freer to experiment with various approaches. Thus I detect a certain past rigidity—albeit unconscious. This has been refreshing and of great benefit to me.

Understanding myself in relation to others in this group was an important first step toward understanding myself in relation to disadvantaged pupils.

RESPONSES REGARDING SCHOOL-COMMUNITY RELATIONS

Another cluster of comments involved the total community: "Understanding school-community relations as they affect the disadvantaged." Among the reactions most frequently expressed were:

Understanding the crucial need for home involvement in order to improve the teaching-learning process for the disadvantaged child.

Understanding the value and availability of community resources.

Recognition of the universality of many of these problems and hence the need for a total community approach.

One participant summed up the reactions of many:

Real and vital relationships cannot be developed by the teacher alone. The development of such relationships requires many people from all walks of life. It involves the home, school, neighborhood and the broader community.

Techniques Amplified

Under the omnibus term "Techniques" a wider range of responses was elicited. Since they are relatively specific, less interpretation of each category will be undertaken.

Instructional strategies and methods that are helpful in working with the disadvantaged incorporated many approaches that are of value in all education but are particularly relevant to the disadvantaged child. A number of them may be summarized:

1. The inductive method, team teaching, role playing, stimulating discovery by the child himself, rather than telling him were among the teaching strategies enumerated.

2. "The importance of and methods for teaching communication skills" evoked a cluster of comments in such proportion that it merits separate treatment. The topic covered all the language arts, both written and oral, with emphasis upon remediation.

3. "Classroom management which will elicit maximum response from the disadvantaged" prompted frequent comments about an informal, permissive atmosphere, but such devices as ungraded classes and small groupings in large classes were also proposed. One partici-

pant related this last-mentioned arrangement to work with the disadvantaged in these words: "I realize now that all the children do not need me all the time, so there will be time for individual work with those who have special needs." Another saw in these approaches a way to "free a child to create and imagine."

4. "Negative of prior statement" was checked by only two people, both of whom deplored so-called democratic procedures in the classroom, which they saw as too lax.

5. "Use and development of instructional materials" included multimedia and various other materials referred to as "hardware"—all concrete and tactile—as well as programmed instruction.

6. "Adaptation of curriculum to the needs and interests of the disadvantaged child" proved to be a category of considerable size despite the minimal weight given to "curriculum revision" by directors in the hierarchy of objectives.

7. "Schoolwide strategies, planning, and organization" elicited comments on the reevaluation of testing procedures, the need for schoolwide planning, the overweening importance of preschool education in the child's adjustment to school, and the need for channels of intercommunication and for sharing of experiences with colleagues.

More participants denied learning any techniques than those who denied gaining understandings, but the number of dissidents was still miniscule, only eight out of more than 1000.

Differentiation of Outcomes by Criterion Groups

The modal analysis of the outcomes of the institutes, as measured by enrollee responses to "Understandings and techniques gained," revealed conceptual growth and procedural lag in the majority opinion. To determine how the reported outcomes varied in different situations, a series of criterion groups was established, differentiated with respect to such factors as inclusion or omission of a practicum, integration or nonintegration of staff, number of enrollees, and scope of the geographical area served (i.e., one school system, one state, or several states). Variations of response between those institutes with a practicum and those without, as defined by the study, were most marked.

COMPARISON OF INSTITUTES WITH AND WITHOUT PRACTICUM

In 17 of the 33 institutes that furnished written responses, there was an opportunity for field teaching experience under intensive supervision.

Institutes with a practicum were compared with those which lacked this feature.

A better balance between understandings and techniques was revealed by institutes with a practicum than by those without, although the major emphasis was still upon understanding in the institutes with a practicum—nearly two to one. The unique dimension of these

TABLE 26 – Differentiation among Institutes, by Inclusion or Omission of Practicum

	Percent of Institutes		
Understandings Gained	*With Practicum (N = 1,072)*	*Without Practicum (N = 1,505)*	*Difference of 10 percent or more*
Understanding developmental aspects	30	42	−12*
Understanding life conditions and cultures	37	32	—
Understandings regarding teaching behavior	24	14	+10
School-community relations	9	12	
No understandings gained	—	—	—
Techniques Gained	*(N = 557)*	*(N = 597)*	
Instructional strategies and methods	28	30	—
Teaching communication skills	26	16	+10
Classroom management	16	21	
Negative of prior statement	—	—	—
Use and development of instructional materials	12	12	—
Adaptation of curriculum to disadvantaged children	12	11	—
Schoolwide planning, organization	6	10	—
No techniques gained	—	—	—

* Minus differential means that the second column (institutes without practicum) has the larger score; plus differential means the opposite.

NDEA institutes was their concern for both knowledge about and empathy with the disadvantaged. The question raised by the participants was one of degree and proportion. (See Table 26.)

A differential of 10 percent or more was revealed between the two groups on three items. One of these three items with a large differential, "Understanding developmental aspects," was theoretical in essence. The institutes *without* a practicum responded with greater frequency to this item.

Two of the items with a large differential were more related to practical application to the classroom. The institutes *with* a practicum gave greater priority to these items: "Understandings re: teaching behavior" and "Teaching communication skills." In other words, the institutes *with* a practicum were less theoretical and more reality-centered.

A significant datum is that the focus upon these two items was proportionately sharper for those institutes which combined two components: (1) a practicum and (2) an integrated staff. In this instance the differential between the two types of institutes for "Understandings regarding teacher behavior" was 17 percent, for "Teaching communication skills " 14 percent.

INSTITUTES WITH ENROLLEES PREDOMINANTLY FROM LOCAL SCHOOL SYSTEM VS. INSTITUTES WITH ENROLLEES FROM A BROAD GEOGRAPHICAL AREA

There was a differential of 15 percent regarding the frequency with which "Understanding the life conditions of disadvantaged children" was mentioned in institutes serving one school system and those serving a broad area. The enrollees in the former type of institute reported more of this understanding gained. Those from a single school system also commented more frequently upon teaching strategies gained and upon improved skills in class management—differentials of 20 percent and 23 percent, respectively.

OTHER CRITERION GROUPS

There were no significant variations with respect to grade span covered, the duration of institutes, or the size of enrollment.

Verbatim Quotes

Once more the quantitative analysis becomes alive and vital when illustrated by the actual words of the respondents. The keen awareness of the need for individualized teaching was a recurrent theme:

To come to a realization that each child in a class has feelings, emotions, anxieties, periods of happiness, sadness, possible depression, is the most important understanding that a teacher can have.

I have achieved a greater awareness of the uniqueness of every individual. Everyone remains a student throughout his life. I have grown in my desire to remain open to the thoughts, emotions, and convictions of others coupled with greater knowledge of self.

This is the key: [the student] . . . being treated as an individual, as a person.

Understanding the life conditions of the disadvantaged was empathetically described by many enrollees, while avoiding the pitfall of creating a new kind of stereotype, which would negate all the understanding gained about the uniqueness of each individual child.

There is a wealth of potential among the disadvantaged and it is the job of creative teachers to bring this forth. Aspirations of this group have turned to frustration.

I gained greater understanding of the "here and now" world of the child.

The "culturally deprived" student is not living a sterile existence because he has no "cultural background." I have become aware of the richness in his life, and the great sensitivity and depth with which this student can interpret art.

The notion of cultural "displacement" rather than cultural disadvantagement seems to me a rather crucial point in understanding the heterocultural community in which I teach.

Inner-city students have a great depth of emotion and a strong sense of living.

Each child brings with him some positive values from his subculture which might be very useful and significant in the various academic disciplines.

Not that we could expect less of some segments of our society but that we should expect more of ourselves in order to bring each individual with whom we work to his own greatest potential.

I have taught in racially mixed schools for seven years but have had more interaction with Negroes and gained more understanding on racial issues here in four weeks than in seven years before.

For me there was reinforcement of ideas of positive values at work in almost any cultural milieu.

The term "educationally unmotivated" might be more appropriate than culturally deprived, because all children have a culture.

A related concept, the overriding necessity for understanding and relating to home and community, was often mentioned:

I realized the importance of interacting with the whole family and working with the children.

The co-partnership of the home and school is the child's hope. Involving the parents is a *must*.

A great focus of attention should be placed *on the community*. We *must* get in to visit homes, speak to parents, see churches, eat at typical disadvantaged establishments, taste their food, etc. I did not like the COOK'S TOUR we were told to take.

Schools and their staffs are so terribly isolated from the communities in which they are located and whom they are supposed to serve.

The involvement of parents is *essential*, even if this means an educational program designed especially to familiarize them with the needs of the children, and of their responsibilities to the school and the school's responsibility to them.

Use customs, activities, and structures in the community as kicking-off points to the study of topics which will extend beyond the community.

The developing role of the school as an institution was frequently cited in relation to social needs.

Curriculum will have to be revised in order that the revolutionary changes arising in society may be met by the schools.

The teacher and the school may be the ones responsible for the culturally disadvantaged children failing in school and eventually dropping out.

The disadvantaged child in American education has been damaged by our inability thus far to communicate with him successfully.

The deprived person is not antagonistic to education but to the schools.

Our present educational system appears to place too much emphasis on the school and the teacher, neglecting the vital human resources in the community. These resources must be tapped if an effective and meaningful curriculum is to be executed.

Working with the culturally deprived children, the school is itself handicapped by home and community conditions and often by its very inheritance of traditional concepts of schooling.

Understanding their own strengths and weaknesses was a unique outcome of the institute in the minds of many enrollees.

The greatest impact of the institute has been the emphasis on looking at oneself, on understanding one's own attitudes, actions, and reactions. I am endeavoring to explore in depth my own biases, misconceptions, also my strengths, which will be helpful in enabling others to reach their greatest potentials.

I learned that I have more strengths and plus factors than I realized. After relating to the institute group my self-image improved.

New concepts of the professional role that is required in working with disadvantaged children and youth were vividly expressed by the enrollees:

Our commitment to the full development of each child has been far too half-hearted. We have accepted failure to reach the child too readily and have been too willing to ascribe it to his lack of motivation rather than to our lack of commitment and our lack of appropriate skills.

Never have I been so much aware of the fact that teaching involves tremendous moral responsibility.

I have learned that achievement is relative.

I have discovered a new meaning for success for each child.

Success is very important to the disadvantaged child even though to the teacher the work may not be significant.

It has been most interesting for me to learn that what these children *want* from life is quite different from what they *expect* from life. I have had time to probe their reactions, feelings, values, outlook on life.

My role as a teacher is to be perceptive enough to discover where a child is, *accept him where he is,* and take him as far as he can go to the best of my ability.

I now perceive that subject matter is not the core of our contributions to children in schools. . . . attitudes, health, freedom to express and act are the important things that children can take away.

We know now that the objectives for the disadvantaged are the same as for all children, but procedures and methods must be altered to meet the cognitive, motor-sensory style of learning.

I am more convinced than ever that the teacher must have a greater voice in planning in her own school.

I would select teachers who were considered "far out," not conventional, that is, those who are willing to experiment and who will not feel lost without a structure from administration.

There were many who specified actual teaching behavior which was consonant with the broader concepts of education developed at the institutes:

Teachers must avoid words or actions which may be interpreted as condescension.

To become involved in an activity with the children is the best way to learn about them.

One successful technique is to let children try more ideas, explore, be able to touch, feel, and make things on their own.

A quiet room is not always the most educational. Create environments in which children feel safe enough to dare.

Look for the positive rather than the negative and build on these.

It is important for teachers of these children to allow them to express themselves in the language that is familiar to them.

Talk less—listen more.

You can teach almost any subject to any child once the avenues of communication have been opened.

Finally, again and again, came the plea that teachers "learn from one another."

REPLIES TO QUESTION 2: "Suggested Changes"

Of the 2,343 recommendations for change, more than half were related to instructional process. The other suggestions for change were divided into three clusters: "Changes in instructional content," "Changes in planning," and "Changes in operation of the program." As many as 46 respondents saw no need for any change in what they deemed a model institute. This contrasts sharply with the minimal response on "No understandings gained" and "No techniques gained." It is significant that the majority were concerned about what they themselves did—not what was done to them.

Table 27 presents the relative importance of these factors in quantitative terms, as gleaned from the answers to the question, "What, if

TABLE 27 – Changes in Program Suggested by Enrollees

	Number of comments (N = 2,343)	*Percent*
Changes in instructional process	1,194	51
Changes in instructional content	425	18
Changes in preplanning	348	15
Changes in operation of program	330	14
No change	46	2

anything, would you change if you were planning such a program?"

Analysis of the subitems in each category is sharply revealing of the focus of the respondents' interests and the areas of greatest need that they identified.

TABLE 28 – Changes in Instructional Process Suggested by Enrollees

	Number (N = 1,194)	*Percent*
Include, expand, improve field teaching experience and informal educational contacts with children	373	31
Use group techniques, small group discussions more extensively and effectively	212	18
Improve, expand, include class observations and demonstrations by master teachers	152	13
Improve and/or increase field work in homes and community	147	12
Negative of prior statement	12	1
Provide more free time for independent study, informal sharing, reflection, and socializing instead of so many formal and written assignments	131	11
Negative of prior statement	21	2
Improve quality and relevance of lectures by outside specialists	116	9
Schedule fewer lectures	30	3

Only two of the suggested changes were mentioned more than 300 times. One was the item with the highest frequency in Table 28, "Include, expand, improve field teaching experience and informal educational contacts with children." The other was the item with the highest frequency in Table 29, "Place more emphasis on strategies, methods, and materials for practical application of new insights to teaching behavior. Such comments constituted 76 percent of all the suggested changes that were related to Instructional Content. These two high-frequency factors are substantively related, since each relates to day-to-day teaching behavior. The message appears to be that enrollees were seeking greater specificity in the implications of the theoretical foundations for their own professional competence, and were also seeking an opportunity for more supervised experimentation in application to the classroom of the new concepts they had gained.

TABLE 29 – Changes in Instructional Content Suggested by Enrollees

	Number of comments (N = 425)	*Percent*
Place more emphasis on strategies, methods, and materials for practical application of new insights to teaching behavior	323	76
Negative of above	11	3
Develop relevant concepts from social-behavioral sciences more effectively	72	17
Negative of above	19	4

Suggested changes in preplanning focused on the clarification of institute goals. Difference of opinion is marked regarding the optimum length of an institute.

Suggested changes in the operation of the program were heavily

TABLE 30 – Changes in Program Preplanning Suggested by Enrollees

	Number of comments (N = 348)	*Percent*
Improve planning and focus or clarify goals	105	30
Improve selection of enrollees	66	19
Improve selection of staff	45	13
Improve facilities	41	12
Increase length of institute	27	8
Decrease length of institute	17	5
Other	47	13

weighted toward changes in scheduling. This confirmed the finding reported in Chapter 6 that the changes most frequently resulting from feedback were in the area of scheduling.

TABLE 31 – Changes in Operation of Program Suggested by Enrollees

	Number of comments (N = 330)	*Percent*
Improve scheduling or reduce over-heavy schedule	138	42
Increase effectiveness of organization and administration	112	34
Place more emphasis on evaluation and follow-up	45	14
Improve staff-enrollee relations	35	10

COMPARISON OF REACTIONS OF ENROLLEES, DIRECTORS, AND AWARE TEAMS REGARDING CHANGES IN CONTENT AND PROCESS

The highly subjective data reported above have more significance and authenticity when cross-checked with the perceptions of others, differentiated by role and responsibility. It was noted already that the change most frequently suggested by the enrollees was, "Include, expand, improve field teaching experience and informal educational contacts with children," mentioned 373 times. This was the highest-frequency item in the category, Instructional Process, for enrollees, directors, and Aware Team members alike. A comparison follows:

Because of the sharp focus on this item, some amplification is in order. The types of comments grouped under this heading are listed

TABLE 32 – Comparison of High-Frequency Scores for Enrollees, Directors, and Aware Team Concerning Suggested Changes in Instructional Process

	Percent of Category		
Suggested Change	*Enrollees (N = 1,194)*	*Directors (N = 83)*	*Aware Teams (N = 85)*
Include, expand, improve field teaching experience and informal educational contacts with children	31	45	32

below in descending order of frequency. They reveal the depth and scope of the enrollees' concern in this area. The code construct follows a similar pattern for the other respondent groups: directors and Aware Team members.

Allow even more time for actual field teaching so as to experiment with new and varied methods of teaching the disadvantaged and the application of institute learnings.

Create teaching opportunities within the informal camping experience with children.

Select pupils in practicum more carefully so as to include the truly disadvantaged in sufficient proportions.

Arrange for more one-to-one and one-to-two contacts with children in the practicum.

Schedule actual practice teaching with children, rather than observation only.

Improve content and planning of informal, educational contacts with children.

Expand Institute control of lab schools to eliminate frictions and restrictions.

Organize field teaching experience better.

Provide closer supervision and analysis of field teaching.

Give greater specificity to field teaching in terms of special content areas.

Plan and execute an institute social-action project as an outcome of field teaching and community contacts.

In the absence of adequate resources for teaching strategies, methods, and materials directly related to work with the disadvantaged, the enrollees appear to be asking for what they would give to the children—an opportunity to "discover" appropriate strategies in field teaching under sensitive and creative supervision.

This was not a request for a shift of emphasis from understandings to techniques but rather for a balanced approach, building upon what had been accomplished and then taking the next step. Understandings and techniques were not seen as dichotomous, but rather as interactive and mutually supportive. Understandings without specific help in translating them into teaching behavior were seen as vague and amorphous gains. Understanding within the context of reality was the essence of the plea for change.

Recommendations for improving programs

CHAPTER 8

To explore *what is* leads inevitably to *what might be*. Out of intensive experimentation in teacher education in a social context have come recommendations for improvement. Moving from a focus upon the child as a separate phenomenon to an understanding of the child within a social setting, both theorists and operationalists recognize new needs and suggest solutions. The recommendations presented in this chapter are made by observers of existing programs and by those who are deeply involved in their development.

The recommendations are directed to several types of programs:

1. Institute-type programs
2. In-service programs in school systems
3. Programs in institutions of higher learning, primarily preservice

Recommendations are directed to all four populations, since OEO- and NDEA-financed programs are combined under the first category, institute-type programs.

The Aware Team's recommendations are based on the site visitations made during July and August, when chiefly institute-type programs were in operation. Therefore, the Team's recommendations are slanted toward the intensive short-term programs during which a relatively small number of enrollees focused attention on one topic exclusively—in this case the preparation of school personnel to work with disadvantaged children and youth. Many of the basic concepts may be applied, however, to in-service and preservice programs.

The recommendations for in-service programs in school systems were drawn from replies by directors of such programs to written questionnaires—in other words, school people speaking to school people. The recommendations to institutions of higher learning were also drawn from the questionnaires, with educators in colleges and universities speaking to their own counterparts in other institutions. In schools, colleges, and universities, the respondents were speaking not only to their counterparts, but also, and more importantly, to themselves.

There was no weighting of the recommendations in terms of frequency of response. Any and all are presented in logical sequence, including the somewhat idiosyncratic along with the virtually unanimous reactions. Only for the Aware Team members was there a feedback from those who had made the proposals concerning the draft formulation of recommendations. The draft was revised accordingly.

RECOMMENDATIONS OF AWARE TEAMS FOR INSTITUTE-TYPE PROGRAMS

The Aware Team members (advisory committee, specialists, and staff) were asked to submit their overall impressions of their site visits and recommendations based on their observations. These written statements were tabulated and served as a point of departure for the discussion at two consultations: one for all Aware Team members, and one for a small group to discuss the major findings and to crystallize further the proposed recommendations.

Out of these written statements and subsequent discussions emerged the following recommendations for more effective preparation of school personnel for working with disadvantaged children and youth in specific programs designed for this purpose alone. After each recommendation, concrete steps for its implementation are proposed.

Recommendations of Aware Teams to Those Planning and Directing Institute-type Teacher Education Programs Based on Foundation or Government Support

RECOMMENDATION 1 *That, in preparing school personnel to work with the so-called disadvantaged, teacher educators should expect the par-*

ticipants to view the learning process of the child in the complete social context of life.

PROPOSED STEPS IN IMPLEMENTATION

a) Analysis of the child's learning in terms of his whole life experiences as well as in relation to the social and economic realities of the larger society.

b) Development of teaching strategies based upon the child's actual learning processes.

c) Study and creation of paradigms for learning environments and school structures which provide the child with the experiences he needs in order to learn.

RECOMMENDATION 2 *That the goals of such programs be expressed in clear, realistic, behavioral terms, not in global abstractions.*

PROPOSED STEPS FOR IMPLEMENTATION

a) Avoidance of a new stereotyped, overgeneralized image of "the disadvantaged child"—one that is conceived with empathy for the disadvantaged, but is nonetheless inimical to individuation.

b) Focus upon real and immediate problems of the specific community and the local school system, or systems, when feasible in terms of geographical coverage.

c) Emphasis not merely upon *why* but also *how to,* and even more specifically upon: *how can the teacher act as an agent for change in his school?*

RECOMMENDATION 3 *That there should be joint planning of and continuing responsibility for each program by the sponsoring institution, the local school system, and the disadvantaged themselves, in each community (when most participants come from one school system or contiguous systems).*

PROPOSED STEPS FOR IMPLEMENTATION

a) Joint planning by college, school, and responsible community representatives *before* the program proposal has been submitted for funding (such as NDEA- or OEO-financed projects visited by Project Aware this summer).

b) Continuing tripartite involvement in and responsibility for the program before, during, and *after* its operation, in order to maximize the impact upon the sponsoring institution, the local school system, and the community in meeting the needs and rising expectations of the disadvantaged.

c) Involvement of the indigenous population served by the school in planning certain aspects of the program.

RECOMMENDATION 4 *That there be flexibility in plan, structure, and administration of programs.*

PROPOSED STEPS FOR IMPLEMENTATION

a) An evolving curriculum responsive to the special needs and interests of participants.

b) Awareness of and responsiveness to the changing needs and climate of the community.

RECOMMENDATION 5 *That experimentation and innovation pervade the program.*

PROPOSED STEPS FOR IMPLEMENTATION

a) Acceptance of the inadequacy of many of the traditional methods of teaching disadvantaged children and youth, as evidenced by the slow learning rate of the majority of these children compared with more advantaged pupils, and the high dropout rate of disadvantaged youth.

b) Familiarity with the findings of the behavioral sciences which have implications for teacher education and an awareness of unique elements of a program for the disadvantaged, i.e., the diagnostic approach and the integration of cognitive and affective aspects.

c) Openness to new ideas at various levels: administrative, teaching, community agencies, and family.

RECOMMENDATION 6 *That intercommunication between staff and participants, as well as between participants and participants, be strengthened by all possible means.*

PROPOSED STEPS FOR IMPLEMENTATION

a) Joint staff-participant curriculum planning.

b) Integrative colloquia at which staff and participants may explore common understandings and clarify basic foci of the program.

c) Scheduled free time for informal sharing of ideas and experiences among participants.

RECOMMENDATION 7 *That racial and ethnic integration be a reality at all levels of operation.*

PROPOSED STEPS FOR IMPLEMENTATION

a) Selection of staff that reflects more than token integration while insuring the competencies needed for each institute.

b) Selection of enrollees in order to achieve racial and ethnic balance where possible.

c) Recruitment of pupils for the laboratory school or practicum in ways that will provide a full complement of both white and non-white children, as well as children of diverse national origins.

RECOMMENDATION 8 *That intensive work with a small group of participants over an extended period of time be a main desideratum.*

PROPOSED STEPS FOR IMPLEMENTATION

a) Limitation of size of institute to not more than 35, to insure maximum involvement of every participant.

b) Duration of at least eight weeks, preferably a whole term, to maximize opportunity for attitudinal and behavioral change.

c) Limitation of span of grade levels to early childhood and elementary, or middle and secondary school.

d) Residential rather than commuting arrangements for at least a portion of the time, preferably for the duration of the program.

RECOMMENDATION 9 *That one criterion for selection of participants be their potential effectiveness as agents for change within their own schools upon their return, at various levels of responsibility: top administrative, supervisory, instructional, special services; and in paraprofessional supportive roles.*

PROPOSED STEPS FOR IMPLEMENTATION

a) Concentration on a single school district for at least a major proportion of participants, to prevent dispersion of impact.

b) Recruitment of a team of participants from a given school, with emphasis on the enrollment of some opinion-makers who will be able to serve as agents of change upon their return.

c) Selection of multilevel personnel as participants, including superintendents, principals, supervisors, teachers, counselors, and auxiliary school personnel.

RECOMMENDATION 10 *That staff be selected with the utmost care in reference to their academic and experiential qualifications.*

PROPOSED STEPS FOR IMPLEMENTATION

a) Appointment of at least some staff members who:
   —Have had recent experience in working with the disadvantaged and know their problems and potentialities.
   —Exemplify in their own behavior the concepts and methodology they teach to others.
   —Are proficient in the behavioral and social sciences.
   —Have themselves experienced disadvantage.
   —Can handle their own feelings and biases.
   —Are thoroughly familiar with current trends in teacher education and with the relevant literature concerning the learning-teaching process.
   —Are cognizant of new research findings in the behavioral and social sciences.

b) Appointment of both academicians and school personnel.

c) Appointment of full-time personnel in large measure to preserve continuity.

d) Appointment of staff with certain special professional competencies, such as:
   —Ability to conduct individual and group counseling.
   —Skill in group development and discussion leadership.
   —Administrative skills needed to relieve the director from routine duties and free him to conduct a catalytic operation.
   —Imagination and creativity which stimulate the disadvantaged child's response to the learning experience.

RECOMMENDATION 11 *That programs be differentiated to meet various levels and styles of needed training.*

PROPOSED STEPS FOR IMPLEMENTATION

a) Advanced institutes for those who have already demonstrated their proficiency in work with the disadvantaged.

b) Workshops for directors before the summer institutes start operation.

c) Subgroups within multilevel institutes (such as institutes for administrators, teachers, and teacher-aides) to provide sharing in self-situational circumstances.

d) Study and adaptation of models hypothesized by major theorists.

RECOMMENDATION 12 *That the fundamental purpose of the institute be interpreted to the broader community, thus upgrading the public image of the teacher of the disadvantaged.*

PROPOSED STEPS FOR IMPLEMENTATION

a) Interpretation through the mass media.

b) Representation at professional conferences.

c) Further utilization of professional journals.

RECOMMENDATION 13 *That the instructional content integrate understanding the disadvantaged with assistance in translating such understanding into teaching behavior.*

PROPOSED STEPS FOR IMPLEMENTATION

a) A cognitive dimension that presents the facts and develops understandings *vis-a-vis* the disadvantaged, moving from myth to reality.

b) A interdisciplinary approach combining sociology, psychology, anthropology, and related social and behavioral studies.

c) Adequate orientation of outside lecturers to avoid repetition and irrelevancy in lecture content.

d) Involvement of the teaching staff in the sociological, anthropological, psychological, and economic content areas in actual school situations and in the community and family life.

e) Greater emphasis on the diagnostic approach, i.e., the analysis of each child's behavior as an individual and not as a member of any group; the possible causes of such behavior; and the teacher's responsibilities regarding child behavior and development.

f) Demonstration of possible strategies, methods, and materials that have special application to working with disadvantaged children and youth.

g) Analysis of demonstrations in terms of their relevance to a wide variety of situations, with emphasis on the necessity for adapting to individual conditions.

h) Participation in curriculum revision, remediation, and development of new materials.

RECOMMENDATION 14 *That instructional process provide opportunity for experiential learnings.*

PROPOSED STEPS FOR IMPLEMENTATION

a) A teaching field experience or practicum that has direction, is involved with children who are truly disadvantaged, and has components of supervision, self-analysis, and reflection.

b) Opportunity for identifying and sharing the contributions of the participants in small-group discussions.

c) Utilizing the leadership skills of participants in conducting discussions, making presentations, and committee activities.

d) Programs of group counseling and sensitivity training to encourage self-understanding and build ego strength in participants.

e) Integration of affective, cognitive, and action components of the program in an effort to achieve behavioral change.

f) Development of more effective supervisory processes.

RECOMMENDATION 15 *That the period of training be extended over three phases: pre-institute, institute, and post-institute, with special reference to the application of learnings to the school program upon the participants' return.*

PROPOSED STEPS FOR IMPLEMENTATION

a) Alerting accepted candidates to methods of preparing themselves for the institute through distribution of bibliographies, basic papers and pamphlets, and assignments, such as the preparation of proposed projects to be developed at the institute.

b) Scheduled time during the institute for planning with others from the same school for specific activities to be undertaken at the school each participant serves during the year.

c) Follow-up after the institute through written reports, week-long seminars later in the year, intervisitation by teams from different schools, supervision and consultation by experts—to help the institute graduates adapt their learnings to their school programs.

RECOMMENDATION 16 *That evaluation be included as an integral part of every program.*

PROPOSED STEPS FOR IMPLEMENTATION

a) Diagnostic measures taken at the beginning and at the end of the institute, and after the participant has returned to his school.

b) Continuing feedback from participants, both written and oral, throughout the institute.

c) Requested evaluation of each participant's performance on the job by his principal and/or supervisor following the institute.

RECOMMENDATION 17 *That greater emphasis be placed on parent participation in the programs and continuing relationships of parents and enrollees in the homes.*

PROPOSED STEPS FOR IMPLEMENTATION

a) Workshops for parents, in which they may share their concern about their children's learnings and hopefully develop a sense of partnership with the school in facilitating the process.

b) Visits by teachers and other school personnel to homes of parents who cannot come to school, so that teachers may learn through actual observation about the life conditions of their pupils.

c) Use of every means of communication to discover the strengths, needs, and interests of parents, and to involve them wherever possible in school planning.

RECOMMENDATION 18 *That facilities and equipment be planned for optimum use.*

PROPOSED STEPS FOR IMPLEMENTATION

a) Convenient access to a well-stocked library.

b) Availability of a wide spectrum of audiovisual equipment.

Recommendations of Aware Teams to Funding Agencies and Organizations for Institutes

RECOMMENDATION 1 *That flexibility of program development be increased without detriment to goals and standards.*

RECOMMENDATION 2 *That follow-up be financed through stipends for regional reunions, travel expenses for intervisitation of teams from different schools, and the assignment of an expert or team of researchers to investigate the effects of this type of education upon teaching behavior.*

RECOMMENDATION 3 *That action research be financed to develop new teaching strategies, methods, and materials in this field and to test their adequacy.*

RECOMMENDATION 4 *That the new paraprofessions of teacher-aides, teacher assistants, and family workers be further explored, evaluated, and expanded, and their functions upgraded.*

RECOMMENDATION 5 *That funds be provided for training superintendents, principals, supervisors, and auxiliary personnel, as well as teachers.*

RECOMMENDATION 6 *That programs be funded to develop family-school-community relationships.*

RECOMMENDATION 7 *That teachers be given preparation for the all-important new function of orchestrating adults (auxiliary personnel) in the classroom to meet the learning needs of pupils as diagnosed by the teachers.*

RECOMMENDATIONS FOR IN-SERVICE PROGRAMS IN SCHOOL SYSTEMS

In the written questionnaires, directors of school programs were asked to answer two open-ended questions calculated to elicit specific recommendations for the improvement and development of their programs:

What kinds of assistance, from what sources, do you need and want in order to improve your program?

If adequate time and money were available, how would you want to evaluate your program—that is to say, what would you consider the optimum method of evaluation?

Sixty-seven of the 89 respondents from school systems submitted suggestions in response to the first question; 74 of the 89 responded to the second. Their comments constitute, in effect, recommendations *to* school officials *from* school officials.

Recommendations of School Administrators to Those Who Plan and Operate In-service Programs

RECOMMENDATION 1 *That program staff be expanded and improved.*

PROPOSED STEPS FOR IMPLEMENTATION

a) Appointment of expert leadership, both internal and external—the latter referring to highly qualified consultants.

b) Appointment of staff members who:

—Have knowledge of and working relationships with community agencies.

—Have interest in and experience with the creative use of teacher-aides.

—Contribute special skills, such as photography and display, for building self-concept.

RECOMMENDATION 2 *That applicants be selected so as to maximize impact of training on the total school situation, i.e., "train the trainers."*

PROPOSED STEPS FOR IMPLEMENTATION

a) Greater emphasis upon training of instructional supervisors.

b) Enrollment of top administrative leadership in school in the same or separate programs.

c) Involvement of parents in at least some aspects of the program.

RECOMMENDATION 3 *That there be closer liaison with local teacher education colleges.*

PROPOSED STEPS FOR IMPLEMENTATION

a) Increased use of educational materials centers, if any.

b) Use of testing and research services.

RECOMMENDATION 4 *That the planners familiarize themselves with promising practices developed in other school systems for teaching of the disadvantaged.*

PROPOSED STEPS FOR IMPLEMENTATION

a) Organization of and participation in, conferences with representatives of other school systems to exchange ideas and experiences, especially about curriculum development and effective use of auxiliary personnel in the classroom.

b) Correspondence with appropriate federal sources for relevant reports and pamphlets, particularly on new developments such as the training and utilization of new subprofessionals and effective methods of achieving desegregation.

c) Development of appropriate bibliographies and library accessions, and their effective use by planners.

RECOMMENDATION 5 *That equipment be expanded and improved.*

PROPOSED STEPS FOR IMPLEMENTATION

a) Develop new instructional materials that have special relevance to teaching the disadvantaged, such as materials which encourage discovery and those which facilitate small-group structuring and flexibility in the classroom.

b) Provide access to these materials.

c) Insure availability of equipment such as tape recorders, cartridge films, film projectors, and video tapes, not only in training programs, but *also in individual schools* for trainees to use upon their return.

RECOMMENDATION 6 *That greater emphasis be placed upon plans for evaluation and follow-up, than has been customary in past institutes.*

PROPOSED STEPS FOR IMPLEMENTATION

a) Visits by trained observation teams to each participant's school, to note institute results not only in the classroom but in the corridors and the lunchroom, in the extent of parent participation, and in all aspects of school life.

b) Comparison of the teaching behavior of the trainees with the behavior of a control nontrained group, before, during, and after period of training. (Interaction analysis might be one method employed.)

c) Observation of changes, if any, in attitudes of trainees toward pupils, parents, supervisors, and peers as a result of participation in the program, and also of any changes in attitude by these different types of school personnel toward the trainees.

d) Quantitative and qualitative evaluation of pupil progress of those taught by enrollees when they return to their respective schools, as measured by standardized tests applied by skilled psychometrists; and of these pupils' behavioral patterns, as reported by teachers and measured by objective criteria, such as mobility, attendance, extent of breakage, career choices.

e) Periodic interviews in depth with participants, and with appropriate colleagues, parents, pupils, community leaders.

f) Group meetings for sharing of experiences.

g) Questionnaires to a representative sampling of participants, nonparticipants, and those affected by the participants.

h) Combination of evaluation by outside experts and internal evaluation by those directly involved.

i) Analysis of tape recordings, planning books, diaries, and new materials developed by participants.

j) Five-year evaluation, based on both immediate and long-range objectives of the program.

RECOMMENDATION 7 *That instructional content incorporate recent research on factors which influence learning and behavior of disadvantaged youth; on guidance, group process, and the development of instructional materials which serve the needs of the disadvantaged.*

RECOMMENDATION 8 *That instructional process include a laboratory for demonstration, development, and evaluation of innovative teaching strategies.*

Recommendations of School Administrators to Internal and External Sources of Funds for In-Service Programs

RECOMMENDATION 1 *That financial support for this type of in-service training be expanded in order to make possible the enrollment of more teachers, supervisors, and teacher-aides as participants, and to provide a higher ratio of staff to enrollees, thus facilitating more small-group work.*

RECOMMENDATION 2 *That such programs either be conducted on released time or that stipends for the participants be granted.*

RECOMMENDATION 3 *That additional funds be provided for field trips by enrollees and for supervision of laboratory experiences, research, and follow-up.*

RECOMMENDATION 4 *That funds be made available for a model school division within each school system.*

RECOMMENDATION 5 *That the value of in-service courses for work with the disadvantaged be interpreted more effectively to the broader community, so that taxpayers will support adequate financing.*

RECOMMENDATIONS FOR PROGRAMS IN INSTITUTIONS OF HIGHER LEARNING, PRIMARILY PRESERVICE PROGRAMS

The directors of programs in institutions of higher learning were asked the same open-ended questions that were asked of the directors of school programs concerning (1) further assistance needed and (2) optimum methods of evaluation. Twenty-four of the 59 directors of college programs replied to the former, 47 to the latter. These suggestions are, in effect, recommendations *to* college and university leadership *from* college and university leadership. To avoid repetition, only those recommendations that were unique to institutions of higher learning are reported here, although all the major categories for the school systems and most of the proposed steps for implementation were also recommended by the colleges and universities.

Recommendations of Teacher Educators to Those Who Plan and Direct Programs in Institutions of Higher Learning

RECOMMENDATION 1 *That the ratio of staff to students be increased, in order to provide more small-group work in year-round programs.*

RECOMMENDATION 2 *That the staff be interdisciplinary, including anthropologists, sociologists, psychologists, and those trained in community experience, group development, medicine, and research.*

RECOMMENDATION 3 *That there be a larger proportion of other school personnel, such as administrators, supervisors, counselors, and curriculum specialists among the enrollees, who are now preponderantly teachers.*

RECOMMENDATION 4 *That teacher-aides be utilized in the programs, both to assist faculty and to demonstrate the value of this paraprofession.*

RECOMMENDATION 5 *That additional scholarships and fellowships be made available for teacher education for work with disadvantaged children and youth.*

RECOMMENDATION 6 *That information about local antipoverty programs be made available to the director and staff so that cooperation with these programs may be fostered.*

RECOMMENDATION 7 *That liaison be established with the local school system, community, agencies, and the indigenous poor.*

RECOMMENDATION 8 *That an educational resources demonstration center be established within the college or university to assist all the departments as well as the community in curriculum development for work with the disadvantaged.*

RECOMMENDATION 9 *That technical equipment be improved, particularly instruments for assessing language development, and research equipment.*

RECOMMENDATION 10 *That plans for evaluation and follow-up be extensive and detailed.*

PROPOSED STEPS FOR IMPLEMENTATION

a) Continuous follow-up for several years of a sample of students graduating from program.

b) Longitudinal evaluation of behavioral change in all concerned, as measured by such factors as career choices, dropouts, and transfers.
c) More experimental studies to test innovative teaching strategies and methods with respect to the pupils' learnings.
d) Identification of carry-over, to the child's family, of values derived by pupils in practicum experience.
e) Studies of perceptions teachers have of their own behavior as teachers of disadvantaged children.
f) Matched-pairs approach, to compare extent of teacher job satisfaction, turnover rate, and change in attitudes toward pupils and toward self, of teachers who have had this type of training with those of teachers who have not.
g) Study of impact of project upon total faculty and upon curriculum development in schools where enrollees teach.

RECOMMENDATION 11 *That instructional content stress teaching as related to personality variables, affective aspects of learning, analysis of the special competencies required for teaching disadvantaged youth, as well as the foundations of the social and behavioral sciences.*

RECOMMENDATION 12 *That instructional process provide smaller classes, additional field experience in disadvantaged areas, and increased, more competent supervision in order to combine field experience with analysis in depth.*

Recommendations of Teacher Educators to Internal and External Sources of Funds for Institutions of Higher Learning

RECOMMENDATION 1 *That more financial support for this program be supplied by the college to assist in its expansion and to give evidence of its importance in the hierarchy of values within the institution.*

RECOMMENDATION 2 *That a combination of federal, state, and private financing be provided to foster cooperation and broad involvement.*

Major findings and implications

CHAPTER 9

Out of innumerable fragments of information and comment, a mosaic of meaning seemed gradually to emerge. Those who had lived with the data found in the thematic patterns of response both reinforcement of long-held convictions and some new and unexpected elements. They were impressed by the values that had been derived thus far from innovative approaches to the preparation of school personnel for work with the disadvantaged and at the same time were alerted to the urgency of unmet needs in this rapidly developing dimension of teacher education.

Major Findings

The purposes of the study, as listed in Chapter 1 were:

1. To describe selected programs designed to improve the knowledge, skills, and attitudes of school personnel for working with disadvantaged children and youth.
2. To identify unique and significant elements of such programs.
3. To develop basic concepts and guidelines for emerging programs of this type.

The major findings are presented below in relation to these objectives.

Purpose 1: *To describe selected programs designed to improve the knowledge, skills, and attitudes of school personnel for working with disadvantaged children and youth.*

The 22 programs described in Chapters 3 and 4 constitute the data related to this purpose. They were selected because they illustrate variety in approach, milieu, and structure. They prepared school personnel to work in urban settings characterized by economic, social, and educational inequality, and in rural areas similarly disadvantaged. They were concerned with low-income Negroes, Indians, Spanish-Americans and Caucasians. They varied in size of enrollment, criteria for enrollee selection, location, grade span covered, number of school systems served, duration of course, and sponsorship. They all had two components in common: (1) They were all institute-type programs—the only type in operation during the period of data collection—and (2) they were all devoted to the common purpose of preparing school personnel to work with disadvantaged children and youth.

The programs described were all financed either by OEO or NDEA funds.

In general the major strengths of the OEO Teacher Education Programs, as perceived by Aware Teams, lay in their high degree of innovation and flexibility and their responsiveness to the needs of both the participants and the community.

The principal weakness identified by the Aware Teams was concerned with management details rather than with conceptualization, apparently related to the haste in planning occasioned by the exigencies getting a new program under way to meet urgent needs.

The innovative aspects of the programs were evident in the development of new dimensions for existing programs as well as in experimentation in preparation of teacher-aides, which gave impetus to the development of a new paraprofession having both educational and economic advantages. The educational advantages lie in freeing the teacher to function at the level of his professional skills and in increasing the proportion of concerned adults to children in the classroom. This is of particular importance to disadvantaged children, for whom individualized concern is essential. The economic advantage lies in the creation of a new job market. Moreover, this type of semiskilled job cannot easily be automated out of existence. Machines can never be substituted for human care of human beings. One difficulty faced by unskilled workers in the past has been that the serving professions have offered few opportunities for any but the highly skilled.

Flexibility—a quality frequently requested by participants in other types of programs studied—was evident not only in the design of the OEO programs but also in the multilevel composition of the enrollee group. No rigid requirements ruled out the combined attendance of administrators, teachers, counselors, and teacher-aides.

The major strength of the NDEA Institutes for Teachers of Disadvantaged Youth, as perceived by Aware Teams, lay in their sharp focus and sense of direction.

These institutes suffered to some extent from the faults of their own virtues. The sound conceptual framework within which they operated appeared to restrict flexibility in some instances. However, directors of NDEA institutes seem to be developing a more liberal interpretation of guidelines.

The NDEA institutes—numerous, varied, structured, and clearly focused—gave new perspective to teacher education.

Government funds from various sources appeared to serve a catalytic function for the reeducation of experienced teachers in school systems and for the preparation of the teachers of tomorrow in colleges and universities. In both in-service and preservice education the teaching role was analyzed within a social context, in tune with the needs of children in a changing world.

Purpose 2: To identify unique and significant elements of these programs.

The written questionnaires, enrollee responses, and reports of site visitations provide various data related to this purpose.

The significance of the programs was found not in disparate elements but rather in the felicitous combination of the cognitive, the affective, and the experiential components of the learnings. The institutes, because of the intensive quality of the experience they made possible, provided an excellent arena in which to observe this integrative process at work.

The following analysis deals first with the basic purposes of the programs as reported by their directors in response to Project Aware questionnaires, next with the directors' plans for implementation of these purposes through instructional content and process. The participants' written responses are then analyzed in relation to these purposes. In other words, the outcomes, as perceived by the participants, are analyzed in terms of the extent to which they appeared to meet the stated goals and also in terms of the relevance and adequacy of instructional content and process toward the achievement of these goals.

A salient finding was that while the majority of directors placed *both* "Understanding the life conditions of disadvantaged groups" *and* "Development of instructional skills, techniques, and materials" among their key objectives, a discrepancy appeared when they were asked to specify how they planned to implement these objectives through instructional content. There was overwhelming response to a question on the relative importance of certain program approaches for suggested items under the first category (Understandings) but meager response for suggested items under the second category (Instructional Skills, Techniques and Materials).

As the categories of possible content areas in the questionnaire became more and more specific in terms of application to teaching behavior, the priority in program emphasis decreased. In essence, then, the directors reported a balanced intent with respect to developing new insights and new teaching behavior, but there was an imbalance with respect to the instructional undergirding of these two purposes.

A crucial test of the balance and impact of the program lies, however, not in the perceptions of the directors, but in the perceptions of the participants themselves. Responding to two questions posed by the Aware Team, more than a thousand participants in 33 NDEA institutes wrote briefly on what they believed they had gained from the experience, and what, if anything, they would like to see changed.

Of the 6,074 comments (approximately six per person), 61 percent indicated positive gains, while only 39 per cent dealt with suggested changes. The response on the positive side gives statistical support for the Aware Team's subjective analysis of the pervasive tone of the institutes visited—a sense of zeal, fervor, and rededication.

In their comments about their personal and professional gains, the participants spoke twice as frequently about new understandings gained than about strategies and methods for applying these understandings to their teaching behavior. This disproportionate response would seem to indicate that in those aspects of the total experience where instructional content was available (i.e., understandings) the program appears to have had an observable impact upon the participants, but in those areas which were not so supported (i.e., practical application to the classroom), the impact was relatively unimpressive.

The participants' suggestions for change reinforced the need for more assistance in translating their understandings into teaching performance. Attitudinal change without behavioral change appeared to them a sterile process. As many as 76 percent of the suggested content changes would place greater emphasis on strategies, techniques, and materials for practical application of new insights to the classroom.

In the absence of content of this type, 31 percent of the comments on procedural change called for closely supervised field experience (practicum). Pending the development of new educational resources for work with the disadvantaged, participants seemed to be requesting more experiential learnings so that they could develop (under skillful supervision) their own strategies, techniques, and materials in an actual teaching situation where innovation would not only be possible but would be encouraged.

This was not a request for a shift of emphasis from understandings to techniques, but rather for a balanced approach, building upon what had been accomplished, and then taking the next step. Understandings and techniques were not seen as dichotomous, but rather as interactive and mutually supportive. Understandings without specific help in translating them into teaching behavior were seen as vague and somewhat amorphous in value. A highly significant datum was that the participants reported more balance between understandings and techniques in those institutes where a practicum was offered than in those institutes lacking a practicum. This differentiation between responses in two types of institutes gives an added dimension to the modal analysis.

***Purpose 3:** To develop basic concepts and guidelines for emerging programs of this type.*

The recommendations in Chapter 8 constitute the data related to this purpose. The findings, summarized above, suggest some new vectors in the preparation of school personnel to work with disadvantaged children and youth. They also suggest three new areas of action research:

1. The development of new strategies, techniques, and materials specifically designed to meet the needs of disadvantaged children in the classroom.
2. Experimentation in the use of such strategies, techniques, and materials in practicums under sensitive supervision.
3. Evaluation of such experiments under scientific controls.

TABLE 33 – Changes in Instructional Process Recommended by Enrollees, Directors, and Aware Teams for NDEA Institutes

	Percent of comments		
Recommended Changes in Process	*Enrollees* (*N* = *1,194*)	*Directors* (*N* = *83*)	*Aware Team* (*N* = *85*)
Include, expand, improve field teaching experience and informal educational contacts with children	31	45	32
Teach group development, use small-group discussions more extensively and effectively	18	23	18
Improve, expand, include class observations and demonstrations by master teachers	13	4	5
Negative of prior statement	1	1	—
Improve, increase field work in homes and community	12	1	9
Schedule more free time for independent study, informal sharing, reflection, and socializing instead of so many formal reading and written assignments	11	17	15
Negative of prior statement, particularly socializing	2	2	—
Improve quality and relevance of lectures	9	1	9
Schedule fewer lectures	3	6	—
Other	—	—	12

N = the number of comments relating to Process, *not* the number of respondents or the total number of comments.

The specific recommendations listed in Chapter 8 were based upon suggestions for change drawn from several sources. Consensus of the need for change was highest with regard to Instructional Process and Instructional Content. In fact, the central tendencies of recommended changes in these two areas were similar for three types of commentators—enrollees, directors, and members of Aware Teams, as they perceived the NDEA institutes (see Tables 33 and 34). The highest-frequency item is identical for all three types of observers for both Process (Table 33) and Content (Table 34).

TABLE 34 – Changes in Instructional Content Recommended by Enrollees, Directors, and Aware Teams for NDEA Institutes

Recommended Changes in Content	*Percent of comments*		
	Enrollees (N = 425)	*Directors (N = 59)*	*Aware Team (N = 28)*
Place more emphasis on strategies, methods, and materials for practical application of new insights to teaching behavior	76	51	43
Negative of prior statement	3	3	—
Develop relevant concepts from social and behavioral sciences more effectively	17	44	41
Negative of prior statement	4	2	—
Other	—	—	15

Responding to these frequently expressed needs, the Aware Team made recommendations for concrete action, with proposed steps for their implementation.

Recommendation on Content*—That the instructional content integrate understanding of the disadvantaged with assistance in translating such understanding into teaching behavior.*

PROPOSED STEPS FOR IMPLEMENTATION

a) A cognitive dimension that presents facts and develops understandings *vis-a-vis* the disadvantaged, and moves from myth to reality.

b) An interdisciplinary approach combining sociology, psychology, anthropology, and related social and behavioral studies.

c) Orientation of outside lecturers to avoid repetition and irrelevancy in lecture content.

d) Involvement of the teaching staff in the sociological, anthropological, psychological, and economic content areas in actual school situations and in the community and family life.

e) More emphasis on the diagnostic approach, i.e., the analysis of each child's behavior as an individual not as a member of any group, the possible causes of such behavior, and the teacher's responsibilities regarding child behavior and development.

f) Demonstration of possible strategies, methods, and materials that have special application to working with disadvantaged children and youth.

g) Analysis of demonstrations in terms of their relevance to a wide variety of situations, with emphasis on the necessity for adaptation to individual conditions.

h) Participation in curriculum revision, remediation, and development of new materials.

***Recommendation on Process**—That instructional process provide opportunity for experiential learnings.*

PROPOSED STEPS FOR IMPLEMENTATION

a) A teaching field experience or practicum that has direction, is involved with children who are truly disadvantaged, has components of supervision, and encourages self-analysis and reflection.

b) Opportunity for identifying and sharing the contributions of the participants in small-group discussions.

c) Utilizing the leadership skills of the participants in conducting discussions, making presentations, and carrying on committee activities.

d) Programs of group counseling and sensitivity training to encourage self-understanding and build ego strength in participants.

e) Integration of affective, cognitive, and action components of the program, in an effort to achieve behavioral change.

f) Development of more effective supervisory processes.

In making these recommendations, Project Aware offers no blueprints for teacher education in today's world. Rather it presents a modal analysis of divergent opinions, theories, and strategies for preparing school personnel to work with disadvantaged children and youth. The majority of teacher-educators, participants, and Aware Team investigators believed that cognitive, affective, and action components can be integrated most effectively through experiential learning, in closely supervised practicums. Nevertheless, teacher-educators, sensitive to the effects of environmental disadvantage upon learning, are seeking and often finding myriad ways of assisting teachers to identify and to develop the latent potential of all children. Most educators see this as a central role of teachers and hence a highly important responsibility of teacher education.

Implications

It is the privilege of individuals who have been involved in a study to review the findings and spell out certain implications. The observations presented here are made in the context of the status of teacher education programs in the country today.

Initially it appears essential that a total restatement of the concept of the disadvantaged child be undertaken. The terms *culturally deprived, socially disadvantaged, environmentally disadvantaged, underprivileged,* and *poor* are all inadequate. One of the outcomes of the new conceptualization should be the evolution of a more accurate description of the total phenomenon of the disadvantaged in the American social scene.

The first focus in this statement of implications is on the content of specific programs for the professional preparation of teachers. With the whole educational spectrum in a state of ferment and with shifts in emphasis and deliberate redesign being undertaken, it would appear essential that teacher education curriculum deal intensively with the processes of change, theoretically and experientially.

Moreover, the growth sciences—all those concerned with the mental, social, and physical aspects of development—need to be taught as integrated constructs, with an emphasis on their significance for the educational process. This may mean an interdisciplinary staff teaching sociology, anthropology, psychology, and human development—a staff which sees all these disciplines as they relate to each other and to the learning-teaching process.

The study of learning and thinking needs to be a basic component of the curriculum. An understanding of the use of langauge and the communication process is of vital significance to learning. New theoretical formulations and recent research in learning in the United States, as well as in Europe, should be incorporated in a curriculum for teachers.

The curriculum for the teachers of the disadvantaged must afford a thorough knowledge of diagnostic principles and skills and their application, enabling the teacher to assess each individual's potential and to use this information as a basis for designing appropriate experiences that will enable him to learn.

A second focus of these implications bears on the instructional process of specific programs designed to improve the knowledge, skills, and attitudes of teachers and other school personnel. The findings certainly imply that the teacher education process itself needs a stronger component of developing professional teaching competencies through a much wider range of practicum, field experiences, and student teaching, or "internships." Such experiential learning must be reinforced by a high quality of supervision and a very close working relationship with the preservice training staff of the institution of higher learning and with the administrative, supervisory, and instructional personnel of the schools. School systems have yet to accept as part of their role, function, and responsibility the provision of supervisory assistance to the practice and field experiences of students. Providing experiences for students learning to be teachers is still considered as a "favor" extended to the teacher education programs of the cooperating colleges.

Another critical element in the development of both teacher and child is an awareness of self and the strengthening of self-concept. The strategies for initiating these processes should be studied by educational psychologists and incorporated in teacher education programs. The teacher who is to help the child develop ego strength must develop awareness of his own person. What is he like? How can he develop self-knowledge and ego strength? Teacher education for school personnel working with the disadvantaged needs to provide the opportunity for teachers in the course of their training to explore "self" through small-group counseling, T-group sessions, or individual counseling. Basically, teacher education must in some ways "transform" a person, and this may be traumatic to the individual. It is when shock occurs that individual counseling is needed as well as group sessions.

The instructional milieu of a program preparing teachers to work with disadvantaged children and youth appears to require a strong component of reality. Extensive participation in community activities and involvement with children and their families in disadvantaged settings is essential for a considerable period of time, to prevent the training from becoming an intellectual exercise on a cultural island and to fit the preparation of teachers to the social context of the times. These experiences, then, need to be related to the child's learning processes. Moreover, the learning-teaching climate can be improved by the teacher who approaches the child in a spirit of openness and demonstrates willingness to learn from the child. The establishment of such a reciprocal relationship, particularly with disadvantaged children, enhances the opportunity for learning for both the child and the teacher.

In addition to specific "institute-type" programs, the school system itself must assume responsibility for the intensive professional development of its teachers and personnel. In a majority of cases in-service training is done in a superficial manner. Rather than a seminar or program at the opening of the school year with a speech by a guest consultant, it requires a cadre of creative, knowledgeable, nonthreatening staff members in consultative, supervisory, and training roles to evolve staff development processes. This will give school personnel the skills, the personal security, ego strength, and basic knowledge to become increasingly effective teachers in today's challenging school situations. Individuals in staff development roles, however, are themselves inadequate in their knowledge of the concepts and processes in the field. Efforts must be made by government and higher education to give advanced training to key school personnel responsible for programs and in-service training.

Continued relationships by teacher education institutions with graduates who are serving as teachers in school systems need to be developed on more than the present pilot scale. One approach is to conceive of the first-year teacher as an apprentice, an assistant, or an associate to an experienced teacher, with the college maintaining its supervisory role. The professional development of school personnel must be seen as a continuing cooperative venture between the institutions of higher learning and the schools.

Another implication of the study is the need to develop a spirit of inquiry, search, and innovation for experimenting with the organization and structure for learning. A possible approach is to evolve different kinds of school structures that are based on differentiated needs of children, such as ungraded classes. The school as a formal institution, operating six hours a day, with the teacher confined to the schoolroom and the counselor confined to the guidance office, no longer serves a high proportion of today's youth. Multilevel cooperation among administrators, teachers, and teacher-aides can give leverage to an otherwise static situation, particularly when the role of the teacher-aide is conceived as more than that of giving custodial services or performing simple clerical tasks.

Actually, an integrative approach to meeting the needs of the child goes deep into the whole fabric of society. It requires the engagement of all segments of the institutional life of the community. Theorists and operationalists need to enter into true dialogue. The involvement of parents is a *sine qua non* of the extended school in the context of reality. Moreover, management, labor, social work, and government all have a common stake with educators in the discovery and development of each child's latent potential.

Integration of all community resources serving children and youth into a single organizational complex is presently supported by the Office of Economic Opportunity Community Action Programs in a number of localities. These experiments in integrating functional components need to be studied and evaluated. Their strengths can then be incorporated in existing school programs, enabling a more effective utilization of all resources in the community that deal with the life and learning of the child. One of these strengths is the concept of planning *with* the disadvantaged, rather than *for* the disadvantaged.

At this time in history the emphasis on special programs for the disadvantaged may have been necessary. However, eventually all teacher education will have to move toward a focus upon meeting the needs of individuals as seen within their social context.

The increasingly recognized need for teacher education which is relevant to the spirit of the age demands a willingness to risk failure in order to broaden the scope of possible alternatives. The depth and pace of change in an atom-triggered world calls for a whole new ethos—one in which rigidity is the prime dysfunction. To learn to live comfortably with ambiguity and yet not succumb to a sense of alienation and anomy is the modern challenge—in school and in society.

Appendices

APPENDIX A

Project Aware Advisory Committee

Mario Anglada
Deputy Secretary of Education
Department of Education
Commonwealth of Puerto Rico
Hato Rey, Puerto Rico

Elmer J. Clark
Dean
School of Education
Southern Illinois University
Carbondale, Illinois

Martin Deutsch
Director
Department of Developmental Studies
New York University
New York, New York

Vernon Haubrich
Professor, Educational Policy
University of Wisconsin
Madison, Wisconsin

William Kvaraceus
Director, Youth Studies
Lincoln Filene Center for Citizenship and Public Affairs
Tufts University
Medford, Massachusetts

Richard E. Lawrence
Associate Secretary
American Association of Colleges for Teacher Education
Washington, D.C.

Samuel Levine
Director
Bureau of Educational Research
San Francisco State College
San Francisco, California

Virginia Love
Professor of Education
Austin College
Sherman, Texas

Bertrand Phillips
Dean of Students
Tuskegee Institute
Tuskegee, Alabama

Daniel Schreiber
Assistant Superintendent for Education of the Disadvantaged
New York City Board of Education
New York, New York

James R. Tanner
Assistant Superintendent
Board of Education
Cleveland, Ohio

Herbert Zimiles
Chairman
Research Programs
Bank Street College of Education
New York, New York

APPENDIX B

Aware Team Specialists

LeRoy Bowman
Professor Emeritus of Sociology
Brooklyn College
Brooklyn, New York

Paul Cooke
Professor of English
District of Columbia Teachers College
Washington, D.C.

Larry Cuban
Project Director
Cardoza Project in Urban Teaching
Board of Education
Washington, D.C.

Robert Groeschell
Director of Elementary Education
Division of Curriculum & Instruction
Office of the Superintendent of Public Instruction
Olympia, Washington

Theresa Held
Administrative Assistant in Charge of Guidance
Canarsie High School
New York City Board of Education
New York, New York

Jacob Landers
Assistant Superintendent in Charge of School Integration
New York City Board of Education
New York, New York

Norman W. Nickens
Assistant Superintendent
Model School Division
Board of Education
Washington, D.C.

Jane O'Connor
Senior Consultant
Educational Resources Center
Bank Street College of Education
New York, New York

Margaret N. Rowley
Director
The Joseph Kaplan Human Relations Program
Morris Brown College
Atlanta, Georgia

APPENDIX C

Staff of Project Aware

Professional Staff of Project Aware

Gordon J. Klopf,* Director
Garda W. Bowman,* Research Coordinator
Lodema Burrows,* Editorial Associate
Clementine Wheeler,* Editorial Associate

Professional Staff for Special Phases of Project

RESEARCH AND EDITORIAL ASSISTANTS

Robert J. Bentley*
Claude A. Burrows
Diana P. Cook
Vida Feinstein
Mildred Huberman*
Douglas O'Connor
Rose Rapoport*
Ruth C. Resch*
Sterling Rogers
Richard Strier
Mignon Swihart*
Leontine Zimiles

CONSULTANTS

John L. Gray
Elizabeth Gilkeson
Martin Haberman
Rose Risikoff
Caryl Steere
Joseph Steere

Secretarial and Clerical Staff of Project

Sonia Bernard
Alan Frisher
Frima Frumes
Mildred Gold
Lillian Lawson
Barbara Pushkin
Elizabeth Rapoport
Jack Reynolds
Fred Richardson
Irene Taylor
Evelyn Tepper

* Served on Visitation Teams.

APPENDIX D

Letter of Transmittal for Questionnaires†

July, 1965

To: Deans of Colleges of Education and Chairmen of Departments of Education (or the Liaison Person Designated for PROJECT AWARE)

From: Gordon J. Klopf, Project Director

As indicated in my memorandum of June 17, the U.S. Office of Economic Opportunity and the staff of the U.S. Office of Education have requested Bank Street College of Education to conduct a study of existing programs designed to improve the knowledge, skills, and understanding of those who work with disadvantaged youth in a school setting. A duplicate copy of the brief description of the Project is enclosed.

One of the four types of programs to be studied is teacher education in institutions of higher learning. We turn to you for information about the nature and extent of the preparation of teachers for work with the disadvantaged, as it has been developed in your institution.

While we are not evaluating your program, we are most interested in your own evaluation of it. We want to share the major strengths of your program, as identified by you, with others who are teaching teachers of the disadvantaged.

We will appreciate your having the enclosed questionnaires filled out by the appropriate person(s) and returned to us no later than August 9. Form A is for the whole institution. Only one copy need be returned to us. Form B is for each *specific* program of this nature. Two copies are sent in the event that you have more than one such program. More copies are available upon request.

Only the overall statistics will be included in the final report. Individual colleges and universities will not be identified without your explicit permission. The name of the respondent is requested in order that we may establish direct communication with you for purposes of follow-up. The general findings will be distributed to education departments and institutions throughout the country.

† The same basic message, with adaptations, was sent to the other populations.

We hope that a descriptive analysis of programs, practices, and concepts in this rapidly developing area of teacher education will be useful as institutions of higher learning develop plans for the spring term of 1966 and the school year of 1966-67. Our final report is due in the fall of 1965. We look forward to hearing from you soon.

Please return questionnaires in enclosed envelopes addressed to Machine Tabulating Company.

APPENDIX E

PROJECT AWARE

Form A: **FOR TOTAL SCHOOL SYSTEM**

conducted for the U.S. Office of Economic Opportunity and the staff of the U.S. Office of Education by Bank Street College of Education

Project location:
103 East 125th Street
New York, N. Y. 10035

A STUDY OF THE PREPARATION OF SCHOOL PERSONNEL FOR WORKING WITH DISADVANTAGED CHILDREN AND YOUTH

Name of Superintendent: ____________________

Name and Address of School System: ____________________

____

____

Number of Pupils in school population.............................. ______

Number of full-time Class-room Teachers.............................. ______

Number of Principals.............................. ______

Please check as many of the following items as apply to the area served by your school system:

1. Urban neighborhoods characterized by low family income, sub-standard and over-crowded housing, and other evidence of economic deprivation. ______
2. Rural communities with similar characteristics.............................. ______
3. Migratory workers.............................. ______
4. Large proportion of various ethnic groups:
   a. Indians.............................. ______
   b. Spanish-speaking Americans.............................. ______
   c. Negroes.............................. ______
   d. Orientals.............................. ______
   e. Others, please specify____________________

Please check as many of the following statements as apply to your school system:

1. We operate special program(s) for preparation of school personnel for working with the disadvantaged.............................. ______
   If checked, how many such programs?.............................. ______
   (Fill out Form B for EACH special program)

2. We incorporate such education into our over-all in-service program... ______

   (If checked, please describe HOW this is done on reverse side of page)

3. We plan to develop a special program for this purpose in: 1965-66 ______
   1966-67 ______

4. We see no need for such education.............................. ______

Name and Title of Respondent: ____________________

Date Questionnaire Completed: ____________________

APPENDIX F

PROJECT AWARE

conducted for the U.S. Office of
Economic Opportunity and the staff of
the U.S. Office of Education by
Bank Street College of Education

Form A: **FOR OVERALL APPROACH OF COLLEGE OR DEPARTMENT**

Project location:
103 East 125th Street
New York, N. Y. 10035

A STUDY OF THE PREPARATION OF SCHOOL PERSONNEL
FOR WORKING WITH DISADVANTAGED CHILDREN AND YOUTH

Name of Dean of College of Education or Chairman of Education Department: ______________

____

Name and Address of Institution of Higher Learning: ______________________

____

____

Number of Students.. ________

Number of full-time Faculty... ________

Please check as many of the following items as apply to the area(s) in which the majority of your students teach after graduation:

1. Urban neighborhoods characterized by low family income, sub-standard and over-crowded housing, and other evidence of economic deprivation. ________
2. Rural communities with similar characteristics........................ ________
3. Migratory workers.. ________
4. Large proportion of various ethnic groups:
   a. Indians.. ________
   b. Spanish-speaking Americans... ________
   c. Negroes.. ________
   d. Orientals.. ________
   e. Other, please specify ______________________________

Please check as many of the following statements as apply to your college or department:

1. We operate special program(s) for preparation of school personnel for working with the disadvantaged ________. If checked, how many such programs? ________. (Fill out Form B for EACH special program)

2. We incorporate such education into our over-all teacher education..... ________ (If checked, please describe how this is done on reverse side of page)

3. We plan to develop a special program for this purpose in: 1965-66 ________ 1966-67 ________

4. We see no need for such education...................................... ________

Name and Title of Respondent: ______________________________

Date Questionnaire Completed: ______________________

APPENDIX G

PROJECT AWARE

conducted for the U.S. Office of Economic Opportunity and the staff of the U.S. Office of Education by Bank Street College of Education

Form B: **FOR SPECIFIC PROGRAMS**
(Prepare separate form for each program)
Project location:
103 East 125th Street
New York, N. Y. 10035

A STUDY OF THE PREPARATION OF SCHOOL PERSONNEL
FOR WORKING WITH DISADVANTAGED CHILDREN AND YOUTH

Title or Description of Specific Program: ____________________
Name and Address of Sponsoring Institution of Higher Learning or School System: ____
____
____

I. RATIONALE FOR PROGRAM

A. Focus: Preparation of School Personnel for Working: (Check as many as apply)
1. In urban areas characterized by low family income, substandard and overcrowded housing, and other evidence of economic deprivation........._____
2. In rural communities with similar characteristics.................._____
3. With migratory workers.._____
4. With various ethnic groups:
a. Indians____ c. Negroes____ e. Other, specify:
b. Spanish-speaking Americans_____ d. Orientals_____ ____________

B. Purpose (Check those which apply to your program. Double check those which are important. Triple check key items)
1. Curriculum development and revision.................................._____
2. Development/improvement instructional skills, techniques and materials.._____
3. Understanding culture and life conditions of various disadvantaged groups..._____
4. Attitudinal and behaviorial change of enrollees......................_____
5. Research......_______. 6. Other, specify____________________
____

II. ORGANIZATIONAL DATA

A. Length and Time of Program
1. # of hours per week......_____
2. (if of brief duration): # of weeks of operation.._____
3. (if of long duration): # of months of operation._____
4. Held during summer, 1965........_____
5. Held during school or college year '64-'65............_____
6. If an on-going program, give date when it started operation.._____

B. Number and Type of Enrollees
1. Total enrollment........._____
2. # of eligible applicants not accepted............_____
3. # of Teachers (accepted).._____
4. # of Administrators............._____
5. # of Counsellors, Social Workers, Psychologists, etc....._____
6. Others, specify____________

C. Selection of Enrollees (Check as many as apply)
1. Criteria for Eligibility and/or Selection
a. Academic record......_____
b. Experience with disadvantaged........_____
c. Appointment to work with disadvantaged...._____
d. Apparent commitment to goals of program......................_____
e. Superior's recommendation......_____
f. Other, specify____________
____
2. Procedure
a. Application form......_____
b. Essay revealing interests, values and personality......_____
c. Interviews......................_____
d. References......................_____
e. Other, specify____________
____

D. Professional Staff Working Directly with Enrollees
1. How many: In all_____ Full time_____ Part time_____ Visiting lecturers_____
2. Ratio full time equivalent professionals to students..................._____
3. Was experience with and knowledge of disadvantaged groups decisive in selection of staff?..................................Yes_____ No_____

E. Credit
1. Is credit given for completion of program?..............Yes_____ No_____
a. Toward Salary Increment..._____
b. Toward Degree..............._____ What Degrees..........._____

F. Source of Funds

Please enter the % of funds provided by each of the following:

1. Government Funds
   a. Federal (specify agency)
   ____________________ .. ______%
   b. State.................. ______%
   c. County.................. ______%
   d. Municipal.............. ______%
2. Foundation Grants............ ______%
3. Sponsoring Institute or Agency...................... ______%
4. Others, specify____________... ______%
   ____________________... ______%

Total Budget $____________________

G. Training of Sub-Professionals (Such as Teacher's Aides)

Do you train sub-professionals to work with the disadvantaged? Yes_____ No_____

If yes, describe:

H. Cooperation with O.E.O. Programs (Such as Headstart and other Community Action Programs, Job Corps, Youth Corps, etc.)

List programs with which you cooperate, if any, and specify forms of cooperation:

III. CONTENT

(Listed below are 7 major content areas with specific aspects under each, as observed by project teams in site visitations. Check those aspects which are covered in your Program. Double check those which are important. Triple check the key items.)

A. Understanding Disadvantaged Children and Youth

1. Culture and traditions of various disadvantaged groups
   a. in general.. ______
   b. for those groups with which majority of enrollees will be working ______
2. Life conditions of economically deprived
   a. the world over.. ______
   b. for those groups with which majority of enrollees will be working ______
3. How environmental conditioning may affect:
   a. Hopes and expectations.. _____
   b. Self-image............. _____
   c. Communication skills.......... ______
   d. Variety of behavior patterns.. ______
4. How accepting or rejecting attitudes of teachers, often at unconscious level, may affect motivation and learning of children and youth.. ______
5. Other, specify____

B. Situational Factors of Concern to Teachers

1. Family life............... _____
2. Peer groups............... _____
3. Social structure and stratification............. _____
4. Community organization..... _____
5. School-community relations. _____
6. Group process.............. ______
7. Analysis of social conflict... ______
8. Youth in an era of rapid technological change.......... ______
9. Other, specify____________________

C. Professional Competence of Teachers of the Disadvantaged

1. The need for self understanding as essential to understanding and relating to others.. ______
2. The need for developing ego strength so as to deal effectively with the wide variety of environmentally conditioned behavior...... ______
3. Self insights as to gratifications and unique satisfactions each individual seeks from teaching.............................. ______
4. Others, specify____

D. Conceptual Framework

1. The interests-and-needs approach.. ______
2. The evolving curriculum based on day-to-day experience.......... ______
3. Strategies for developing values consistent with the needs of present-day democratic society.. ______
4. Strategies for bringing about behavior changes consonant with such values.. ______
5. Use of symbolism in instructional materials........................ ______
6. Emphasis upon discovery by children through experiments and problem solving as opposed to being told......................... ______

7. Attention to individual growth patterns.............................______
8. Concept that every teacher is also a counselor.....................______
9. Others, specify____
____

E. Instructional Techniques

1. Team teaching..............______
2. Teacher-pupil planning and evaluation............______
3. Establishing the work climate..................______
4. Field trips.................______
5. Project-centered learning..______
6. Committee activity and special assignments........______
7. Discussion techniques.........______
8. Programmed teaching...........______
9. Role playing..................______
10. Structured and dramatic presentations................______
11. Films, television and other media..................______
12. Others, specify__________________

F. Instructional Materials

1. Testing existing materials.______
2. Developing new materials...______
3. Other, specify__________________

G. Special Subject Matter Enrollees Are Being Prepared to Teach

1. Reading....................______
2. English as a Foreign Language..................______
3. Modern Foreign Languages...______
4. Social Studies.............______
5. Science....................______
6. Mathematics..................______
7. Geography....................______
8. Educational Media............______
9. Other, specify__________________

H. Other Major Content Area(s) Specify:

IV. INSTRUCTIONAL PROCESS

(Listed below are some instructional procedures observed by project teams in site visits. Check those which are used in your Program. Double check those which are important. Triple check those which are key items.)

A. Specific Procedures

1. Lectures by visitors............______
2. Lectures by Program faculty......______
3. General discussion...............______
4. Small group discussion...........______
5. Group counseling sessions........______
6. T-groups for self awareness......______
7. Field trips for observation of community....................______
8. Field experience with involvement in community activities..........______
9. Field experience in teaching.....______
10. Practicum (Closely supervised teaching and/or counseling)......______
11. Home visits...............______
12. Case studies..............______
13. Research..................______
14. Reports of reading........______
15. Preparation of papers.....______
16. Preparation of daily log..______
17. Individual conferences....______
18. Scheduled study time......______
19. Free time for socializing and recreation............______
20. Other, specify__________________

B. Which of the above do you use to help enrollees perceive the relationship of new concepts to new experiences, thus integrating them into a meaningful whole? (Give numbers for A above) ______________________________
Other methods, specify ______________________________

V. METHODS OF PROGRAM EVALUATION USED

(Check as many as apply)

A. Feed-Back from Enrollees during Program

1. Written.......______ How often______
2. Discussion....______ How often______
3. Faculty present? Yes_____ No_____

Is feed-back an important consideration in developing Program? Yes_____ No_____
If Yes, what specific changes resulted?

B. Plan for Follow-Up with Enrollees after Program (Check as many as apply)

If you have a plan for follow-up, does it include:

1. Personal contacts.................____ 4. Group reunion..............____
2. Letter or questionnaire...........____ 5. Other, specify____________
3. Class visitation..................____

Is follow-up an important consideration for future Program development?

Yes____ No____

C. Evaluation of Program by Professional Staff

1. Written............................____ How often________
2. In staff meetings..................____ How often________

Is staff evaluation an important consideration in developing Program?

Yes____ No____

If Yes, what specific changes resulted?

D. Optimum Method of Evaluation

If adequate time and money were available, how would you want to evaluate your Program?

TITLE OF PROGRAM:________________________
SCHOOL OR INSTITUTION:________________________
COMMUNITY:________________________

VI. EVALUATION OF PROGRAM BY ADMINISTRATOR

A. What do you see as the main strengths of your Program?*

B. What, if anything, would you add, omit or change if you were starting again?

C. Why would you make such changes?

D. What kinds of assistance, from what sources, do you need and want in order to improve your Program?

(Attach additional sheets, if necessary)

NAME OF RESPONDENT: ________________________ DATE QUESTIONNAIRE

TITLE OF RESPONDENT: ________________________ COMPLETED:__________

*A purpose of the study is to share the strengths of each program, as identified by its administrator, with others responsible for similar approaches to teacher education.

APPENDIX H

Guidelines for Aware Team Site Visits

I. *Use of Interview Schedules*

The climate is essential. Though the team chairman's introduction would hopefully establish rapport, it is the responsibility of the whole team to maintain a nonthreatening atmosphere.

The basic questions will undoubtedly lead to many subquestions and to a general give and take.

All basic questions should be covered eventually, in whatever order seems best.

The questions should be expressed, in the interviewer's own words, to fit the situation. All that matters is that the content be covered for the purposes of reporting.

The minimum time for the interview with enrollees is one hour—preferably one and a half to two hours.

The minimum time for the interview with the professional staff is two hours—preferably two and a half hours.

To avoid broad generalizations, it is important to ask for *concrete examples*. The reverse is also effective, moving from the specific to the theoretical. In either sequence, *specificity is essential.*

Within these limits, the interviewers should allow the interviews to be free flowing and should conduct them, in their own style, in the light of the local situation.

II. *Group Interview with Professional Staff*

First, establish rapport.

Then ask group to identify themselves by name, professional role, and the nature and extent of their experiences with the disadvantaged.

A. Basic Questions for Discussion

1. Do you think the actual program has been effectively related so far to the stated objectives and to the needs and expectations of the enrollees?

   Some possible subquestions:

   a. On what changes in behavior do you base these judgments?
   b. Which of your purposes can be analyzed objectively?
   c. Have any basic needs of the teachers of the disadvantaged, not previously perceived or anticipated, been identified?
   d. How were these needs assessed?

e. What changes were made in program objectives and procedures as a result of this assessment?
f. What provisions for follow-up do you have?
2. In what ways do you think this program differs from effective teacher education in general?
3. What do you see as the main strengths of the program?
4. What would you change if you were starting again?

B. POSSIBLE QUESTIONS IF RESPONSE WARRANTS DEEPER PROBING:

On Organization—
a. How many eligible candidates had to be turned away, if any?
b. Did you get the kind of information needed to select participants?
c. Were internal procedures for screening applicants adequate?

On Content—
a. What would you add or omit in content covered?
b. Were the various fields of study presented integrated into a meaningful whole? How?
c. Was there an emphasis on the need to develop ego strength so as to deal effectively with the wide variety of environmentally conditioned behavior?
d. What is the role of the committed innovator in the field?

On Affect—
a. Do you believe the concepts and experiences have been internalized by the enrollees to any extent thus far?
b. Do any of them voice new questions, express new concepts, show evidence of any new self-awareness? If so, give examples.

III. *Group Interviews with Enrollees*

Preferably not more than ten in a group.

No staff or faculty present.

Team chairman's introduction should establish a climate valuing direct, honest communication and counteracting the image of an "inspector general."

Group may be asked to introduce themselves, when and if appropriate.

A. BRIEF WRITTEN RESPONSES (not more than ten minutes in all). *Before* discussion begins, written response to the following questions should be requested:
1. List understandings and techniques you have gained thus far.
2. What changes would you make if you were planning such a program?

B. BASIC QUESTIONS FOR GENERAL DISCUSSION

Amplification of above, then:
1. What did you expect or hope to get out of this experience?
2. What do you see as the main strengths of this program?
3. What specific kinds of help, if any, would you like to have after the program, when you try to put your new knowledge into day-by-day practice?

C. RATIONALE FOR QUESTIONS

The written questions serve to provide a direct response from each enrollee, uninfluenced by the first respondents, who tend to set the tone. *Please send these written responses with your report.*

Answers to the question about understandings and techniques may be revealing in terms of which of the two parts of the question the respondents stress in their replies.

IV. *Aware Team's Reactions to Program in Action*

This is not an evaluation of the program as good, bad, or indifferent. It is an analysis of the various elements of the program as they relate to (1) the stated objectives, and (2) the apparent needs and expectations of the enrollees. This constitutes the Team's perception of the program, based on both observations and interviews.

A. TOPICS TO COVER IN REPORT

1. *Main Strengths of Program*
2. *Aspects of Program Which Might Be Changed—and Why*
3. *Conditions* (Ratio of Staff to Enrollees, Span of Grade Levels, Length of Program, etc.) *as Related to Purpose and Needs*
4. *Cognitive Aspects of Program as Related to Purpose and Needs*
5. *Affective Aspects* (i.e., the Total Experience and Its Apparent Relationship to Enrollee's Attitudes and Behavior)
6. *A Frankly Subjective Analysis of the Tone of the Program*
7. *Other Comments or Recommendations*

B. OTHER INSTRUCTIONS

When Team's perception of any aspect of the program differs substantially from that of enrollees and/or staff, this difference should be indicated and possible causal factors suggested.

APPENDIX I

Project Aware Site Visits

I. *Office of Economic Opportunity Teacher Education Programs—Sponsoring Institutions*

ARIZONA
Arizona State College
Tempe

CALIFORNIA
University of California Extension
Riverside
Santa Clara County Economic Opportunity Commission
San Jose

MASSACHUSETTS
Harvard University and Action for Boston Community Development
Boston
Garland Junior College and Action for Boston Community Development
Boston

MICHIGAN
Wayne State University and Detroit School System
Detroit

NEW JERSEY
Princeton University and Trenton School System
Trenton

NEW YORK
Syracuse Crusade for Freedom
Syracuse

OREGON
University of Oregon[1]
Tongue Point, Astoria

PENNSYLVANIA
University of Pittsburgh and Pittsburgh Public Schools
Pittsburgh

TENNESSEE
George Peabody College
Nashville

WISCONSIN
Dominican College[2]
Racine
University of Wisconsin
Stevens Point

[1] Job Corps Center. (Visited, though *not* a teacher education program, to observe another dimension of the needs of disadvantaged youth.)
[2] Financed by OEO and NDEA.

II. *National Defense Education Act Institutes for Teachers of Disadvantaged Youth—Sponsoring Institutions*

ALABAMA
Tuskegee Institute
Tuskegee

CALIFORNIA
California State College
Los Angeles
College of Notre Dame
Belmont
San Diego State College
San Diego
San Fernando Valley State College
Northridge
San Francisco State College
San Francisco

DISTRICT OF COLUMBIA
District of Columbia Teachers College
Washington

FLORIDA
Bethune-Cookman College
Daytona Beach
University of Miami
Coral Gables

ILLINOIS
Northwestern University
Evanston

INDIANA
Ball State University
Muncie

KANSAS
Washburn University of Topeka
Topeka

MAINE
University of Maine
Orono

MARYLAND
Coppin State College
Baltimore
Goucher College
Towson
University of Maryland
College Park

MASSACHUSETTS
Tufts University
Medford

MICHIGAN
Wayne State University
Detroit

MISSISSIPPI
Jackson State College
Jackson

MISSOURI
Washington University
St. Louis

MONTANA
Western Montana College
Dillon

NEBRASKA
Municipal University of Omaha
Omaha

NEW JERSEY
Glassboro State College
Glassboro

NEW YORK
City University of New York
Brooklyn College
Brooklyn

City University of New York
Hunter College
Manhattan
Hofstra University
Hempstead
New York Medical College
Manhattan

NORTH CAROLINA
Western Carolina College
Cullowhee

OHIO
Bowling Green State University
Bowling Green

PENNSYLVANIA
Pennsylvania State University
University Park

PUERTO RICO
University of Puerto Rico
Rio Piedras

RHODE ISLAND
Rhode Island College
Providence

TEXAS
University of Texas
Austin

WASHINGTON
Western Washington State College
Bellingham

WISCONSIN
Dominican College[3]
Racine

III. *In-Service Programs in School Systems*

CALIFORNIA
Los Angeles Board of Education
San Francisco Board of Education

ILLINOIS
Chicago Board of Education

MASSACHUSETTS
Boston (A.B.C.D.) and Boston Schools

MICHIGAN
Detroit Board of Education

OHIO
Cleveland Board of Education

PENNSYLVANIA
Pittsburgh Board of Education

PUERTO RICO
Commonwealth of Puerto Rico, Department of Instruction

TEXAS
Fort Worth, Texas, Board of Education

IV. *College and University Programs*

MASSACHUSETTS
Harvard University—Center for Research and Development on Educational Differences, Cambridge

OHIO
John Carroll University, Cleveland

TENNESSEE
University of Tennessee, Knoxville

[3] Financed by both OEO and NDEA.

APPENDIX J

NDEA Institutes for Teachers of Disadvantaged Youth: A Summary of Directors' Final Reports, Summer 1965

by Louis Urgo and Roderick Hilsinger

During the summer of 1965 the U.S. Office of Education contracted with 61 institutions of higher education for the operation of Institutes for Teachers of Disadvantaged Youth, under Title XI of the National Defense Education Act, 1964 Amendments. Upon completion of each institute the director submitted a Final Report to the Division of Educational Personnel Training, U.S.O.E. In addition to supplying statistical information, each director was requested to use the report as "an opportunity to make a full statement on and appraisal of his institute." By categorizing their statements according to the comments most frequently expressed, we have attempted to summarize their evaluations. Interpretations and judgments about their comments have been avoided wherever possible.

QUANTITATIVE CHARACTERISTICS

General Classification

The 61 summer institutes can be readily classified in four ways.

1. *School population served by participants:*	
urban	42
rural	7
urban and rural	12
2. *Participant groups in institutes:*	
teachers and supervisors	30
teachers only	31
3. *Grade level served by participants:*	
preschool	6
preschool through grade 6	17
preschool through grade 9	8
preschool through grade 12	16
grades 7 through 12	14
4. *Major curricular focus of institutes:*	
language arts, English and/or reading	10
other academic fields (mathematics, social studies, Spanish, and various combinations of these with language arts)	5
general (not focused on specific instruction in subject matter fields)	46

Participants

1. *Applications:*	
inquiries	40,606
applications sent out	33,834
applications completed	16,268
institute participants	2,290*
percent applying to only one NDEA institute	70
percent applying to two NDEA institutes	15
percent applying to three NDEA institutes	8
2. *Age ranges:*	
20 to 29	26%
30 to 34	21%
35 to 44	32%
over 45	21%
3. *Sex and marital status:*	
females	59%
males	41%
married	69%
single	31%
4. *Previous education:*	
less than a bachelor's degree	1%
bachelor's degree	66%
master's degree	26%
more than a master's degree	2%
5. *Previous employment:*	
a. Years of teaching experience	
less than 3 years	20%
four to 5 years	16%
six to 10 years	27%
more than 10 years	37%
b. School enrollments represented by participants	
less than 500	30%
500 to 1,000	31%
more than 1,000	39%
c. Type of schools represented by participants	
public school	95%
private school	5%
6. *Academic credit and advanced degrees:*	
working for academic credit	96%
apply institute credit toward degree	46%

* Based on 59 Final Reports received out of a possible 61. The two institutes not included had 98 participants. The true number of participants is actually 2,388, but percentages are based on the 2,290 figure.

Faculty

1. *Source of Faculty:*	
institution of higher education	66%
other (elementary or secondary school, state or private agencies)	34%
institution conducting institute	50%
visiting faculty from other institutions	50%
2. *Percent of faculty participation in institutes:*	
full-time in institute	50%
part-time (range: 1/8 to 4/5)	50%
3. *Faculty-student ratios:*	
mean ratio of full-time equivalent faculty members to participants	1:10
range of full-time equivalent faculty to participants	1:4 to 1:28
4. *Visiting lecturers or consultants:*	
mean number of visiting lecturers per institute	9
range of visiting lecturers per institute	2 to 23

DIRECTORS' COMMENTS

Since the primary purpose of the final report was to obtain the director's evaluation of his institute, freedom was given to each director to select those aspects which he felt most pertinent to his evaluation. The U.S. Office of Education memorandum dealing with the final report did suggest 20 items as examples of relevant evaluative issues, but it did not restrict the director to that list. While most directors followed the suggested 20 items, many initiated their own revisions, allocating great differences in the space and emphasis they gave to each. In this appendix attention is focused on those issues that were repeatedly stressed by directors or on which there was a substantial amount of disagreement.

The issues that dominated the directors' discussion are divided into two categories: Personnel and Program. The numbers in parentheses after each of the following headings indicate how many directors responded to the issue.

Personnel

A. *Participants*

1. QUALITY OF PARTICIPANTS (25): Twenty-two directors expressed concern for the lack of intellectual sophistication of school teachers and had major reservations about the selection process used to choose their participants. They indicated that recommendations from supervisors were

too general and usually omitted any weakness. They wanted a more scientific screening device with more precise questions. They preferred personal interviews with their final candidates and more evidence of each applicant's ability to express himself in writing. They questioned the idea of selecting on the basis of "paper credentials," in favor of recruitment of promising individuals. Five felt that younger teachers profited more from the institutes, and three thought their high admission standards eliminated the very teachers they were contracting to help—those in the poorer schools.

2. LOCAL VS. NATIONAL SELECTION (35): Twenty-eight directors indicated that selecting a team of participants (principals, counselors, key teachers) from each of several selected local schools is preferable to a national representation because it promotes better preplanning, establishes more lasting school-college cooperation, eliminates the necessity of selection solely by "paper credentials," greatly increases reinforcement during and after the institute, and allows for a more effective follow-up.

Five directors thought that national representation of individuals was superior because of its cross-fertilizing effects. Two would use teams of teachers and supervisors from the same schools but would have a national representation of schools.

3. SUPERVISORS AND TEACHERS VS. TEACHERS ONLY (34): Thirty directors would add more supervisors and administrators in another institute; most would team these with teachers from the same school. Two saw a need for a separate institute for administrators, and two thought that administrators should be excluded from institutes.

B. Faculty

1. INSTITUTE STAFFING PATTERNS: Ten directors would have included more secondary school "master" teachers on their faculty. Six emphasized that the major strength of the institute was the interdisciplinary nature of its faculty. Seven felt that visiting staff members are necessary but stressed that they should be full-time in the institute; one said that "qualifications are more important than the question of visiting vs. local faculty." Two indicated that local staff facilitated preplanning and follow-up.

2. FULL-TIME VS. PART-TIME FACULTY (24): Twenty-four directors preferred full- to part-time faculty because they were more available to participants, provided better integration of courses, facilitated a "total institute experience," could be more easily oriented in a team approach, and insured easier communication. These directors felt that part-time faculty had difficulty in identifying with the institute. Three required all staff to be present at all institute courses and activities.

3. GUEST LECTURERS (24): While the average institute had nine guest lecturers for a day or less, ten directors felt that fewer outside lecturers for longer periods of time would be more beneficial. Eleven others, along with most of the previous ten, stressed that speakers should be scheduled more appropriately so that their contributions could coincide with the current phase of the institute's instruction. They also felt that lecturers should

have advance notice of what this phase would be, and that participants should have better preparation on the lecturer's background and writings before his presentation.

Program

A. Institute Grade Span, Size, and Duration

1. GRADE SPAN (19): Generally, those with a large grade span would decrease it. Nine would decrease their grade spread, four would increase it, and six would keep it the same. Only three directors who conducted a K-12 institute would repeat it. The rest would either decrease the spread or have some separate courses for elementary and secondary teachers.

2. SIZE: Most directors thought the number of participants in their institute represented an ideal size. The central mode across all institutes was 30–40 participants. One stated, "The number of participants is of no consequence if the teacher-student ratio is around 1 to 10 (the median ratio among all institutes).

3. DURATION: Directors generally agreed that six to seven weeks during the summer was optimum because of such factors as the availability of participants, commitments of faculty, the necessity for summer vacations, and institute fatigue. Twelve directors who opened their institutes in June recommended a later starting date to give teachers a breather between the end of the school year and the beginning of the institute.

B. Instructional organization

1. COURSE WORK AND RELATED ACTIVITIES (59): Institutes averaged 30 scheduled hours per week, 15 in didactic instruction and 15 in related activities. All institutes had at least one course or instructional unit in Sociology, Psychology, and Curriculum or Materials. The typical Sociology course consisted of Urban, Rural, or General Sociology of the Disadvantaged, with some modifications such as Anthropology, or Literature as a Source of Understanding. Most Psychology courses dealt with psychological foundations of the disadvantaged with such variations as: Diagnosis of Learning Difficulties, Guidance, Mental Health, and the Psychology of Reading. Curriculum or Materials courses centered on the teaching-learning factors of the disadvantaged, such as, Readings for Disadvantaged Children, Remedial Reading, Linguistics, and the teaching of English, Social Studies, Mathematics, or any one specific content area to disadvantaged youth.

The other half of the scheduled time was dominated by some form of involvement activity with disadvantaged children, their parents, or fellow teachers in the institute. Experiences requiring the most direct involvement were the supervised classroom teaching, observation, and field trips; case studies of individuals, groups, or families; individual or small-group tutoring; team-teaching; role-playing; T-group discussion; laboratory demonstration; and home visits. A somewhat lesser degree of personal involvement was also evidenced in such instructional units as: conferences with faculty, community power studies, curriculum projects, construction of teaching materials, and independent study or research.

Twenty-four directors commented on the use of new teaching materials. Seven expressed appreciation for such materials as films, programmed materials, transparencies, individual laboratory kits, tapes, newer books and readers, and techniques for group interaction. Six reported that the development of new materials by participants was a unique feature. Three indicated that having teachers bring to the institute and demonstrate material that they had developed or found effective was most beneficial. Eight thought that the materials available were inadequate or that they would spend more time in another institute developing their own materials.

2. Practicum (47): Twenty-four directors expressed the need for more practice teaching under supervision, stressing the communication problems in the teaching-learning process and more demonstrations of effective teaching practices. Typical recurring comments: "need children who are really disadvantaged," "demonstration classes were too artificial," "lack of superior master teachers, specialists, and supervisors," and "lack of teaching centers on campus."

Fourteen directors stated that the intense, supervised practicum was a definite strength in their institute. They attributed practicum success to the quality of the supervisors, the availability of school facilities, and working within the context of small-group teaching. Nine were appreciative of the cooperation afforded by a preschool program in Head Start, a desegregation program, a Community Action or other O.E.O. program, or any privately operated program for disadvantaged youth. Only one director thought there was "too much observation for experienced teachers."

3. Field trips (30): Even though the average was one field trip per week, 22 directors stated that there were not enough of the type needed. What they seemed to advocate were fewer field trips with greater depth, closer coordination and advance planning with community agencies, better supervision, and more effective matching of field trips and didactic theory.

Five directors stressed the importance of more effective supervision in unifying field trips with interviews, home visits, and research surveys. Three wanted a greater variety of field experiences.

4. Scheduling of participants' time and the necessity of continuous evaluation (49): Thirty-four directors criticized participants' schedules as overstructured, leaving insufficient time for reading, study, research, informal seminars, small-group work, and social activities. Most directors favored "trying to cover less but in more depth." Fifteen others, and many of the above, stated that built-in flexibility contributed to the success of their institute. All recommended some form of continuous evaluation or feedback, such as participant representatives meeting regularly with the institute staff, weekly diaries or logs, or informal feedback through seminar discussions. But most indicated that such evaluations must result in curriculum changes during the institute if they are to be worthwhile.

5. COMMUNICATIONS (43): Thirty-eight directors observed some lack of communication both before and during the institute with participants, staff, lecturers, outside agencies, or with personnel in different components of the program. The need for advanced distribution of reading lists and statements of specific objectives, more thorough preplanning and orientation, more small-group discussion and integrating seminars, and better overall coordination of all facets of the program was made abundantly clear.

Five directors stated that the success of their institute was a result of the close communication among staff and participants. One attributed his success to "having a staff which has been totally involved with the plans of the institute from the start."

6. CONTENT VS. METHODOLOGY, AND THE NEED FOR INTERDISCIPLINARY INTEGRATION: Thirty-eight directors discussed the content vs. method issue, 25 advocating integration, balance, or interaction between the two, using such phrases as "Practicum should be illustrative of theory." Six would emphasize more academic substance, six more teaching skills, and one concluded that "content vs. methods depends on the experiences of the participants."

Twenty-three directors discussed the need for a broader interdisciplinary approach in teacher education, using such phrases as "integration of field work, supervised teaching, demonstration classes, and course work; each demanding experts in different areas." Two said that the major weakness of their institute was "insufficient interdisciplinary integration."

CONCLUSION

In this first summer of NDEA Institutes for Teachers of Disadvantaged Youth, 61 directors found 61 varieties of approach to the challenge in the NDEA legislation: "to offer a specialized program of instruction designed to assist such teachers in coping with the unique and peculiar problems involved in the teaching of such youth." None was content that he had found the answer. All were stimulated by the experience and most suggested substantial modifications for future institute programs. The variety of their approaches and the range of their recommendations indicate that NDEA Institutes are indeed something quite different from the regular summer teaching education programs and supports the contention that we do not yet have a universally accepted model for the education of teachers of disadvantaged youth.

If a synthesis is to be drawn, however, it is the opinion of the authors that institute directors fundamentally agree on the characteristics that distinguish NDEA Institutes from regular university summer courses and further agree on the basic necessities for successful education programs for teachers of the disadvantaged. Directors' recommendations tended to support the original description of the "Distinguishing Characteristics of an Institute" as stated in *NDEA, Title XI, Institutes for Advanced Study,*

A Manual for the Preparation of Proposals, Summer 1966, Academic Year 1966–67. There also was substantial agreement that successful programs for teachers of disadvantaged youth should be based on the following concepts in various organizational patterns:

1. Communication and cooperation among all staff involved is vital—from the planning stages through to completion of the program.

2. Careful attention must be given to the selectiin of participants, since the success of the program depends as much on the intellectual ability and motivation of its students as on the knowledge and energy of its faculty.

3. Both staff and students should understand the objectives of the program and engage in continuous evaluation, which should result in actual curricular organizational adjustments during the course of the program.

4. Some continuous supervised involvement with disadvantaged youth is essential. The proportion of didactic content and theory to practicum will vary according to the objectives of the program, the abilities of the faculty, and the availability of facilities. However, too much of one element, or an inadequate integration of the two, seriously weakens the effectiveness of the program.

APPENDIX K

Responses to Questionnaires

		N = 61	N = 89	N = 59	N = 209
		NDEA[1] *Institutes* (%)	*School Systems* (%)	*Colleges and Universities* (%)	*Total Group* (%)
I. *Rationale of Program*					
A. *Focus: Preparation of school personnel for working—*					
1. In urban areas characterized by low family income, substandard and overcrowded housing, and other evidences of economic deprivation	*N.A.*	16	11	17	14
	Applies	84	89	83	86
2. In rural communities	*N.A.*	66	94	58	76
	Applies	34	6	42	24
3. With migratory workers	*N.A.*	89	97	83	90
	Applies	11	3	17	10
4. With various ethnic groups					
a. Indians	*N.A.*	89	92	80	88
	Applies	11	8	20	12
b. Spanish-speaking Americans	*N.A.*	61	47	59	55
	Applies	39	53	41	45
c. Negroes	*N.A.*	29	8	34	22
	Applies	71	92	66	78
d. Orientals	*N.A.*	96	89	90	91
	Applies	4	11	10	9
e. Other	*N.A.*	74	55	85	69
	Applies	26	45	15	31

[1] NDEA = National Defense Education Act.

Legend: N.A. = No answer
1 = Applies to Program
2 = Important in Program
3 = Key Item in Program

		N = 61 NDEA Institutes (%)	N = 89 Schools (%)	N = 59 Colleges (%)	N = 209 Total Group (%)
B. Purpose					
1. Curriculum development and revision	*N.A.*	29	27	31	29
	1	34	34	32	33
	2	30	23	25	26
	3	7	16	12	12
2. Development/improvement instructional skills, techniques, materials	*N.A.*	2	6	4	4
	1	20	29	27	26
	2	28	29	42	33
	3	50	36	27	37
3. Understanding culture and life conditions of various disadvantaged groups	*N.A.*	—	9	3	5
	1	6	28	24	21
	2	42	32	32	34
	3	52	31	41	40
4. Attitudinal and behavioral change of enrollees	*N.A.*	—	14	7	8
	1	16	33	32	28
	2	17	19	25	20
	3	67	34	36	44
5. Research	*N.A.*	70	67	54	65
	1	23	22	29	24
	2	7	5	12	7
	3	—	6	5	4
6. Other	*N.A.*	81	83	81	82
	1	8	13	14	11
	2	3	1	2	2
	3	8	3	3	5

II. *Organizational Data*

		NDEA Institutes (%)	Schools (%)	Colleges (%)	Total Group (%)
A. Length and time of program					
1. Number of hours per week	*N.A.*	14	38	44	32
	1– 9	2	33	9	17
	10–19	—	5	4	4
	20–29	8	12	16	11
	30–39	42	8	13	20
	40–49	30	1	12	12
	50 and over	4	3	2	4

		N = 61 NDEA *Institutes* (%)	N = 89 *Schools* (%)	N = 59 *Colleges* (%)	N = 209 *Total Group* (%)
2. Number of weeks of operation					
	N.A.	6	60	49	41
	1– 9	94	32	42	52
	10–19	—	7	7	5
	Over 20	—	1	2	2
3. Number of months of operation (if of long duration)					
	N.A.	97	70	74	77
	1– 9	3	9	12	9
	10–19	—	19	10	11
	Over 20	—	2	4	3
4. Held during summer 1965					
	N.A.	6	69	42	43
	Yes	94	31	58	57
5. If ongoing program, date when it started operation					
	N.A.	97	52	49	64
	1932	—	—	2	1
	1933	—	—	2	1
	1942	—	1	—	1
	1954	—	—	2	1
	1957	—	—	2	1
	1959	—	3	2	2
	1960	—	6	2	3
	1961	—	3	—	1
	1962	—	2	2	1
	1963	—	10	8	6
	1964	—	14	12	9
	1965	3	9	17	9
B. Number and type of enrollees					
1. Total enrollment[2]	*N.A.*	—	18	2	8
	Under age 20	2	12	12	9
	20–29	6	10	12	9
	30–39	33	10	20	20
	40–49	35	1	8	13
	50–59	12	5	15	9
	60–69	10	5	3	6
	70 and over	2	39	28	26

[2] The total enrollment was 23,109, with a "No Answer" of 9%. Since the N.A. was larger for the typology of enrollment, the total for various types of enrollees is smaller than the overall total. Extrapolation of 23,109 (91% response) gives an estimated 25,395.

		N = 61 NDEA Institutes (%)	N = 89 Schools (%)	N = 59 Colleges (%)	N = 209 Total Group (%)
				Number	*%*
2. Type of enrollees					
a. Teachers				15,073	73
b. Administrators				2,157	10
c. Counselors, social workers, psychologists				604	3
d. Other school personnel				2,993	14
			Totals:	20,827	100
C. Selection of enrollees					
1. Criteria for eligibility and/or selection					
a. Academic record	*N.A.*	31	90	49	61
	Yes	69	10	51	39
b. Experience with disadvantaged	*N.A.*	16	58	68	49
	Yes	84	42	32	51
c. Appointment to work with disadvantaged	*N.A.*	8	45	56	37
	Yes	92	55	44	63
d. Apparent commitment to goals of program	*N.A.*	12	46	29	31
	Yes	88	54	71	69
e. Superior's recommendation	*N.A.*	6	49	53	38
	Yes	94	51	47	62
f. Other	*N.A.*	59	64	63	62
	Replies	41	36	37	38
2. Procedures for selection of enrollees					
a. Application form	*N.A.*	4	62	22	34
	Yes	96	38	78	66
b. Essay revealing interests, values, and personality	*N.A.*	51	94	80	78
	Yes	49	6	20	22
c. Interviews	*N.A.*	83	71	42	66
	Yes	17	29	58	34
d. References	*N.A.*	23	74	54	54
	Yes	77	26	46	46

		N = 61 NDEA Institutes (%)	N = 89 Schools (%)	N = 59 Colleges (%)	N = 209 Total Group (%)
e. Other	*N.A.*	74	67	64	68
	Yes	26	33	36	32
D. Professional staff working directly with enrollees					
1. Total staff					
	1– 9	45	53	46	49
	10–19	39	8	19	20
	20–29	7	7	7	6
	30–39	2	3	2	3
	Over 40	3	7	3	5
2. Full-time staff					
a. Percent	*N.A.*	5	42	17	24
	1– 9	88	47	73	66
	10–19	5	5	5	5
	20–29	—	2	3	2
	30–39	—	—	—	—
	Over 40	2	4	2	3
b. Number	*N.A.*	3	37	10	50
	1– 9	252	121	129	502
	10–19	32	47	32	111
	20–29	—	42	52	94
	30–39	—	—	—	—
	Over 40	40	1161	44	1,245
	Totals:	324	1371	257	1,952
3. Ratio, full-time staff to enrollees[3] One full-time staff person to every 9.8 enrollees (approximately 1 to 10)					
E. Credit					
1. Is credit given for completion of program?	*N.A.*	3	7	5	5
	Yes	93	31	80	63
	No	4	62	15	32
a. Toward salary increment	*N.A.*	63	73	80	68
	Yes	37	27	20	32
b. Toward degree	*N.A.*	32	90	44	60
	Yes	68	10	56	40

[3] This figure is based upon the extrapolation of 23,109 enrollees (91% response) to 25,395 enrollees, and the extrapolation of 1,952 staff (76% response) to 2,569 staff.

		N = 61 NDEA *Institutes* (%)	N = 89 *Schools* (%)	N = 59 *Colleges* (%)	N = 209 *Total Group* (%)
F. *Financing*					
Total budgets[4]:	NDEA				$ 2,775,980.00
	Schools				14,340,376.00
	Colleges				2,398,107.00
	Total:				$19,514,463.00
Per-capita cost[5] (rough approximation)					$ 1,130.00
G. *Training of subprofessionals* (such as teacher-aides)					
Do you train subprofessionals to work with the disadvantaged?	*N.A.*	2	16	10	11
	Yes	9	42	17	25
	No	89	42	73	64

III. *Instructional Content*

		NDEA Institutes	Schools	Colleges	Total Group
A. *Understanding disadvantaged children and youth*					
1. Culture and traditions of various disadvantaged groups					
a. In general	*N.A.*	4	32	22	21
	1	49	38	37	41
	2	25	20	27	24
	3	22	10	14	14
b. For those groups with which majority of enrollees will be working	*N.A.*	9	25	19	19
	1	14	24	20	20
	2	22	27	17	23
	3	55	24	44	38
2. Life conditions of economically deprived					
a. The world over	*N.A.*	62	75	69	70
	1	36	20	31	28
	2	2	4	—	2
	3	—	1	—	—

[4] Of 209 programs reporting, 64 (32%) did not reply to this question.
[5] This figure is based on the extrapolation of the total budgets from $19,514,000 (68% response) to $28,697,000, and the extrapolated total enrollment from 23,109 (91% response) to 25,395.

		N = 61 NDEA *Institutes* (%)	N = 89 *Schools* (%)	N = 59 *Colleges* (%)	N = 209 *Total Group* (%)
b. For those groups with which majority of enrollees will be working					
	N.A.	3	16	10	11
	1	27	37	25	31
	2	25	27	31	27
	3	45	20	34	31
3. How environmental conditioning may affect—					
a. Hopes and expectations					
	N.A.	3	12	11	9
	1	19	38	32	31
	2	35	27	32	31
	3	43	23	25	29
b. Self-image	*N.A.*	1	10	7	7
	1	11	29	29	24
	2	30	23	35	28
	3	58	38	29	41
c. Communication skills					
	N.A.	—	9	2	4
	1	2	24	27	19
	2	32	21	34	28
	3	66	46	37	49
d. Variety of behavior patterns					
	N.A.	2	14	6	9
	1	17	30	31	26
	2	37	35	36	35
	3	44	21	27	30
4. How accepting or rejecting attitudes of teachers, often at unconscious level, may affect motivation and learning of children and youth					
	N.A.	—	12	5	7
	1	6	19	27	18
	2	23	25	22	23
	3	71	44	46	52
5. Other	*N.A.*	92	92	93	92
	1	3	4	4	3
	2	—	1	—	1
	3	5	3	3	4
B. Situational factors of concern to teachers					
1. Family life	*N.A.*	—	13	5	7
	1	24	39	37	35
	2	30	33	34	32
	3	46	15	24	26

		N = 61 NDEA Institutes (%)	N = 89 Schools (%)	N = 59 Colleges (%)	N = 209 Total Group (%)
2. Peer groups	*N.A.*	11	20	12	15
	1	26	40	39	36
	2	40	23	35	31
	3	23	17	14	18
3. Social structure and stratification	*N.A.*	4	25	12	15
	1	26	45	34	37
	2	32	19	39	28
	3	38	11	15	20
4. Community organization	*N.A.*	2	33	22	21
	1	38	36	44	39
	2	45	16	25	27
	3	15	15	9	13
5. School-community relations	*N.A.*	4	15	15	12
	1	13	36	42	31
	2	46	30	24	33
	3	37	19	19	24
6. Group process	*N.A.*	12	35	17	23
	1	33	30	46	35
	2	30	22	20	24
	3	25	13	17	18
7. Analysis of social conflict	*N.A.*	12	47	31	32
	1	46	38	39	41
	2	20	8	20	15
	3	22	7	10	12
8. Youth in an era of rapid technological change	*N.A.*	25	45	27	34
	1	35	30	42	35
	2	25	13	19	18
	3	15	12	12	13
9. Other	*N.A.*	89	97	90	92
	1	5	3	7	5
	2	3	—	—	1
	3	3	—	3	2
C. *Professional competence of teachers of the disadvantaged*					
1. The need for understanding self as essential to understanding and relating to others	*N.A.*	—	12	10	8
	1	17	39	32	31
	2	26	24	29	26
	3	57	25	29	35
2. The need for developing ego strength so as to deal					

		N = 61 NDEA *Institutes* (%)	N = 89 *Schools* (%)	N = 59 *Colleges* (%)	N = 209 *Total Group* (%)
effectively with the wide variety of environmentally conditioned behavior	*N.A.*	8	20	17	15
	1	29	44	37	38
	2	28	17	31	24
	3	35	19	15	23
3. Self insights as to gratifications and unique satisfactions each individual seeks from teaching	*N.A.*	7	26	15	17
	1	45	37	46	42
	2	18	21	20	20
	3	30	16	19	21
4. Other	*N.A.*	89	93	96	93
	1	—	6	—	2
	2	3	—	2	2
	3	8	1	2	3
D. *Conceptual framework*					
1. The interests-and-needs approach	*N.A.*	6	25	14	16
	1	30	23	30	27
	2	38	37	34	37
	3	26	15	22	20
2. The evolving curriculum based on day-to-day experience	*N.A.*	12	29	25	23
	1	27	28	44	32
	2	30	25	21	25
	3	31	18	10	20
3. Strategies for developing values consistent with the needs of present-day democratic society	*N.A.*	7	28	15	19
	1	30	31	34	31
	2	42	24	36	32
	3	21	17	15	18
4. Strategies for bringing about behavior changes consonant with such values	*N.A.*	11	31	15	21
	1	23	35	27	29
	2	43	19	39	32
	3	23	15	19	18
5. Use of symbolism in instructional materials	*N.A.*	34	55	32	42
	1	30	25	37	30
	2	20	12	17	16
	3	16	8	14	12

		N = 61 NDEA *Institutes* (%)	N = 89 *Schools* (%)	N = 59 *Colleges* (%)	N = 209 *Total Group* (%)
6. Emphasis upon discovery by children through experiments and problem solving, as opposed to being told	*N.A.*	6	24	15	16
	1	15	30	34	27
	2	23	17	25	21
	3	56	29	26	36
7. Attention to individual growth patterns	*N.A.*	4	20	4	11
	1	21	36	41	33
	2	22	18	36	24
	3	53	26	19	32
8. Concept that every teacher is also a counselor	*N.A.*	21	18	20	20
	1	32	43	63	45
	2	28	27	8	22
	3	19	12	9	13
9. Other	*N.A.*	92	97	95	94
	1	2	1	2	2
	2	4	—	—	2
	3	2	2	3	2
E. *Instructional techniques*					
1. Team teaching	*N.A.*	29	56	42	44
	1	25	28	31	28
	2	27	7	17	15
	3	19	9	10	13
2. Teacher-pupil planning and evaluation	*N.A.*	24	39	17	29
	1	30	33	49	36
	2	30	12	22	20
	3	16	16	12	15
3. Establishing the work climate	*N.A.*	17	29	20	23
	1	27	28	36	30
	2	18	20	25	21
	3	38	23	19	26
4. Field trips	*N.A.*	7	27	15	18
	1	32	39	37	37
	2	26	20	24	23
	3	35	14	24	22
5. Project-centered learning	*N.A.*	37	42	20	35
	1	21	34	43	33
	2	25	17	20	20
	3	17	7	17	12

	N = 61 NDEA *Institutes* (%)	N = 89 *Schools* (%)	N = 59 *Colleges* (%)	N = 209 *Total Group* (%)
6. Committee activity and special assignments				
N.A.	24	47	27	35
1	30	36	49	38
2	25	9	15	15
3	21	8	9	12
7. Discussion techniques				
N.A.	9	24	10	16
1	20	36	44	34
2	30	16	32	24
3	41	24	14	26
8. Programmed teaching				
N.A.	52	67	56	60
1	36	25	37	31
2	10	6	5	7
3	2	2	2	2
9. Role playing *N.A.*	20	36	29	30
1	33	41	42	39
2	22	17	17	18
3	25	6	12	13
10. Structured and dramatic presentations *N.A.*	41	48	46	45
1	26	34	30	30
2	23	11	12	15
3	10	7	12	10
11. Films, television, and other media *N.A.*	14	24	15	18
1	35	44	49	43
2	23	20	19	21
3	28	12	17	18
12. Other *N.A.*	84	83	85	84
1	—	17	10	10
2	1	—	—	—
3	15	—	5	6
F. Instructional materials				
1. Testing existing materials				
N.A.	27	50	29	37
1	38	31	46	37
2	22	11	17	16
3	13	8	8	10
2. Developing new materials				
N.A.	24	40	20	30
1	28	26	46	32
2	16	16	15	16
3	32	18	19	22
3. Other *N.A.*	86	90	85	87
1	4	10	12	9
2	3	—	3	2
3	7	—	—	2

		N = 61 NDEA Institutes (%)	N = 89 Schools (%)	N = 59 Colleges (%)	N = 209 Total Group (%)
G. *Special subject matter enrollees are being prepared to teach*					
1. Reading	*N.A.*	39	51	44	46
	1	23	27	32	27
	2	15	7	5	9
	3	23	15	19	18
2. English as a foreign language	*N.A.*	91	86	80	86
	1	3	7	15	8
	2	3	2	—	2
	3	3	5	5	4
3. Modern foreign languages	*N.A.*	96	91	80	89
	1	2	9	15	9
	2	—	—	3	1
	3	2	—	2	1
4. Social studies	*N.A.*	54	68	39	56
	1	31	25	46	32
	2	7	2	10	6
	3	8	5	5	6
5. Science	*N.A.*	71	75	46	66
	1	19	19	44	26
	2	7	2	7	5
	3	3	4	3	3
6. Mathematics	*N.A.*	65	65	44	59
	1	18	24	42	27
	2	12	—	9	6
	3	5	11	5	8
7. Geography	*N.A.*	84	85	63	79
	1	11	14	32	18
	2	3	1	3	2
	3	2	—	2	1
8. Educational media	*N.A.*	87	84	71	81
	1	7	9	22	12
	2	4	5	2	4
	3	2	2	5	3
9. Other	*N.A.*	79	82	66	76
	1	11	17	29	19
	2	—	1	—	1
	3	10	—	5	4

IV. *Instructional Process*

A. *Specific procedures*

1. Lectures by visitors	*N.A.*	—	32	10	16
	1	24	45	46	39
	2	41	13	25	25
	3	35	10	19	20

		N = 61 NDEA *Institutes* (%)	N = 89 *Schools* (%)	N = 59 *Colleges* (%)	N = 209 *Total Group* (%)
2. Lectures by program faculty	*N.A.*	4	36	17	21
	1	16	35	29	28
	2	27	16	37	25
	3	53	13	17	26
3. General discussion	*N.A.*	3	13	—	7
	1	24	42	37	35
	2	40	16	32	27
	3	33	29	31	31
4. Small-group discussion	*N.A.*	3	14	5	9
	1	10	29	27	23
	2	33	24	34	29
	3	54	33	34	39
5. Group counseling sessions	*N.A.*	47	63	56	57
	1	28	18	34	25
	2	12	14	5	11
	3	13	5	5	7
6. T-groups for self-awareness	*N.A.*	72	79	78	77
	1	10	15	12	12
	2	8	4	7	6
	3	10	2	3	5
7. Field trips for observation of community	*N.A.*	6	46	18	27
	1	29	28	41	32
	2	33	19	22	24
	3	32	7	19	17
8. Field experience with involvement in community affairs	*N.A.*	42	66	49	55
	1	13	18	24	18
	2	10	9	12	10
	3	35	7	15	17
9. Field experience in teaching	*N.A.*	35	73	47	54
	1	13	15	17	15
	2	12	4	9	8
	3	40	8	27	23
10. Practicum (closely supervised teaching and/or counseling)	*N.A.*	43	74	46	58
	1	5	7	10	7
	2	15	4	10	9
	3	37	15	34	26

		N = 61 NDEA *Institutes* (%)	N = 89 *Schools* (%)	N = 59 *Colleges* (%)	N = 209 *Total Group* (%)
11. Home visits	*N.A.*	40	57	59	53
	1	16	21	24	21
	2	27	16	10	17
	3	17	6	7	9
12. Case studies	*N.A.*	38	59	39	47
	1	27	24	44	31
	2	20	11	12	14
	3	15	6	5	8
13. Research	*N.A.*	59	63	51	58
	1	23	27	29	26
	2	15	8	10	11
	3	3	2	10	5
14. Reports of reading	*N.A.*	29	52	34	40
	1	31	30	44	34
	2	22	15	12	16
	3	18	3	10	10
15. Preparation of papers	*N.A.*	22	76	42	51
	1	37	15	29	25
	2	23	7	20	15
	3	18	2	9	9
16. Preparation of daily log	*N.A.*	63	76	66	70
	1	15	17	19	17
	2	8	7	7	7
	3	14	—	8	6
17. Individual conferences	*N.A.*	17	48	19	31
	1	33	27	32	30
	2	33	15	29	24
	3	17	10	20	15
18. Scheduled study time	*N.A.*	60	85	73	75
	1	23	14	20	18
	2	17	1	5	7
	3	—	—	2	—
19. Free time for socializing and recreation	*N.A.*	19	76	54	54
	1	46	23	31	31
	2	27	—	12	11
	3	8	1	3	4
20. Other	*N.A.*	89	87	76	84
	1	3	12	12	10
	2	1	1	3	2
	3	7	—	9	4

		N = 61 NDEA Institutes (%)	N = 89 Schools (%)	N = 59 Colleges (%)	N = 209 Total Group (%)
V. *Methods of Program Evaluation Used*					
A. *Feedback from enrollees during program*					
1. Written	*N.A.*	3	34	19	21
	Yes	97	66	81	79
2. Discussion	*N.A.*	2	13	12	10
	Yes	98	87	88	90
3. Faculty present?	*N.A.*	8	35	10	20
	Yes	84	56	85	72
	No	8	9	5	8
4. Is feedback an important consideration in developing program?	*N.A.*	4	12	9	9
	Yes	94	82	86	87
	No	2	6	5	4
B. *Plan for follow-up with enrollees after program*					
1. Personal contracts	*N.A.*	31	38	37	36
	Yes	69	62	63	64
2. Letter or questionnaire	*N.A.*	23	66	58	51
	Yes	77	34	42	49
3. Class visitation	*N.A.*	61	48	64	56
	Yes	39	52	36	44
4. Group reunion	*N.A.*	54	76	71	68
	Yes	46	24	29	32
5. Other	*N.A.*	89	90	80	87
	Replies	11	10	20	13
6. Is follow-up an important consideration for future program development?	*N.A.*	12	26	19	20
	Yes	86	70	69	74
	No	2	4	12	6
C. *Evaluation of professional staff*					
1. Written	*N.A.*	39	54	51	49
	Yes	61	46	49	51
2. In staff meetings	*N.A.*	4	29	32	23
	Yes	96	71	68	77
3. Is staff evaluation an important consideration in developing program?	*N.A.*	1	21	25	17
	Yes	99	79	75	83
	No	—	—	—	—

APPENDIX L

Relative Importance of Instructional Content and Process Areas (Form B)

	Percent of those who judged items important (double- or triple-checked)			
	N = 61 NDEA Institutes (%)	N = 89 School Systems (%)	N = 59 Colleges and Universities (%)	N = 209 Total Group (%)
III. *Instructional Content*				
A. *Understanding disadvantaged children and youth*				
1. Culture and traditions of various disadvantaged groups				
a. In general	47	30	41	38
b. For those groups with which majority of enrollees will be working	77	51	61	61
2. Life conditions of economically deprived				
a. The world over	2	5	—	2
b. For those groups with which majority of enrollees will be working	70	47	65	58
3. How environmental conditioning may affect				
a. Hopes and expectations	78	50	57	60
b. Self-image	88	61	64	69
c. Communication skills	98	67	71	77
d. Variety of behavior patterns	81	56	63	65
4. How accepting or rejecting attitudes of teachers, often at unconscious level, may affect motivation and learning of children and youth	94	69	68	75
5. Other	5	4	3	5

	Percent double- or triple-checked			
	N = 61 NDEA *Institutes* (%)	N = 89 *Schools* (%)	N = 59 *Colleges* (%)	N = 209 *Total Group* (%)
B. Situational factors of concern to teachers				
1. Family life	76	48	58	58
2. Peer groups	63	40	49	49
3. Social stratification	70	30	54	48
4. Community organization	60	31	34	40
5. School-community relations	83	49	43	57
6. Group process	55	35	37	42
7. Analysis of social conflict	42	15	30	27
8. Youth in an era of technological change	40	25	31	31
9. Other	6	—	3	3
C. Professional competence of teachers of the disadvantaged				
1. The need for understanding self as essential to understanding and relating to others	83	49	58	61
2. The need for developing ego strength so as to deal effectively with the wide variety of environmentally conditioned behavior	63	36	46	47
3. Self insights as to gratifications and unique satisfactions each individual seeks from teaching	48	37	39	41
4. Other	11	1	4	5
D. Conceptual framework				
1. The interests-and-needs approach	64	52	56	57
2. The evolving curriculum based on day-to-day experience	61	43	31	45
3. Strategies for developing values consistent with the needs of present-day democratic society	63	41	51	50
4. Strategies for bringing about behavioral changes consonant with such values	66	34	58	50

	Percent double- or triple-checked			
	N = 61 NDEA *Institutes* (%)	N = 89 *Schools* (%)	N = 59 *Colleges* (%)	N = 209 *Total Group* (%)
5. Use of symbolism in instructional materials	36	20	31	28
6. Emphasis upon discovery by children through experiments and problem solving as opposed to being told	79	46	51	57
7. Attention to individual growth patterns	75	44	55	56
8. Concept that every teacher is also a counselor	47	39	17	35
9. Other	6	2	3	4
E. *Instructional techniques*				
1. Team teaching	46	16	27	28
2. Teacher-pupil planning and evaluation	46	28	34	35
3. Establishing the work climate	56	43	44	47
4. Field trips	61	34	48	45
5. Project-centered learning	42	24	37	32
6. Committee activity and special assignments	46	17	24	27
7. Discussion techniques	71	40	46	50
8. Programmed teaching	12	8	7	9
9. Role playing	47	23	29	31
10. Structured and dramatic presentation	33	18	24	25
11. Films, television, and other media	51	32	36	39
12. Other	6	—	5	6
F. *Instructional materials*				
1. Testing existing materials	35	19	25	26
2. Developing new materials	48	34	34	38
3. Other	10	—	3	4
G. *Special subject matter enrollees are being prepared to teach*				
1. Reading	38	22	24	27

	Percent double- and triple-checked			
	N = 61 NDEA *Institutes* (%)	N = 89 *Schools* (%)	N = 59 *Colleges* (%)	N = 209 *Total Group* (%)
2. English as a foreign language	6	7	5	6
3. Modern foreign languages	2	—	5	2
4. Social studies	15	7	15	12
5. Science	10	6	10	8
6. Mathematics	17	11	14	14
7. Geography	5	1	5	3
8. Educational media	6	7	7	7
9. Other	10	1	5	5
IV. Instructional Process				
A. *Specific procedures*				
1. Lectures by visitors	76	23	44	45
2. Lectures by program faculty	80	29	54	51
3. General discussion	73	45	63	58
4. Small-group discussion	87	57	68	68
5. Group counseling sessions	25	19	10	18
6. T-group for self-awareness	18	6	10	11
7. Field trips for observation of community	65	26	41	41
8. Field experience with involvement in community	45	16	27	27
9. Field experience in teaching	52	12	36	31
10. Practicum (closely supervised teaching and/or counseling)	52	19	44	35
11. Home visits	44	22	17	26
12. Case studies	35	17	17	22
13. Research	18	10	20	16
14. Reports of reading	40	18	22	26
15. Preparation of papers	41	9	29	24
16. Preparation of daily log	22	7	15	13
17. Individual conferences	50	25	49	39
18. Scheduled study time	17	1	7	7
19. Free time for socializing and recreation	35	1	15	15
20. Other	8	1	12	6

Bibliographies

A Selected Bibliography on the Preparation of School Personnel for Working with Disadvantaged Children and Youth

Books

Action for Improvement of Teacher Education: Proceedings of the 18th Annual Meeting of the American Association of Colleges of Teacher Education, Washington, D.C., 1965, pp. 111–125.

Taking its discussion points from a synthetic proposal for teacher preparation to work with disadvantaged children distributed earlier, a panel of experienced educators raises questions and formulates some tentative programmatic approaches to be tried in institutes preparing teachers for schools in deprived communities. Among approaches discussed are: joint planning by teachers and administrators, school-community liaison, the use of nonprofessionals in the classroom, and the identification of methods and materials most appropriate for work with the disadvantaged.

Ashton-Warner, Sylvia: TEACHER, Simon & Schuster, New York, 1963.

An unusual teaching method for reading based on the emotional needs of the individual child, which was successfully used by the author with Maori children in New Zealand, has implications for the teaching of the disadvantaged.

Chandler, B. J. *et al.:* EDUCATION IN URBAN SOCIETY, Dodd, Mead, & Co., New York, 1962, pp. 226–229.

In this book of essays describing the forces which influence the schools, the authors describe how Chicago helps its inexperienced new teachers in slum schools.

CHANGES IN TEACHER EDUCATION: AN APPRAISAL, National Commission on Teacher Education and Professional Standards, Washington, D.C., 1963, pp. 228–239, 323–241.

Two articles deal with attempts by city colleges and universities to find better ways to prepare teachers for disadvantaged schools.

Clift, V. A., Anderson, A. W., and Hullfish, H. G. (eds.): NEGRO EDUCATION IN AMERICA, Harper & Row, New York, 1962, pp. 78–81.

A description is presented of what the Negro colleges are contributing to the area of teacher education.

Greene, Mary Frances, and Ryan, Orletta: THE SCHOOL CHILDREN, Pantheon Books, New York, N.Y., 1965.

In this record of day-to-day life in classrooms in East Harlem and Harlem, two teachers vividly report both the problems children in the ghetto face and their coping strategies. The book raises the question, what should the role of the teacher become so as to ameliorate some of the problems faced by schools in the ghetto?

Havighurst, Robert J.: THE PUBLIC SCHOOLS OF CHICAGO, Chicago Board of Education, 1964, pp. 338–354, 411–422.

An assessment is made by the author of the current situation in the schools in Chicago and recommendations for action are presented. Included is a study of the Chicago teacher and his view of his job, with implications for teacher education.

Hodenfield, G. K., and Stinnett, T. M.: THE EDUCATION OF TEACHERS, Prentice-Hall, Englewood Cliffs, N.J., 1961, pp. 66–68, 86–87.

A summary of three conferences of the NCTEPS refers to teacher preparation for big city schools.

Hunnicutt, C. W. (ed.): URBAN EDUCATION AND CULTURAL DEPRIVATION, Syracuse University School of Education, Syracuse, N.Y., 1964.

Proceedings of a conference held at Syracuse University in the summer of 1964. Part IV, "The School," presents a program by Frank Riessman giving a five-part plan for the training of both preservice and inservice teachers of urban disadvantaged youth. Among these are attitude change through interest, the use of appropriate teaching technologies, and the special significance of role-playing for the disadvantaged student.

Jewett, Arno, Mersand, Joseph, and Gunderson, Doris V. (eds.): IMPROVING ENGLISH SKILLS OF CULTURALLY DIFFERENT YOUTH IN LARGE CITIES, U.S. Department of Health, Education, and Welfare, Office of Education Bulletin No. 5, Government Printing Office, Washington, D.C., 1964.

The authors deal with the selection and preparation of teachers, and the professional and personal qualifications needed in order to serve effectively in schools for disadvantaged youth.

Kerber, August, and Bommarito, Barbara (eds.): THE SCHOOLS AND THE URBAN CRISIS, Holt, Rinehart & Winston, New York, 1965, pp. 219–221, 230–237, 256–257.

Implications for teacher preparation for working in slum schools thread the entire book, especially Chapter V, "The Teacher and the Urban School."

Klopf, Gordon J., and Laster, Israel A. (eds.): INTEGRATING THE URBAN SCHOOL, Teachers College, Columbia University, New York, 1963, pp. 18–25.

Six contributors make 30 recommendations for overall consideration relating to urban education, including those for the preparation of teachers for inner-city schools.

Kornberg, L. (ed.): BRIDGES TO SLUM-GHETTO CHILDREN, Queens College (A BRIDGE Project publication, No. 3), New York, 1962.

Teachers-in-training for slum schools relate their experiences in student-teaching.

Landes, Ruth: CULTURE IN AMERICAN EDUCATION, John Wiley & Sons, Inc., New York, N.Y., 1966.

This is a report of an experimental teacher training program in areas with minority group students which is based on an anthropological and social work approach.

Language Programs for the Disadvantaged, Report of National Council for Teachers of English Task Force on Teaching English to the Disadvantaged, Champaign, Illinois, 1965.

In the chapter, "Teacher Education," Task Force members report a lack of congruence in teacher preparation for work with the disadvantaged, and biases relating to culture, norms, and course content. Remedies attempted in programs such as the NDEA Institutes for Teachers of the Disadvantaged are described. Recommendations made by the Task Force emphasize inservice preparation, background training in sociological learnings, and the use of appropriate literature in classes containing disadvantaged children.

Masoner, Paul H.: A DESIGN FOR TEACHER EDUCATION, University of Pittsburgh Press, 1963.

The author describes the total educational experience leading to entry into the teaching profession and to preparation of the candidate for current and future changes and needs of children. This book is oriented to the education of teachers for the disadvantaged.

McGeogh, Dorothy, *et al.:* LEARNING TO TEACH IN URBAN SCHOOLS, Teachers College, Columbia University, New York, 1965.

Four second-year teachers describe their experiences in New York City schools for the disadvantaged. Dr. McGeogh points out implications for preparation of teachers in similar schools.

Miller, Harry B., and Smiley, Marjorie R. (eds.): EDUCATION AND THE METROPOLIS: A BOOK OF READINGS, Hunter College (Project TRUE), New York, 1964.

Part III discusses the challenge to the teacher in teaching in urban schools.

Moore, G. Alexander, Jr.: URBAN SCHOOL DAYS, Hunter College, (A Project TRUE publication), New York, 1964.

This is a teacher trainee handbook based on field observations of classroom behavior for the prospective teacher entering urban disadvantaged schools for the first time.

Noar, Gertrude: TEACHING AND LEARNING THE DEMOCRATIC WAY, Prentice-Hall, Englewood Cliffs, N.J., 1963, pp. 119–121.

The chapter, "Facts Teachers Need," has implications for the preparation of those who will be working in disadvantaged schools.

Passow, A. Harry (ed.): EDUCATION IN DEPRESSED AREAS, Teachers College, Columbia University, New York, 1963, pp. 243–277.

Part II, "Teachers for Depressed Areas," presents suggestions for changes in teacher preparation to meet today's conditions in big city schools, and discusses what strategies teachers must learn.

The Preparation of Teachers for Schools in Culturally Depressed Neighborhoods, Queens College of the City University of New York (The BRIDGE Project), 1965.

Chapters 3 and 11 discuss the teacher preparation program for urban teaching and the important role of the coordinator as a resource person for the beginning teacher.

Riessman, Frank: The Culturally Deprived Child, Harper & Row, New York, 1962, pp. 81–97.
The author describes the kind of teacher who works successfully with the disadvantaged child and illustrates the methods used.

Strom, Robert S.: Teaching in the Slum School, Charles E. Merrill Books, Inc., Columbus, Ohio, 1965, pp. 30–46, 99–107.
The author offers many ideas for the improvement of teacher preparation in order to effect a reversal "from deprivation to dignity" in the slum schools.

——— (ed.): The Inner-City Classroom: Teacher Behaviors, Charles E. Merrill Books, Inc., Columbus, Ohio, 1966.
In this series of essays describing teacher behavior in classrooms of inner-city schools, various authors make proposals for needed changes.

Sutton, Elizabeth: Knowing and Teaching the Migrant Child, National Education Association, Department of Rural Education, Washington, D.C., 1962.
This book, an outgrowth of a special project in Virginia and Florida on the education of the children of agricultural migratory workers, offers the conclusions of the supervisor and the teachers involved as they relate to procedures for teaching migrant children and suggestions for preparing teachers to work with them.

Urban School Days, Hunter College of the City University of New York (Project TRUE), 1964.
An introduction is given to first-year teachers and prospective teachers in inner-city schools about what to expect and how to cope with problems.

Wood, Helen Cowan: Teaching Children Who Move with the Crops, Fresno County Project, The Educttional Program for Migrant Children, Office of the County School Superintendent, Fresno, Calif., 1955.
Directed to teachers of migrants and prospective teachers, this book suggests techniques that have proved effective for working successfully with migrant children and offers suggestions for teacher preparation programs.

Usdan, Michael D., and Bertolaet, Frederick (eds.): Teachers of the Disadvantaged, Follett Publishing Co., Chicago, Ill., 1966, pp. 59–92.
A report of Task Force II of the School-University Teacher Education Project of the Research Council of the Great Cities Program for School Improvement in Cooperation with Northwestern University contains position papers on new methods to prepare teachers for urban schools by Harry Rivlin and Martin Haberman. Five major changes are suggested in areas of pretenure and continuing education, undergraduate focus on specific skills, assignment of selected school personnel, renumeration, and school-college cooperation, as well as four critical areas to be evaluated in the professional sequence for urban teacher preparation.

Articles in Journals and Periodicals

Arnez, N. L.: "Effect of Teacher Attitudes on the Culturally Different," *School and Society,* Vol. 94, March 19, 1966, pp. 149–152.

In this article an experienced teacher points up the need for change in attitude on the part of those working or preparing to work with the disadvantaged. His thesis is that curriculum modification must follow, not precede, attitude change.

Asbell, Bernard: "Not Like Other Children," *Redbook*, October 1963, pp. 65, 114–118, 120.

The author describes several teaching methods effective with disadvantaged children.

Ellis, Richard R.: "Looking toward Desired Behavior in Teachers of the Disadvantaged," *Urban Education*, Vol. I, No. 2, Winter, 1965.

This article, in a brief overview of the sociological and psychological research findings of the Institute for Developmental Studies and other programs, yields implications for training and orientation of teachers to work with disadvantaged children.

Fink, D. R., Jr.: "Selection and Training of Teachers for Teams," *National Elementary School Principal*, January 1965, pp. 54–59.

There are special advantages which team teaching holds for the disadvantaged, according to the author, who enumerates them.

Frazier, Alexander: "Teaching the Culturally Deprived," *National Elementary School Principal*, February 1963, pp. 16–19.

This article is based on a study guide developed for use with staffs of selected elementary schools and illustrates what teachers should be aware of when teaching the disadvantaged.

Frost, J. L.: "Schools and the Migrant Child," *Childhood Education*, November 1964, pp. 129–132.

Educational programs built on the life experiences of migrant children are urged by the author, who offers some guidelines for the teacher.

Gage, N. L.: "Desirable Behaviors of Teachers," *Urban Education*, Winter, 1965, pp. 85–94.

The author cites teacher behaviors required for satisfactory teacher performance in disadvantaged urban schools.

———: "Psychological Research on Teacher Education in the Great Cities," *Urban Education*, Vol. I, No. 3, Spring, 1965, pp. 175–195.

In addition to research based upon pupil characteristics, teaching methods, and teacher personality, the author suggests other pertinent areas and methodology such as a survey of student attitudes in teacher education programs. He advocates implementation of "practical wisdom" to help ease teacher shortage for work in disadvantaged urban neighborhoods.

Goldberg, Miriam L.: "Adapting Teacher Style to Pupil Differences: Teachers for Disadvantaged Children," *Merrill Palmer Quarterly*, April 1964, pp. 162–178.

A hypothetical model of a teacher for the disadvantaged is drawn by the author.

Gordon, Edmund W.: "A Review of Programs of Compensatory Education," *American Journal of Orthopsychiatry*, Vol. XXXV, No. 4, July 1965.

After an examination of current approaches to "compensatory education" for disadvantaged children, among them improved teacher recruitment and training, the author reports the lack of truly innovative approaches in the areas of improving teacher competence and behavior. He states the most productive approach as that which emphasizes provision of new and improved methods and techniques for teachers. It is difficult for teachers to remain indifferent when their efforts meet with success. Responsibility for success in the academic venture must be placed where he believes it belongs—not on the learner, but on the school system.

Greene, M.: "Teacher and the Negro Child: Invisibility in the School," *Educational Forum,* March 1965, pp. 275–280.
The author suggests how teachers can better prepare themselves to recognize the meaning and pain of "facelessness," as experienced by the Negro child.

Groff, Patrick J.: "Dissatisfactions in Teaching the Culturally Different Child," *Phi Delta Kappan,* November 1963, p. 76.
Analyzing the responses of 294 teachers in 16 schools serving Negro and Mexican-American ghettos, the author gives reasons for the large turnover of teachers in slum areas.

Haubrich, Vernon F.: "The Culturally Different: New Context for Teacher Education," *Journal of Teacher Education,* June 1963, pp. 163–168.
The author presents a description of the special Hunter College teacher preparation program for teachers of the disadvantaged, and calls for the revision of professional preparation for teachers of these children.

———: "The Culturally Disadvantaged and Teacher Education," *The Reading Teacher,* March 1965, pp. 499–506.
Guidelines for effective teacher preparation are furnished, with special recommendations for institutions that prepare teachers to work with disadvantaged children and youth.

Hayes, Charles: "Team Teaching in Culturally Deprived Areas," *National Elementary School Principal,* January 1965, pp. 60–65.
An analysis of team-teaching organization in Pittsburgh that spells out the roles of the teacher personnel involved is presented by the author.

Hott, Irving: "School Administrator and the Educationally Disadvantaged Child," *Bulletin of the National Association of Secondary School Principals,* March 1964, pp. 85–98.
The author maintains that the efforts of the school administrative staff, pupil-personnel staff, and instructional staff must be coordinated in order to meet the needs of the disadvantaged child.

Johnson, G. Orville: "Organizing Instruction and Curriculum Planning for the Socially Disadvantaged," *Journal of Negro Education,* Summer, 1964, pp. 260–263.
Asserting that no dichotomy exists between instruction and curriculum, as they are interdependent, the author pleads for carefully designed programs for children whose educational needs are unique and lists factors that are important in the teaching of the disadvantaged.

Kavaraceus, William C.: "Programs for the Disadvantaged: Promise or Pretense?" *National Elementary Principal,* Vol. 45, February 1966, pp. 64–69.

The author stresses the need for teachers to carry on their own action-research, citing 12 operational principles found to be effective, and discusses the "instructional interview," whereby the teacher, making a task analysis, enables teacher and learner to enter a dialogue leading to a more accurate diagnosis of learning needs.

Kirman, Joseph M.: "Teacher Survival in Difficult Schools," *High Points,* No. 4, 1964, pp. 69–70.

The author presents useful techniques to the teacher to replace unsuccessful middle-class-oriented approaches to disadvantaged children.

Kornberg, Leonard: "Slum Children and New Teachers," *Journal of Negro Education,* Spring, 1964, pp. 74–81.

This report of a "case conference" in supervision in a difficult school demonstrates the type of inservice training which creates a bridge between the new teacher in the slum and the professor of education.

Landers, Jacob: "The Responsibilities of Teachers and School Administrators," *Journal of Negro Education,* Summer, 1964, pp. 318–332.

Schools must be organized and teachers prepared to "redress the social balance for the disadvantaged," asserts the author, setting forth the necessary tasks in order for that result to be achieved.

Loretan, J. O.: "Problems in Improving Educational Opportunities for Puerto Ricans in New York," *High Points,* May 1963, p. 31.

In describing the educational program for the over 100,000 Puerto Rican children in the elementary and junior high schools of New York City, the author outlines the special teacher training project that is part of the program.

Mayer, Martin: "Schools, Slums, and Montessori," *Commentary,* June 1964, pp. 33–39.

The author recommends the Montessori method as one approach for teachers to use with slum children.

McCreary, Eugene: "Learning To Teach Deprived Children," *Integrated Education,* April 1963, pp. 38–40.

This is a description of an extension course entitled "Problems of the Culturally Handicapped Child," for the experienced teacher as well as the supervisor.

Rabinow, Barney: "Training Program for Teachers of the Emotionally Disturbed and Socially Maladjusted," *Exceptional Children,* February 1960, pp. 287–293.

Eight fields of training for "special" teachers in both content and method are surveyed by the author with implications for teachers of the disadvantaged.

Riessman, Frank: "Some Suggestions for Teaching the Culturally Deprived," *National Education Association Journal,* April 1963, pp. 20–22.

Teachers who are successful with the disadvantaged generally combine the traditional concept of order and the newer "learning by doing" approach, in the view of the author.

Rivlin, Harry H. (ed.): "Teacher and Teacher Education for Urban Disadvantaged Schools," *Journal of Teacher Education,* June 1965, pp. 135–192.

Teachers and administrators contribute to the special section in this issue and discuss effective ways of dealing with problems of the disadvantaged. In addition, two professors of education analyze the contributions and make recommendations for schools of education.

Smiley, Marjorie B.: "Who Would Teach Here," *PTA Magazine,* September 1963, pp. 16–19.

Quoting from Walt Whitman, "Who would teach here must well prepare himself, body and mind," the author pleads for better preparation for teachers of the disadvantaged.

Strickler, Robert W.: "Follow Through with the First-Year Teacher," *Educational Administration and Supervision,* January 1950, pp. 1–6.

". . . the degree to which adjustment is satisfactory to the individual first-year teacher . . . affects the quality of his service to the school, his decision to remain in the system, and may determine whether or not he continues in the profession." Suggestions are made for intensive inservice education specifically and solely for the first-year teacher, particularly in disadvantaged schools.

Tenenbaum, Samuel: "The Teacher, the Middle Class, the Lower Class," *Phi Delta Kappan,* November 1963.

A teacher educator explains why it is difficult for a middle class teacher to teach lower class children, emphasizing several important issues.

Tomlinson, Loren R.: "A Preservice Experience in Teaching the Educationally Disadvantaged Child," *Journal of Teacher Education,* March 1965, pp. 100–101.

The author examines an experimental course that provides an opportunity for the undergraduate student in elementary education to explore the teaching of the disadvantaged through study, observation, and participation.

Vontress, Clement E.: "Our Demoralizing Slum Schools," *Phi Delta Kappan,* November 1963, pp. 77–81.

The Negro teacher and administrator have special problems when working in slum schools, asserts the author, who describes what they must know and do.

Voss, Elsa: "On Making the Image Three-Dimensional," *High Points,* No. 1, 1964, pp. 59–63.

The teacher's role in trying to strengthen the self-image of the disadvantaged child in order to enable him to function better is described by the author.

Walker, Edith V.: "Inservice Training of Teachers To Work with the Disadvantaged," *The Reading Teacher,* March 1965, pp. 493–498.

Preservice preparation for teachers, plus follow-up internship (school-university program), is suggested for teachers in slum schools.

Wayson, William W.: "Teachers in Slum Areas," *Scholastic Teacher,* February 11, 1965, pp. 4-T, 8-T.

A summary and an analysis are given of the study of the Mid-West Administration Center of the University of Chicago to determine why some teachers remain in slum schools while others do not.

———: "Expressed Motives of Teachers in Slum Schools," *Urban Education,* Vol. I, No. 4, 1965.

This article describes the problem of securing competent teachers to work in low socioeconomic areas, stating that after assignment some stay, while others are eager to leave. Investigation indicates differences in teacher definitions of the teaching role, with those who stayed more "pupil-centered" in their role perception than those who left. Implications for teacher educators seem to be to manipulate the work environment rather than attempt to change pupils and parent problems in the slum school.

Wilkerson, Doxey A.: "Prevailing and Needed Emphasis in Research on the Education of Disadvantaged Children and Youth," *Journal of Negro Education*, Summer, 1964, pp. 346–358.

An area needing research, states the author, is that of teacher behavior, characteristics, and education, to determine what makes a teacher notably effective with disadvantaged pupils.

Williams, Catherine P.: "The Fifth Year Makes the Difference," *American Education*, May 1965, pp. 6–9.

This description of the fifth-year internship program in teacher preparation at the University of Pittsburgh stresses its value for the teacher. Implications for teachers of the disadvantaged are discussed.

Wood, Helen C.: "Teachers Are Important to Migrant Children," *Childhood Education*, October 1965, pp. 72–76.

Several techniques are offered to train teachers of migrant children who "move with the crops" every few weeks.

Wood, Nancy: "Summer School Help for Migrant Workers' Children," *National Education Association Journal*, (May, 1962), p. 18.

A brief reference to the way teachers are trained to teach migrant children is made in this article.

Pamphlets

Alessandro, Joseph: *School for Migrant Children*, Pennsylvania State University, University Park, Pa., 1955, pp. 4–5.

This report describes a school for migrant children and explains how teachers were trained on the job.

American Education and the Search for Equal Opportunity: Educational Policies Commission, National Education Association, Washington, D.C., 1965, pp. 14–22.

The chapter, "The Education of Teachers of the Disadvantaged," summarizes the role of the principal and administrator and the preparation necessary for the teacher of the disadvantaged.

Buchheimer, Naomi, and Buchheimer, Arnold: *Equality Through Education*, Anti-Defamation League of B'nai B'rith, New York, N.Y. (not dated).

A detailed description of one of the first attempts in integration (1951), this account of the Greenburgh School District No. 8, in New York, explains how teachers were prepared to contribute to its success.

Campus-School Exchange: Board of Education, Division of Elementary Schools, New York, N.Y., 1965.

One of the objectives of the program of campus schools is to insure preservice and on-the-job professional growth and development of teachers through co-operation between the public schools and the colleges and universities in the Greater New York area.

Decade of Experiment 1951–61: Fund for the Advancement of Education, New York, N.Y., 1961, pp. 25–43, 34–69.

Two chapters that deal with the preparation of teachers for working with disadvantaged children and youth, "More and Better Teachers" and "Efficient Use of Teachers' Time and Talents" are pertinent.

Education and the Disadvantaged American: Educational Policies Commission, National Education Association, Washington, D.C., 1962, pp. 19–22, 23–25.

What teachers and supervisors should be taught to know and do when working with the disadvantaged is set forth in this pamphlet.

Education of the Deprived and Segregated: Report of a seminar conducted by Bank Street College of Education, Bank Street College of Education, New York, N.Y., 1965, pp. 32–35.

Improvements are needed in teacher preparation if teachers are to be effective in teaching in disadvantaged urban areas, concludes the working group on teacher education at this seminar. Concrete suggestions are offered for the improvement of teacher preparation.

Fishman, Joshua A.: "Project Beacon: A Project Addressed to the Needs of the Socially Disadvantaged," (Reprint from *Pioneer Ideas in Education,* Washington, D.C.: Committee on Education and Labor of the House of Representatives, 88th Congress, First Session, September 1963), New York, N.Y.

This reprint describes training programs for psychoeducational specialists for leadership responsibilities in working with socially and culturally disadvantaged children and youth.

Human Relations in the Classroom: A Study of Problems and Situations Reported by 1,075 Second Year Secondary School Teachers, North Central Association, Chicago, Ill., 1963.

Teachers were asked to evaluate the methods used in their training institutions to prepare them to deal with human relations problems. The findings have implications for schools of education preparing teachers to work with disadvantaged children and youth.

Innovation and Experiment in Education: Panel of Educational Research and Development for the President's Science Advisory Committee, Government Printing Office, Washington, D.C., March 1964.

In the chapter, "The Deprived and the Segregated," an analysis is made of slum schools and teacher education, and suggestions are offered for current needs in both areas.

Nix, Elmer: *The Keys to Indian Education,* Arizona State University, College of Education, Tempe, Ariz., 1962, pp. 28–42.

This report of a workshop on Indian education for teachers, counselors, and administrators contains a section on the orientation of teachers.

Noar, Gertrude: *Information Is Not Enough:* The Implementation of Human

Relations Education in the Classroom, Anti-Defamatation League of B'nai B'rith, New York, N.Y., 1961.

Examples of techniques for teachers that should help them strengthen the self-concept of their pupils are offered.

———: *The Times Call for Courage,* Anti-Defamation League of B'nai B'rith, New York, N.Y., 1964.

The author suggests that colleges which prepare teachers for urban schools should include in their pre- and inservice courses techniques for effective change in teacher attitudes that will lead to an understanding and acceptance of different cultures.

Performance Objectives for Interns: Urban Teacher Preparation Program, Syracuse University, Syracuse, N.Y., 1964.

The objectives of the Urban Teacher Preparation Program are set up in performance teams, which are described herein.

Peterson, Jacqueline L., *et al.: A Guide To Using Assistant Teachers in the Public Schools:* 1964–65 School Assistants Program Report, Associated Community Teams (ACT), New York, N.Y., 1965.

A report by an agency about the recruitment and preparation of highly motivated persons to serve as preprofessional assistants in the Harlem schools.

Potts, Alfred M. (ed.): *Developing Curriculum for Indian Children,* The Center for Cultural Studies, Alamosa State College, Alamosa, Colo., 1964.

A workshop for teachers reports the elements that are essential in educating the Indian child. What the teachers must know in order to create truly affirmative learning is presented, with implications for teacher education.

Promising Practices from the Projects for the Culturally Deprived: Research Council of the Great Cities Program, Chicago, Ill., 1964.

Several of the promising practices submitted by the Directors of the projects in the Great Cities involve special preparation of teachers—the Cleveland internship program for prospective teachers, the Preschool Institute for "special service" schools, and Philadelphia's inservice education are described.

Rivlin, Harry N.: *Teachers for Our Big City Schools,* Anti-Defamation League of B'nai B'rith, New York, N.Y., 1962.

The author describes the kinds of special-preparation programs for teachers in big city schools through pre- and inservice courses.

Rosecrance, F. C.: *Research Seminar on Teacher Education,* U.S. Office of Education Cooperative Research Project No. 6-011, Government Printing Office, Washington, D.C., 1963.

In the chapter, "Teacher Education for Metropolitan Areas," suggestions are offered on how teachers may be prepared for urban school assignments and how effective inservice courses can be maintained.

Schueler, Herbert: *Teachers and Resources for Urban Education, An Urban University Meets a Challenge,* Hunter College of the City University of New York, 1963.

A description of Project 120, a realistic preparation program for student teachers to equip them for teaching in the inner city, is presented.

Some Principal Educational Needs of Children in Disadvantaged Areas and Illustrative Teacher Behavior Required To Meet These Needs, Milwaukee Public Schools, Great Cities Improvement Program, Milwaukee, Wisc., 1964.
A worksheet developed by a task force of the School-University Teacher Education Project deals with the subject of the title.

Storen, H. F., and Edgar, R. W.: *Learning To Teach in Difficult Schools,* Queens College of the City University of New York (A BRIDGE Project publication, No. 4), 1963.
A booklet, prepared for classes in methods of teaching in the secondary schools, highlights the difficulties of beginning teachers and indicates the measures taken to assist them.

Teacher Education for Human Relations in the Classroom: Report of the Teacher Education Committee and Subcommittee on Human Relations in the Classroom, North Central Association of Colleges and Secondary Schools, Chicago, Ill., 1962.
A survey of 1,108 college professors reports what teacher education institutions are doing to sensitize prospective teachers about human relations problems in the classroom.

Teacher Education Project Follow-up of Selected Practices: The Research Council of the Great Cities Program for School Improvement, Chicago, Ill., 1963.
This follow-up report offers a more detailed description of the practices offered in the Preliminary Survey.

Teacher Education Project Progress Report: The Research Council of the Great Cities Program for School Improvement, Chicago, Ill., 1963.
The report is a summary of the returns received in response to the Preliminary Survey of Existing Practices in Teacher Education, including 23 from the Great Cities and 36 from colleges and universities.

Training Programs in Project BEACON: Ferkauf Graduate School of Education, Yeshiva University, New York, 1963, pp. 103–111.
The program for the preparation of preservice and inservice personnel to work in grades one through six in socially disadvantaged schools is described.

Zavitkovsky, Docia: *The Prevention of Failure,* National Education Association, Washington, D.C., 1965.
In the chapter, "The Education of Teachers," the author discusses the wide range of understandings needed by teachers of the disadvantaged and suggests the type of inservice preparation that would prove useful to them.

Papers and Addresses

Goldberg, Miriam L.: "Methods and Materials for Educationally Disadvantaged Youth," an address delivered at the Ohio State University Post-Doctoral Seminar, Columbus, Ohio, October 1964.

Hess, R. D., Jackson, J. D., and Shipman, Virginia: "Communication Styles in Teachers: An Experiment," unpublished manuscript, The University of Chicago, Chicago, Ill., 1965.

Kerber, August: "An Experimental Project To Improve the School Experiences of Culturally Deprived Children and the Inservice Education of Their Teachers," a mimeographed memorandum. Wayne State University College of Education Detroit, Mich. (not dated).

Koenigsberg, S. P.: "Teaching in Lower Socio-Economic Area Schools: The Classroom Activities of Seventh Grade Teachers in New York City Judged Effective by their Principals," unpublished doctoral dissertation, Columbia University, New York, N.Y., 1962.

Marburger, Carl L.: "Eliminating Disadvantage Through Education," paper presented at a conference on the disadvantaged). Tuskegee Institute Press, Tuskegee, Ala., 1964.

Miller, Harry L.: "The Effect of Information on Student Beliefs about the Slum Schools," paper, Hunter College (Project TRUE), New York, N.Y., 1963.

Riessman, Frank: "Action Principles for Working with Low Income Families," paper delivered to staff of Mobilization for Youth, Mobilization for Youth, New York, N.Y., 1962.

———: "Alternative Strategies for the Education of the Disadvantaged," paper delivered to staff of Mobilization for Youth, Mobilization for Youth, New York, N.Y., 1962.

———: "Curriculum for Training Indigenous Nonprofessionals," paper delivered to staff of Mobilization for Youth, Mobilization for Youth, New York, N.Y., 1963.

Schueler, Herbert: "The Development of Teachers for Urban Service," paper presented to the Associated Organizations for Teacher Education in Washington, D.C., October 1963.

Stratmeyer, Florence B.: "Perspective on Action in Teacher Education," address to the 17th Annual Meeting of the AACTE in Chicago, Ill., February 1965.

A Bibliography of Bibliographies Concerned with the Educational Development of Disadvantaged Children and Youth

American Association of Colleges for Teacher Education, Subcommittee on Urban Teacher Education, 1201 Sixteenth Street, NW, Washington, D.C.: *Sources of Bibliographic Information on the Preparation of Teachers for Urban Areas,* 1964.

American Library Association, 50 East Huron Street, Chicago, Ill.: *The Culturally Disadvantaged Child* (annotated bulletin), 1964.

Anti-Defamation League of B'nai B'rith, 315 Lexington Avenue, New York, N.Y.: *Education and the Disadvantaged,* June 1965.

Bank Street College of Education, 69 Bank Street, New York, N.Y.:
1) *Brief Bibliographical References on Special Aspects of Work with the Disadvantaged,* 1964.
2) *List of Publications Related to the Education of the Disadvantaged,* 1965.

City College of the City University of New York, Convent Avenue & 139th Street, New York, N.Y.: *A Selected Bibliography of Societal Factors and Urban Revival in Education,* 1964.

Commonwealth of Pennsylvania, Department of Public Instruction, 1400 Spring Garden Street, Philadelphia, Pa.: *Human Relations: Guide to Intergroup Education in Schools,* 1964.

Federation Employment and Guidance Services, 215 Park Avenue South, New York, N.Y.: *A Guide to Resources for Anti-Poverty Programs: A Selected Bibliography,* 1964.

Hunter College of the City University of New York, 695 Park Avenue, New York, N.Y.:
1) *Urban Education, An Annotated Bibliography,* 1963.
2) *Supplement I* (to Urban Education), 1964.

Institute for Developmental Studies, Department of Psychiatry, New York Medical College, 23 East 105th Street, New York, N.Y.: *Selected Bibliography of Societal Factors Related to Learning,* 1965.

Mobilization for Youth, 214 East 2nd Street, New York, N.Y.: *Bibliography of Papers, Published, Unpublished, and Presented at Conferences,* 1965.

National Committee on the Education of Migrant Children, 145 East 32 Street, New York, N.Y.: *Selected References on Migrant Children's Education,* 1954.

National Conference of Christians and Jews, 43 West 57th Street, New York, N.Y.: *To the Teacher: A Bibliography,* 1964.

National Education Association of the U.S.A., 1201 Sixteenth Street, NW, Washington, D.C.: *References on the Education of the Disadvantaged,* 1963.

New York State Education Department, Division of Inter-Cultural Relations in Education, State Campus Building, Albany, N.Y.: *Intercultural Relations: A Suggested Reading List,* 1964.

New York Public Library, Fifth Avenue at 42nd Street, New York, N.Y.: *The Negro in the United States: A List of Significant Books,* 1965.

New York University, School of Education, Department of Secondary Education, Washington Square, New York, N.Y.: *Selected References Which Have Implications for the Education of the Culturally Deprived,* 1964.

Ohio Civil Rights Commission, 240 Parsons Avenue, Columbus, Ohio:
1) *Bibliography for Intergroup Relations,* 1964.
2) *Education in Depressed Areas: Suggested Readings,* 1965.

Syracuse University Youth Development Center, Syracuse, N.Y.: *School Dropouts: A Commentary and Annotated Bibliography,* 1964.

Union Theological Seminary, Urban Education College, Auburn Collection, Broadway and 120th Street, New York, N.Y.: *Urban Education: An Introduction to the Literature of Research and Experimentation,* 1964.

U.S. Government, Department of Health, Education, and Welfare, Children's Bureau Research Division, Washington, D.C.: *A Selected Bibliography: Economic and Social Deprivation: Its Effects on Children and Families in the U.S.,* 1964.

U.S. Government, Department of Health, Education, and Welfare, Division of Elementary and Secondary Education, Washington, D.C.: *Publications Pertaining to or Applicable to Education in Rural and Small Communities,* 1964.

U.S. Government, Department of Health, Education, and Welfare, Office of Education, Washington, D.C.: *Selected References on Migrant Education,* 1965.

University of Chicago, Chicago, Ill.: *Selected Annotated Bibliography of Research Relevant to Education and Cultural Deprivation,* 1965. *Inventory of Compensatory Education Projects,* 1965.

University of the State of New York, Bureau of Child Development and Parent Education, State Campus Building, Albany, N.Y.: *A Selected Bibliography on the Education of Young Children in Disadvantaged Areas,* 1964.

University of the State of New York, Bureau of Guidance, State Campus Building, Albany, N.Y.: *Selected References for the Education of Culturally Disadvantaged Groups,* 1965.

Yeshiva University, Ferkauf Graduate School of Education, 55 Fifth Avenue, New York, N.Y.:
1) *Bibliography on the Education of Socially Disadvantaged Children and Youth,* 1964.
2) *Guidance of Socially Disadvantaged Children,* 1964.
3) *Socially Disadvantaged Children, A Brief Bibliography,* 1965.

Teacher Education in a Social Context *was produced for the Bank Street College of Education by the Mental Health Materials Center, Inc., New York.*

Designed by Gayle A. Jaeger.